The Essential
CHAUCER

*an annotated bibliography
of major modern studies*

A
Reference
Publication
in
Literature

James L. Harner
Editor

The Essential
CHAUCER

an annotated bibliography
of major modern studies

MARK ALLEN
and
JOHN H. FISHER

G.K.HALL &CO.
70 LINCOLN STREET, BOSTON, MASS.

Library of Congress Cataloging-in-Publication Data

Allen, Mark (Mark Edward)
  The essential Chaucer.

  (A Reference publication in literature)
  Includes index.
  1. Chaucer, Geoffrey, d. 1400—Bibliography.
  2. Chaucer, Geoffrey, d. 1400—Criticism and interpretation.
  I. Fisher, John H.   II. Title.
  III. Series.
  Z8164.A43 1987 [PR1905]   016.821'1   87-17682
  ISBN 0-8161-8739-8

Contents

Contents

Canterbury Tales

Contents

Contents

The Authors

Mark Allen, educated at St. Norbert College, Arizona State University, and the University of Illinois at Urbana, where he received his Ph.D. in 1982, is assistant professor of English in the Division of English, Classics, and Philosophy at the University of Texas at San Antonio. He has published in the fields of Old and Middle English and fantasy literature, having contributed to several books, and having had essays appear in <u>Studies in the Age of Chaucer</u> and <u>Literary Onomastic Studies</u>.

John H. Fisher, B.A. from Maryville College, M.A. and Ph.D. from University of Pennsylvania, has held professorships at New York University, Duke University, and Indiana University, and is currently John C. Hodges Professor of English at the University of Tennessee in Knoxville. Among his books are <u>John Gower: Moral Philosopher and Friend of Chaucer</u> (1964) and editions of <u>The Tretys of Loue</u> (EETS, 1951), <u>The Complete Poetry and Prose of Geoffrey Chaucer</u> (1977), and <u>An Anthology of Chancery English</u> (1984). He has served as executive secretary of the MLA and editor of <u>PMLA</u> (1963-72), and is currently executive director of the New Chaucer Society and editor of its <u>Chaucer Newsletter</u>.

Preface

    The Essential Chaucer is a guide to twentieth-century Chaucer studies, intended primarily as a research tool for students, but also as convenient reference for scholars and critics. It includes 925 studies of Chaucer written between 1900 and 1984, selected for their value in helping us to understand Chaucer and his works, and annotated to identify their content and methodologies.

    Each entry is listed once, alphabetically, under an appropriate topic heading or under the title of the Chaucerian work it treats most directly. These topics are arranged intuitively from general to specific, preceding the Chaucerian titles that are arranged by their importance (Canterbury Tales, first, Troilus and Criseyde, second, etc.). The categories are further subdivided. See the table of contents for the complete classification.

    Cross-referencing augments the classifications. Within the annotations, references are made to parallel studies or critical disagreements. The lists of cross-references that appear at the end of most sections cite entries on related subjects or refer the user to subjects analyzed in the index. The index lists names, topics, and titles not specified in the taxonomy.

    The annotations provide bibliographic information, identify the primary focus of the item annotated, and summarize its contents—all with an eye to clarifying the work's contribution to the study of Chaucer. They combine description and evaluation, although description dominates since the selection process itself was, by nature, evaluative. Choosing from the vast field of Chaucer scholarship and criticism was difficult, but we hope that the books and essays selected interpret Chaucer's works in the ways that have proved most fruitful, that is, those that are built on time-tested methods, explicate familiar and unfamiliar details of Chaucer's language and style, and place his works in their literary and historical contexts.

    The selection is, in a word, conservative, emphasizing traditional approaches and including items readily accessible in college and university libraries and through interlibrary loan services. The majority of the entries have been published in the last twenty-five years, superseding earlier works by being built upon them. Works that address specific topics outnumber more global studies; what they lack in range, they gain in focus, ennabling users to identify more clearly the important issues. The general studies included are notable for their influence and good sense.

The bibliography in the seventh printing of John Fisher's <u>The Complete Poetry and Prose of Geoffrey Chaucer</u> (entry 15) formed the basis of this selection. Its sixteen hundred items, selected from among studies written before 1979, were winnowed and updated to 1984, and annotated by Mark Allen. In the stages of this selective process, effort was made to include representative studies of all of Chaucer's works. The number of entries is in ratio to the importance of the piece. For example, thirty-five items are listed for the Wife of Bath's Tale, eight for the Manciple's Tale, and one apiece for the Cook's fragment and <u>Boece</u>. Yet there are some imbalances: although the Miller's Tale is certainly more important than the Physician's Tale, it has fewer entries. This is rectified in part by the cross-referencing. Because the Miller's Tale is treated so much more often than the Physician's Tale in other essays (in general studies of the <u>fabliaux</u>, for example), it is cross-referenced many more times, so that the total of its citations is greater. The length of the annotations depends in part upon the length of the annotated item but also in part upon its importance. So the more important works by Chaucer are distinguished by some combination of more annotations, more cross-references, and a tendency to longer annotations. With the exceptions of a few scholarly compilations (e.g., entries 47 and 252) collections of critical essays are not included because the important essays from such collections are annotated individually. Dissertations and book reviews are not included either, and with one exception (Koch, entry 17), entries are restricted to works written in English or available in translation. One final exception must also be noted: in deference to its importance to future Chaucer studies, the new <u>Riverside Chaucer</u> (entry 19), published in 1987, has been included even though it follows our <u>terminus ad quem</u> of 1984.

Selection, arrangement, cross-referencing, and indexing are intended to be convenient and, above all, useful. Students will, we hope, find the work a reliable handbook to Chaucerian study, guiding their reading for both discussion and research. Experienced Chaucerians will, no doubt, disagree with some of the inclusions and miss some omissions, but the information provided will, we hope, prove helpful to them in recalling the outlines of familiar books and articles.

The staff of the library and the interlibrary loan service at the University of Texas at San Antonio deserve special thanks for their contributions to the completion of this book, particularly Anita Brown, Leonard De Leon, David Garcia, Maggi Joseph, Kathy McCabe, and, especially, Sue McCray. The project was aided by financial support

Preface

from the UTSA which helped to defray the costs of copying and travel.
For this, too, we are grateful.

Mark Allen
University of Texas at San Antonio
San Antonio, Texas

John H. Fisher
University of Tennessee
Knoxville, Tennessee

General Treatments

1   COGHILL, NEVILL. <u>The Poet Chaucer</u>. 2d ed. Oxford Paperback
Series, no. 23. London: Oxford University Press, 1967,
156 pp.
      Traces the chronological growth of Chaucer's poetry and
comic genius, discussing how his life affected his works, and, at
much greater length, his improving technique from poem to poem.
Chaucer investigated the closed form of dream allegory in <u>Book of
the Duchess</u>, <u>House of Fame</u>, and <u>Parliament of Fowls</u>, although
each is progressively less conventional. In <u>Troilus and Criseyde</u>
he creates a tragedy of character, a new literay form. When rep-
rimanded by the queen for his characterization of Criseyde, he
ironically returns to dream vision in <u>Legend of Good Women</u>, mean-
while discovering the "new shape of a poem" that was to blossom
in the crowning achievement of <u>Canterbury Tales</u>. The General
Prologue and tales reflect most clearly the wide embrace of
Chaucer's comic, Christian view.

2   CORSA, HELEN STORM. <u>Chaucer: Poet of Mirth and Morality</u>.
Notre Dame, Ind.: University of Notre Dame Press, 1964, 247
pp.
      Develops the argument that Chaucer's "mirth reveals his
moral premises." <u>Book of the Duchess</u>, <u>House of Fame</u>, and
<u>Parliament of Fowls</u> are "preludes" to Chaucer's mature comic
style, "intimations" of the mixture of philosophical order and
human diversity that typify <u>Troilus and Criseyde</u> and <u>Canterbury
Tales</u>. <u>Troilus</u> is a realization of a high order that renders
comic its hero's tragedy. The Tales of Canterbury demonstrate
human variety within overarching justice: the Host's game of
mirth is under constant threat of descending to mere contentious-
ness, but such figures as the Knight, Franklin, and Parson assert
providential order in the face of such struggle.

3   GARDNER, JOHN CHAMPLIN. <u>The Poetry of Chaucer</u>. Carbondale:
Southern Illinois University Press, 1977, 408 pp.
      Discusses Chaucer's corpus by isolating two major poles:
Neoplatonic Christianity and nominalistic uncertainty. Early
experimentation with rhetoric and ornament typify <u>Book of the</u>

<u>Duchess</u>, the lyrics, and with increasing structural sophistica-
tion, <u>Parliament of Fowls</u>. <u>Troilus and Criseyde</u> offers a tragic
clash between the two poles; <u>House of Fame</u> (here thought to be
composed about the time of <u>Troilus</u>) contrasts the two subordinate
themes of authority and experience; <u>Legend of Good Women</u> comi-
cally privileges Neoplatonic love. <u>Canterbury Tales</u> embraces
both poles, encompassing Christian unity and philosophical
diversity, authority and experience, medieval representationalism
and modern realism.

4   HALLIDAY, F.E. <u>Chaucer and His World</u>. London: Thames &
     Hudson, 1968, 144 pp.
         A discursive, generously illustrated introduction to
Chaucer, his literature, and the social conditions and events of
his age, interspersed with quotation from his poetry. Chrono-
logically arranged, critical description of the poetry and
biographical information clarify the interrelationships between
Chaucer's art and times. Includes some two hundred black and
white photographs of architecture, statuary, manuscript illumina-
tion, and other medieval materials.

5   HOWARD, EDWIN J. <u>Geoffrey Chaucer</u>. Twayne's English Authors
     Series, no. 1. New York: Twayne, 1964, 219 pp.
         An informative introduction to Chaucer's biography and
cultural context, and an analytic summary of his works. Except
for certain groups of lyrics (complaints, ballads, envoys), each
work is described individually, beginning with a plot summary and
moving to commentary on chronology, versification, theme, and
characterization. Devotes most attention to <u>Canterbury Tales</u>,
considering it fragment by fragment in the Ellesmere order, and
concludes with an historical survey of Chaucer's poetic
reputation.

6   HUSSEY, S.S. <u>Chaucer: An Introduction</u>. 2d ed. London:
     Methuen, 1981, 245 pp.
         Surveys Chaucer's biography and poetry, combining plot sum-
mary with traditional critical concerns. Reads Chaucer's dream
visions against the backdrop of <u>Roman de la rose</u> and courtly
love. Assesses the characters and Boethian philosophy of <u>Troilus
and Criseyde</u> in contrast to Boccaccio's <u>Filostrato</u>, reading
<u>Troilus</u> as a high tragedy that sophisticates the techniques and
concerns of the dream visions. Defines the literary genres
(romance, <u>fabliau</u>, saint's life, didactic forms) collected in
<u>Canterbury Tales</u>, discussing representative tales and describing
the style and function of General Prologue. Comparisons with
John Gower, William Langland, and the <u>Pearl</u> poet clarify the
nature of Chaucer's narrative voice, his realism, and his sensitive portrayals of love.

7   KANE, GEORGE. <u>Chaucer</u>. Past Masters. New York: Oxford
     University Press, 1984, 122 pp.

A compact assessment of Chaucer, his poetry, and his intellectual achievement, describing the development of his idea of
poetry and the subsequent growth of his art. Biographical
detail, comparison to continental contemporaries, and summary of
intellectual tradition serve as background for a chronological
survey of his poetry, from his novel use of French convention and
the English language in Book of the Duchess, to his exploration
of poetic identity in House of Fame and his conflation of love,
poetry, and philosophy in Parliament of Fowls. The greatness of
Troilus and Criseyde lies in its investigation of the relation
between sexuality and personality and its generalized representation of the "human predicament." Canterbury Tales reflects
contemporary issues and thought, and the human impulses of
sexuality and acquisitiveness. These motifs compose a tragi-
comedy of human ideals and the failure to achieve them.

8   KEAN, P.M. Chaucer and the Making of English Poetry. 2
     vols. London: Routledge & Kegan Paul, 1972, 482 pp. 1 vol.
     abridged ed. 1982, 327 pp.
     Evaluates Chaucer's status as the father of English poetry,
reading his works for their relation to literary tradition,
emphasizing his appropriation of English and continental literature, and identifying his self-consciousness about his poetry and
its place in tradition. In Book of the Duchess and the short
poems, he developed an "urbane" style, dependent upon tradition
but freshly aware of audience. More rich philosophically and
more conscious of their status as poetry, Parliament of Fowls and
House of Fame explore, respectively, the contrasts of love and
the relation of poetry to tradition. Troilus and Criseyde draws
its audience into the experiences of love and of philosophy by
capturing them in the "intrigue and cross purposes" of the
characters. Canterbury Tales incorporates a huge array of
sources and reflects Chaucer's exploitation and manipulation of
comedy, religion, rhetoric, and narrative variety. Chaucer's
various contributions were apparent to his fifiteenth-century
followers, even though the metaphors of their criticism obscure
this fact.

9   KITTREDGE, GEORGE LYMAN. Chaucer and His Poetry. Cambridge
     Mass.: Harvard University Press, 1915. Reprint. 1970, 266
     pp.
     An important work of interpretive criticism that has done
much to influence twentieth-century understanding of Chaucer.
The progress of Chaucer's career, the breadth of his appeal, and
attention to irony and characterization typify the six included
essays, notable for their insight, intellectual grace, and
exposure of critical illusions. Chaucer was not naive: a naive
"Collector of Customs would be a paradoxical monster." Book of
the Duchess benefits from Chaucer's naive pose and "is really
like a dream." House of Fame surveys the "whole world of mortal
endeavor," and Troilus and Criseyde is "the first novel, in the
modern sense, that was ever written," presenting fully developed

psychological characters. <u>Canterbury Tales</u> is a "human comedy"
in which the tales are "long speeches" that dramatize the characters of the tellers. Such seminal observations have provoked
positive and negative response from Chaucer critics for several
generations.

10   LAWLOR, JOHN. <u>Chaucer</u>. London: Hutchinson University
     Library, 1968, 181 pp.
        Assesses the ongoing struggle between experience and
authority in Chaucer's narrative poetry, exploring the ways in
which his narrative poses, his sense of literary tradition, and
his sensitivity to his audience reflect his concern with both
poetic freedom and the human freedom of his characters. In his
early dream visions, Chaucer confronts the relations between
bookish authority and dream experience. In <u>Troilus and Criseyde</u>,
his transformations of Boccaccio's <u>Filostrato</u> emphasize the
pathos of the characters' submission to convention and the
narrator's submission to poetic tradition. <u>Legend of Good Women</u>
defines the gap between poetic theory and practice, and
<u>Canterbury Tales</u> explores the problem through various situations.
Reads the Marriage Group as the culminating treatment of the
theme.

11   LOOMIS, ROGER SHERMAN. <u>A Mirror of Chaucer's World</u>.
     Princeton: Princeton University Press, 1965, n.p.
        Collects some two hundred portraits of Chaucer and his
contemporaries, photographs of places he frequented and common
objects from his life, and manuscript illustrations of details or
scenes in his writings. Arranged according to the pieces they
illustrate, the pictures are accompanied by Chaucerian quotations
and helpful bibliography.

12   LOUNSBURY, THOMAS R. <u>Studies in Chaucer: His Life and
     Writings</u>. New York: Harper & Brothers, 1892. Reprint. 3
     vols. New York: Russell & Russell, 1962, 1607 pp.
        An early, scholarly compendium of Chaucer's biography,
canon, and poetic achievement, valuable for its summary of
previous scholarship and criticism, particularly the "legendary
biography." Describes the difficulty of establishing Chaucer's
canon, applying various tests of genuineness to eliminate
spurious works and <u>Romaunt of the Rose</u>. Examines Chaucer's
learning and gauges his contributions to linguistic history.
Studies his allusions, identifying his "errors" in using them,
and assesses his vocabulary. Comments upon Chaucer's religious
convictions, viewing him as an early Protestant, and explores his
literary achievement by analyzing his self-consciousness, experimentation, and originality.

See also entries 57, 58, 66, 201, 229.

Editions and Editing

13   BLAKE, N.F., ed. The "Canterbury Tales" by Geoffrey Chaucer:
      Edited from the Hengwrt Manuscript. York Medieval Texts, 2d
      ser. London: Edward Arnold, 1980, 713 pp.
          Edits Chaucer's Canterbury Tales, following the Hengwrt
      manuscript for both text and tale-order, and emending it only
      conservatively except when introducing modern punctuation and
      paragraphing. The introduction defines editorial practice,
      describes the habits of the scribe, and defends the use of
      Hengwrt as a base text. Brief notes and glosses clarify archaic
      words and phrases, and occasionally identify sources. Includes a
      brief bibliography and glossary, a note on language, and un-
      glossed appendixes of Ellesmere materials not in Hengwrt or added
      to it late, that is, links between tales and Canon's Yeoman's
      Prologue and Tale.

14   DONALDSON, E. T[ALBOT], ed.   Chaucer's Poetry: An Anthology
      for the Modern Reader. 2d ed. New York: Ronald Press Co.,
      1975, 1179 pp.
          Includes selected poetic tales of Canterbury, Troilus and
      Criseyde, and a judicious selection of the early poems and
      lyrics. Normalized spelling, modern punctuation, helpful
      glosses, and short explanatory notes ease modern reading, but
      more importantly, the extensive commentary on each work and on
      miscellaneous topics provides insightful discussion of Chaucer's
      poetry. The glossary, short bibliography, and especially the
      commentary are a good point of departure for any first-time
      investigation of Chaucer and valuable touchstones for more
      advanced criticism.

15   FISHER, JOHN H., ed. The Complete Poetry and Prose of
      Geoffrey Chaucer. New York: Holt, Rinehart & Winston, 1977.
      Reprint (with revised bibliography) 1982, 1047 pp.
          The most recent edition of Chaucer's prose and poetry, com-
      plete with the traditional corpus, Equatorie of the Planets, and
      Romaunt of the Rose. Each text is drawn from a base manuscript
      (Ellesmere for Canterbury Tales), emended conservatively from the
      collations of Manly and Rickert (entry 31), Root (entry 20), or

Koch (entry 17). Includes select variants, explanatory notes, and glosses, emphasizing ease of use rather than absolute thoroughness. Helpful essays introduce individual works and discuss Chaucer's poetic contribution, his life, and his language and versification. The full bibliography and small glossary combine with the editing, the commentary, and the format to make this the most useable edition of Chaucer.

16   GUNTHER, R.T. Chaucer and Messahalla on the Astrolabe. Early Science in Oxford, no. 5. Oxford: Printed for the subscribers, 1929, 242 pp.
        A translation and partial edition of Chaucer's unfinished Treatise on the Astrolabe, most valuable for reproduction of the sixty-two illustrations that accompany the treatise in MS Cambridge Dd.3.53. Includes facsimiles and translation of Massahalla's illustrated Astrolabe, which was probably a source for Chaucer, and the text and translation of non-Chaucerian materials similar to those with which he planned to conclude his treatise.

17   KOCH, JOHN, ed. Geoffrey Chaucer: Kleinere Dichtungen: nebst Einleitung Lesarten, Anmerkungen und einem Worterverzeichnis. Englische Textbibliothek, no. 18. Heidelberg: Carl Winter, 1928, 268 pp.
        Edits all of Chaucer's poems except Troilus and Criseyde and Canterbury Tales, following the canon established by Brusendorff (entry 26). Valuable primarily for its lists of textual variants in the early poems and lyrics. Introduction and apparatus written in German. See entry 28.

18   PRICE, DEREK J., ed. The Equatorie of the Plantis: Edited from Peterhouse MS 75.I. Cambridge: Cambridge University Press, 1955, 230 pp.
        A facsimile reproduction, transcription, and modern English translation of Equatorie of the Planets that ascribes the text to Chaucer, describes the manuscript and its provenance, discusses the astrological tables that accompany the text, and explains the Ptolemaic planetary system and the history of equatoria. Includes a linguistic analysis by R.M. Wilson that supports the ascription to Chaucer, an analysis of the script believed to be Chaucer's own, a comparison with Chaucer's Treatise on the Astrolabe, and a glossary.

19   ROBINSON, F.N., ed. The Works of Geoffrey Chaucer. New Cambridge Edition. 2d ed. Boston: Houghton Mifflin Co., 1957. Revised as The Riverside Chaucer, ed. Larry D. Benson (Boston: Houghton Mifflin Co., 1987), 1327 pp.
        The best known, most frequently quoted edition of Chaucer's works. Based upon preferred manuscripts of the works (Ellesmere for Canterbury Tales), the eclectic text, as well as the introductory essays and the textual and explanatory notes, have made this the standard edition of Chaucer for several

generations. A team of thirty-three experts have recently reedited the texts (complete corpus except for Equatorie of the Planets), rewritten the apparatus and introductory essays, and expanded the bibliography and glossary. Brief glosses for unfamiliar words are provided at the foot of each page and the format has been made more attractive and readable.

20   ROOT, ROBERT KILBURN, ed. The Book of Troilus and Criseyde, by Geoffrey Chaucer. Princeton: Princeton University Press, 1926, 663 pp.

Long regarded as the best edition of Troilus and Criseyde but recently challenged for its questionable textual theory (see Windeatt, entries 24 and 693; and Hanna, in entry 21). The text is based on the assumption that Chaucer revised the poem extensively. Hence, the textual apparatus provides only limited variants, assuming that the others were expunged by the poet. The explanatory introduction discusses the sources of the poem, and Chaucer's learning, and describes the manuscripts and previous major editions. The extensive annotations underlie all later discussions of the poem. Especially good are the philological comments.

21   RUGGIERS, PAUL G., ed. Editing Chaucer: The Great Tradition. Norman, Okla.: Pilgrim Books, 1984, 310 pp.

Collects twelve essays on the major editors of Chaucer between the invention of printing and the first half of the twentith century. Includes essays on Caxton by Beverly Boyd, Thynne by James E. Blodgett, Stow by Anne Hudson, Speght by Derek Pearsall, Urry by William L. Anderson (exerpted from entry 193), Tyrwhitt by B.A. Windeatt, Wright by Thomas Ross, Furnivall by Donald C. Baker, Skeat (entry 23) by A.S.G. Edwards, Root (entry 20) by Ralph Hanna III, Manly and Rickert (entry 31) by George Kane, and Robinson (entry 19) by George F. Reinecke.

22   _____. A Variorum Edition of the Works of Geoffrey Chaucer. Norman: University of Oklahoma Press, 1979–.

Intended to present fresh texts from the best manuscripts, variants from the important manuscripts and editions down to the present, textual and explanatory notes summarizing the scholarship and criticism to ca. 1980–85, and introductory surveys of the criticism and textual tradition. Published so far: vol. 1 (entry 33); vol. 2, p. 3: The Miller's Tale, ed. Thomas W. Ross, 1983; vol. 2, p. 9, The Nun's Priest's Tale, ed. Derek Pearsall, 1984; vol. 2, p. 10, The Manciple's Tale, ed. Donald C. Baker, 1984; vol. 5, The Minor Poems, ed. George B. Pace and Alfred David, 1982 (Contains Truth, Gentilesse, Lak of Stedfastnesse, The Former Age, Adam Scrivyn, Envoy to Bukton, Envoy to Scogan, To Rosemounde, Merciles Beaute, Womanly Noblesse, Against Women Unconstant, Proverbs). For editorial principles, see vol. 1 (entry 33).

23   SKEAT, WALTER W., ed. <u>The Complete Works Of Geoffrey Chaucer:</u>
      <u>Edited from Numerous Manuscripts</u>. 2d ed. 7 vols. Oxford:
      Clarendon Press, 1899-1900, 4274 pp.
          The "Oxford" Chaucer; the first complete, modern edition of
      Chaucer's prose and poetry based on manuscripts rather than
      earlier editions. Because emended eccentrically, the text is
      outdated, but the glossary is detailed and extensive. The schol-
      arly notes form the basis of modern understanding of Chaucer and
      must be consulted by student and scholar alike. With few excep-
      tions the canon is standard. Adjusts the Ellesmere manuscript to
      follow the Chaucer Society order of <u>Canterbury Tales</u>. The
      seventh, supplementary, volume is the best available collection
      of Chaucer apocrypha.

24   WINDEATT, B[ARRY] A. <u>Troilus & Criseyde: A New Edition of</u>
      <u>"The Book of Troilus."</u> London: Longman, 1984, 596 pp.
          A conservative, scholarly edition of the Corpus Christi
      manuscript of <u>Troilus and Criseyde</u>, including a complete record
      of substantial variants in the manuscripts and first three
      printed editions of the poem. Presents the text alongside the
      Italian of Boccaccio's <u>Filostrato</u>, Chaucer's source, and provides
      extensive scholarly and critical notes that gloss hard words,
      survey criticism, and clarify Chaucer's relations to his sources.
      The introductory material describes the poem's manuscripts and
      meter, theorizes about Chaucer's techniques of translation (see
      entry 704) and scribal treatment of the poem (see entry 692), and
      challenges Root's theory (entry 691) of multiple versions of the
      text (see entry 693).

          See also entries 28, 33, 122, 913.

Manuscripts and Texts

25   BLAKE, N.F. "Geoffrey Chaucer: The Critics and the Canon." Archiv für das Studium der Neueren Sprachen und Literaturen 221 (1984):65-79.

Confronts the traditional assumption that Chaucer left incomplete many of his works, and argues that manuscript transmission probably accounts for the appearance of incompleteness. Criticism should not, therefore, date Chaucer's works by their apparent state of completion nor attribute it to Chaucer's habits or conditions of composition.

26   BRUSENDORFF, AAGE. The Chaucer Tradition. London: Oxford University Press, 1925, 510 pp.

Examines fourteenth- and fifteenth-century references to Chaucer's poetry as they relate to the poet's biography and his canon. Attributions and notations by John Shirley and anonymous scribes, and quotations from Chaucer and his literary contemporaries and descendants (Usk, Gower, Hoccleve, and Lydgate) test traditional hypotheses about Chaucer's corpus and his relations with his patrons. Omits Equatorie of the Planets and attributes to Chaucer the Middle English Romaunt of the Rose. Otherwise, poem by poem analysis establishes the canon that is accepted today, with a few exceptions among the lyrics. Discusses lost works and apocrypha.

27   DONALDSON, E. T[ALBOT]. "The Manuscripts of Chaucer's Works and Their Use." In Geoffrey Chaucer. Edited by Derek Brewer. Writers and their Background. London: G. Bell & Sons, 1974. Reprint. Athens: Ohio University Press, 1976, pp. 85-108.

Surveys the essential problems of editing medieval literature from manuscripts and describes the available manuscripts of Chaucer's works, demonstrating how editions simplify the complexities of reading Chaucer and make readers more certain than they should be about Chaucer's actual words.

28   DOYLE, A.I., and PACE, GEORGE P. "A New Chaucer Manuscript." PMLA 83 (1968):22-34.

Describes and analyzes the long-lost Coventry manuscript that includes texts of six of Chaucer's lyrics unavailable to Koch (entry 17) and modern editors: <u>An ABC</u>, <u>Lenvoy to Bukton</u>, <u>Complaint of Chaucer to His Purse</u>, <u>Gentilesse</u>, <u>Lak of Stedfastnesse</u>, and <u>Truth</u>. Transcribes the Chaucerian poems of the manuscript and correlates them with standard stemmata.

29   DOYLE, A.I., and PARKES, M.B. "The Production of Copies of the <u>Canterbury Tales</u> and the <u>Confessio Amantis</u> in the Early Fifteenth Century." In <u>Medieval Scribes, Manuscripts & Libraries: Essays Presented to N.R. Ker</u>. Edited by M.B. Parkes and Andrew G. Watson. London: Scolar, 1978, pp. 163–210.

Analyzes the execution and consistency of several manuscripts to argue that early fifteenth-century manuscript production was "a bespoke trade consisting of independent craftsmen working to specific commissions." Compares facsimile pages of the Hengwrt and Ellesmere manuscripts of the <u>Canterbury Tales</u>, assessing the layout of these manuscripts by the same scribe. The headings and glosses of the Hengwrt are afterthoughts, while the Ellesmere reflects the scribe's intention to, in effect, edit the text.

30   <u>The Ellesmere Chaucer: Reproduced in Facsimile</u>. 2 vols. Manchester: University Press, 1911, n.p.

A facsimile reproduction of the most opulent manuscript of Chaucer's <u>Canterbury Tales</u>, once owned by the earl of Ellesmere. The illustrations of each pilgrim tale-teller, lavish borders at the beginning of each tale, rubrics, and decorated initials that accompany the text are clear, as are marginal glosses in Latin and English, indicating textual divisions or identifying allusions and sources.

31   MANLY, JOHN M., and RICKERT, EDITH, eds. <u>The Text of the "Canterbury Tales," Studied on the Basis of All Known Manuscripts</u>. 8 vols. Chicago: University of Chicago Press, 1940, 4758 pp.

A complete account of the the text of the <u>Canterbury Tales</u>; the fullest source available for its textual materials. The description of the manuscripts and the collations are standard and not likely to be superseded. However, the text, a recension from questionable manuscript stemmata, has less authority than more recent, "good" manuscript editions.

32   PACE, GEORGE B. "Speght's Chaucer and MS Gg.4.27." <u>Studies in Bibliography</u> 21 (1968):225–35.

Identifies the copy text for Speght's printed edition of Chaucer's <u>An A.B.C.</u> as Cambridge University Library MS Gg.4.27, thereby supporting Speght's claim that the poem was written for Blanche, duchess of Lancaster.

33   RUGGIERS, PAUL G., ed. The "Canterbury Tales": A Facsimile
      and Transcription of the Hengwrt Manuscript, with Variants
      from the Ellesmere Manuscript. Variorum Edition of the Works
      of Geoffrey Chaucer, vol. 1. Norman: University of Oklahoma
      Press; Folkestone: Wm. Dawson & Sons, 1979, 1077 pp.
          The base text for the variorum edition of Canterbury Tales:
      a clear, slightly reduced, black-and-white facsimile of the
      Hengwrt manuscript, with facing-page transcription of the text
      and variants from the Ellesmere manuscript. Ruggiers's editor's
      preface gives the editorial principles of the variorum Chaucer
      (entry 22), its goals, and a short history of the project.
      Donald C. Baker's introduction explains the relation of edited
      texts of Canterbury Tales to the Hengwrt and justifies its use as
      a base text. A.I. Doyle's and M.B. Parkes's paleographical in-
      troduction describes the Hengwrt (construction, hands, punctua-
      tion, decoration, binding, etc.), conjectures about scribal
      method and sequence of copying, and defines the relationship
      between the Hengwrt and Ellesmere.

34   SILVIA, DANIEL S. "Some Fifteenth-Century Manuscripts of the
      Canterbury Tales." In Chaucer and Middle English Studies in
      Honour of Rossell Hope Robbins. Edited by Beryl Rowland.
      London: George Allen & Unwin, 1974, pp. 153-63.
          Analyzes the contents of manuscripts containing some or all
      of the Canterbury Tales. Complete versions of the Tales are most
      numerous, but select "courtly" or "moral" tales were collected
      with similar non-Chaucerian works, indicating their topical
      popularity.

35   TATLOCK, J.S.P. "The Canterbury Tales in 1400." PMLA 50
      (1935):100-139.
          Amplifies Brusendorff's discussions (entry 26) of Chaucer's
      working habits, the scribal practices of his day, and the likely
      condition of Canterbury Tales at his death. Suggests that
      Chaucer left no "fair copy" of the poem and that extant
      manuscripts reflect the "commercialization" of the book trade.
      Attributes much of the confusion about links, genuine and spuri-
      ous, to scribal practice and argues that the order of the frag-
      ments in the manuscripts has no authority. Appends a lengthy
      note that asserts the value of the Hengwrt manuscript and
      describes its relation to scribal practice.

          See also entries 18, 22, 36, 99, 105. For Canterbury
      Tales: 263, 265, 267, 271, 403, 413, 424, 601, 613, 628, 675;
      Troilus and Criseyde: 691-93; Book of the Duchess: 813; Legend
      of Good Women: 887; short poems: 903, 916.

Canon, Apocrypha, and Lost Works

36   BONNER, FRANCIS W. "The Genesis of the Chaucer Apocrypha."
      Studies in Philology 48 (1951):461-81.
         Blames historically inaccurate attributions of works to
      Chaucer upon misinterpretation of the lists left by him and his
      contemporaries--Gower, Lydgate, and Shirley. Chaucer's reputa-
      tion as a love poet and fifteenth-century methods of manuscript
      compilation also contributed to such apocryphal attributions.

37   LEWIS, ROBERT ENZER. "What Did Chaucer Mean by Of the Wretched
      Engendrynge of Mankynde?" Chaucer Review 2 (1968):139-58.
         Assesses Chaucer's reference to his now-lost Of the
      Wretched Engendrynge of Mankynde in the Legend of Good Women,
      comparing the title with various titles ascribed to Pope Innocent
      III's De miseria conditionis humana (De contemptu mundi) and
      suggesting that the lost work was a prose translation of
      Innocent's work.

38   MOORE, ARTHUR K. "Chaucer's Lost Songs." JEGP: Journal of
      English and Germanic Philology 48 (1949):198-208.
         Considers Chaucer's use of the word "song" as applied to
      poetry, assessing his short poems and the lyrics embedded in
      longer works, and studying the contemporary habits of Machaut and
      Deschamps to conclude that Chaucer's lost verse, however
      "recitative," was probably not musical.

39   RUUD, JAY. "Against Women Unconstant: The Case for Chaucer's
      Authorship." Modern Philology 80 (1982):161-64.
         Traces the image of the mirror of the mind in Against Women
      Unconstant to Chaucer's gloss in Boece, rendering Chaucer's pos-
      sible authorship of the lyric less "doubtful" than has been
      claimed.

40   SKEAT, WALTER W. The Chaucer Canon: With a Discussion of the
      Works Associated with the Name of Geoffrey Chaucer. Oxford:
      Clarendon Press, 1900, 178 pp.
         Establishes Chaucer's canon by applying various tests of
      grammar and rhyme, accepting only those works that reflect habits

similar to those of <u>Canterbury Tales</u>. Uses Squire's Tale as the
basis for comparison and examines all works attributed to Chaucer
in early editions. Identifies three distinct parts of <u>Romaunt of
the Rose</u>, accepting Fragment A as Chaucerian, but rejecting B and
C. Modern scholarship accepts the canon established here with
minor variations: expunging Fragment A of <u>Romaunt of the Rose</u>,
adding <u>Equatorie of the Planets</u>, and leaving several lyrics
doubtful.

41   WIMSATT, JAMES I. <u>Chaucer and the Poems of "Ch" in University
      of Pennsylvania MS French 15</u>. Chaucer Studies, no. 9.
      Cambridge: D.S. Brewer; Totowa, N.J.: Rowman & Littlefield,
      1982, 136 pp.
          Edits a portion of Pennsylvania MS French 15, containing
      the fifteen French love poems signed "Ch." Suggests that, if not
      by Chaucer, the poems clarify the "poetic mode" of Chaucer's
      early career. Analyzes the contents of the complete manuscript
      and suggests that Oton de Granson anthologized the collection.

          See also entries 12, 23, 26, 45, 203, 913.

Bibliographies

42   BAIRD, LORRAYNE Y. A Bibliography of Chaucer: 1964-1973.
      Reference Guides in Literature. Boston: G.K. Hall, 1977, 311
      pp.
           The standard Chaucer bibliography for 1964-73. Follows the
      format of Griffith (entry 44) and Crawford (entry 43), but num-
      bers the entries and adds several categories of classification.
      Entries are cross-referenced by number rather than page. Lists
      recordings, films, and filmstrips under a single heading.
      Entries are lightly annotated and indexed by subject as well as
      author.

43   CRAWFORD, WILLIAM R. Bibliography of Chaucer: 1954-63.
      University of Washington Publications in Language and
      Literature, no. 17. Seattle: University of Washington Press,
      1967, 188 pp.
           The standard bibliography for 1954-63, continuing
      Griffith's bibliography (entry 44), following its format, and
      updating some of its entries. The large number of citations
      indicates the blossoming of Chaucer studies, and an important in-
      troductory essay, "New Directions in Chaucer Criticism," dis-
      cusses major trends and representative works, emphasizing the
      struggle between close reading of Chaucer's works and study of
      their historical context.

44   GRIFFITH, DUDLEY DAVID. Bibliography of Chaucer: 1908-1953.
      University of Washington Publications in Language and
      Literature, no. 13. Seattle: University of Washington Press,
      1955, 416 pp.
           The standard Chaucer bibliography for 1908-53, arranging
      studies of Chaucer alphabetically under topical headings:
      bibliographies, manuscripts, editions, biography, individual
      works, etc.--twenty categories in all. Nearly one half of the
      citations pertain to individual works by Chaucer; criticisms of
      three or more works are listed separately, as are linguistic,
      background, and stylistic studies. The section "Influence and
      Allusion" updates Spurgeon's work (entry 202), as the entire
      volume continues Hammond's (entry 45). Lists reviews of book-

length studies. Citations are cross-referenced, lightly annotated, and indexed by author.

45   HAMMOND, ELEANOR P. <u>Chaucer: A Bibliographical Manual</u>. New
     York: Macmillan Co., 1908. Reprint. New York: Peter Smith,
     1933. 589 pp.
         Lists and analyzes Chaucer scholarship to 1906. Ignores
     "literary" or critical discussions, but prints and comments upon
     early accounts of Chaucer's life, and discusses his canon, its
     chronology, and the editions of his works. The largest section
     pertains to <u>Canterbury Tales</u>—its sources, arrangement,
     manuscripts, selections, translations, editions for children,
     chronology of the composition of the tales, and the frame and
     narrative context for each tale. Similar sections treat
     Chaucer's other works and printed apocrypha. A separate section
     discusses Chaucer's verse and poetic style, listing appropriate
     studies (1847-1906) and glossaries. The final chapter decribes
     major British libraries, offers short biographies of important
     Chaucerians, fully describes the publications of the Chaucer
     Society, and concludes with a reference list of the most impor-
     tant Chaucer scholarship. This is an important handbook to the
     early study of Chaucer and the best bibliography of the time.

46   PECK, RUSSELL A. <u>Chaucer's Lyrics and "Anelida and Arcite":
     An Annotated Bibliography 1900 to 1980</u>. Chaucer
     Bibliographies. Toronto: University of Toronto Press, 1983.
     246 pp.
         An expansive bibliography of scholarship and criticism of
     Chaucer's twenty-two short poems, extensively annotated. Some
     one hundred fifty citations describe important textual, prosodic,
     and general studies. The other four hundred twenty-five entries
     annotate studies of individual poems. Since the general studies
     are reannotated under several headings, cross-referencing is
     minimal. Throughout, annotations are lengthy, generously quoting
     the original.

47   ROWLAND, BERYL, ed. <u>Companion to Chaucer Studies</u>. Rev. ed.
     New York: Oxford University Press, 1979. 526 pp.
         Presents twenty-two bibliographic essays by eminent
     Chaucerians, surveying the history and dominant trends of Chaucer
     criticism from its beginnings. Each essay defines its topic,
     epitomizes the critical concerns that have shaped its discussion,
     and provides selected bibliography. The index makes it possible
     to trace topics and scholars through the separate essays. Essays
     include "Chaucer the Man," by Albert C. Baugh; "Chaucer, the
     Church, and Religion," by Robert W. Ackerman; "Chaucer and the
     Art of Rhetoric," by Robert O. Payne; "Chaucer's Prosody," by
     Tauno F. Mustanoja; "Chaucerian Narrative," by Robert M. Jordan;
     "Chaucer's Imagery," by Beryl Rowland; "The French Influence on
     Chaucer," by Haldeen Braddy; "The Italian Influence on Chaucer,"
     by Paul G. Ruggiers; "The Influence of the Classics on Chaucer,"
     by Richard L. Hoffman; "Chaucer and Astrology," by Chauncey Wood;

"The Design of the Canterbury Tales," by Charles A. Owen, Jr.;
"The General Prologue," by Thomas A. Kirby; "The Tales of
Romance," by J. Burke Severs; The Fabliaux, by D.S. Brewer;
"Allegory in the Canterbury Tales," by Robert P. Miller; "Modes
of Irony in the Canterbury Tales," by Vance Ramsey; "The Lyrics,"
by Rossell Hope Robbins; "The Book of the Duchess," by D.W.
Robertson, Jr.; "The House of Fame," by Laurence K. Shook; "The
Parliament of Fowls," by Donald C. Baker; "Troilus and Criseyde,"
by John P. McCall; and "The Legend of Good Women," by John H.
Fisher.

Dictionaries

48 DAVIS, NORMAN; GRAY, DOUGLAS; INGHAM, PATRICIA; and WALLACE-
    HADRALL, ANNE. A Chaucer Glossary. Oxford: Clarendon Press,
    1979, 205 pp.
      A glossary of Chaucer's words and phrases unfamiliar to
    modern readers, providing definitions, etymologies, parts of
    speech, and selective references to Chaucer's use. The word-list
    is based upon the Tatlock-Kennedy concordance (entry 53),
    covering Chaucer's corpus and Romaunt of the Rose Fragment A, but
    omitting Equatorie of the Planet and some lyrics. The defini-
    tions are succinct, often a single word or phrase, and occasional
    quotations illustrate idiomatic, phrasal, or metaphoric usage.
    Appends a short list of names of persons and places.

49 DILLON, BERT. A Chaucer Dictionary: Proper Names and
    Allusions, Excluding Place Names. Boston: G.K. Hall, 1974,
    283 pp.
      Alphabetically catalogs and locates by line numbers proper
    names, references, and allusions in Chaucer's corpus (excluding
    Equatorie of the Planets), identifying them with short descrip-
    tions, and indicating major critical discussions. Complements
    Magoun's Gazetteer (entry 50). A clear system of abbreviation
    identifies the nature of Chaucer's references (direct or in-
    direct) and their sources (e.g., Bible chapter and verse or
    classical author and text). Entries for passing references offer
    simple identifications and locations, while those for seminal
    sources like Boccaccio's works or Roman de la rose provide sec-
    tion and line references that comprise an index for source study
    as well as a dictionary.

50 MAGOUN, FRANCIS P., Jr. A Chaucer Gazeteer. Chicago:
    University of Chicago Press, 1961, 173 pp.
      Alphabetically lists "all geographical names and names
    (uncapitalized) of geographical origin or with geographical
    connections" in the works of Chaucer (except Equatorie of the
    Planets), identifying provenance, etymology, and literary
    tradition. Includes indirect references in which Chaucer does

17

not use the actual name. Citations range from simple identifica-
tions to discursive explanations.

51   ROSS, THOMAS. Chaucer's Bawdy. New York: E.P. Dutton & Co.,
      1972, 256 pp.
          An alphabetical dictionary of Chaucerian references to sex
      and scatology, including punning terms, direct references, and
      allusions. Individual entries explain the terms, cite scholarly
      authorities and critical interpretations, and describe the mean-
      ing and use of the terms in Chaucer's works. The introduction
      discusses Chaucer's risqué language and its comic value.
      Includes fifteen illustrations and a line-index to bawdry in
      Chaucer's works.

52   SCOTT, A.F. Who's Who in Chaucer. New York: Taplinger
      Publishing Co., 1974, 145 pp.
          A dictionary of the historical and fictional characters and
      the animals referred to in Chaucer's major works, divided into
      two parts: (1) Canterbury Tales and (2) other major works.

53   TATLOCK, JOHN S.P., and KENNEDY, ARTHUR G. Concordance to the
      Complete Works of Chaucer and to the "Romaunt of the Rose."
      1927. Reprint. Gloucester, Mass.: Peter Smith, 1963, 1123
      pp.
          Alphabetical list of all but the most common words (e.g.,
      and, but, his) in Chaucer's works (except Equatorie of the
      Planets) and the Romaunt of the Rose. Individual entries include
      every occurrence of a word in the corpus, quotation of the whole
      line for each instance, and citation of line numbers. Some
      variant spellings included. Although based on the outdated Globe
      edition of Chaucer's works, edited by Alfred Pollard and others
      (Macmillan & Co., 1913), this is the standard concordance to
      Chaucer's works.

Contemporary Social Conditions

54   AERS, DAVID. <u>Chaucer, Langland, and the Creative Imagination</u>.
      London: Routledge & Kegan Paul, 1980, 248 pp.
         Describes the ideological plurality of the late fourteenth
      century, demonstrating Chaucer's sensitivity to the tension be-
      tween individual need and social tradition. Through the Wife of
      Bath and Pardoner, Chaucer presents authority in the mouths of
      very human speakers, disclosing the limitations of authority.
      Through Criseyde, Chaucer subverts the received idea of woman.
      The Marriage Group examines marital ideologies and leaves them
      unresolved. Through Knight's Tale, Chaucer exposes the weakness
      of idealized order by having Theseus employ reified abstractions
      (order, necessity, love) in ways that encourage "critical dis-
      crimination" of the value of such abstractions.

55   BENNETT, H.S. <u>Chaucer and the Fifteenth Century</u>. Oxford
      History of English Literature, no. 2, p. 1. Oxford:
      Clarendon Press, 1947. Reprint 1979, 348 pp.
         Introduces in helpful, general terms the literary and
      social milieu of Chaucer's age, setting a biographical reading of
      his poetry against a discussion of city, court, and religious
      life, and using the poet's works to illuminate details of this
      society. Examines Chaucer's contributions to the development of
      English poetic diction and imagery, prosody, and verse forms,
      showing how Chaucer adumbrates fifteenth-century literature,
      discussed here as emulation of his genius. Includes a valuable
      essay on "The Author and His Public" in English medieval
      tradition, summaries of the verse and prose of the fifteenth
      century, chronological tables, and a dated but useful
      bibliography of the literature and its context.

56   BENNETT, J.A.W. <u>Chaucer at Oxford and Cambridge</u>. Oxford:
      Oxford University Press; Toronto: University of Toronto
      Press, 1974, 131 pp.
         From university and shire records, documents the historical
      accuracy of the local color in Miller's Tale and Reeve's Tale.
      Substantiates Chaucer's familiarity with Oxford, Cambridge, and
      their locales (but does not argue for Chaucer's attendance at

either university), indicating that Chaucer's poetic technique
was affected by the life around him as well as the conventions of
the fabliau. Examines the library records of Merton College,
Oxford, to clarify what resources were available in Chaucer's
day, especially those that relate to Treatise on the Astrolabe
and Equatorie of the Planets.

57   BOWDEN, MURIAL. A Reader's Guide to Geoffrey Chaucer. New
      York: Farrar, Straus & Giroux, 1964, 220 pp.
          Surveys in introductory fashion the part that "environment
      played in Chaucer's poetry" and shows how fourteenth-century life
      and thought infuse it. Short, discursive essays identify
      Chaucer's use of contemporary science, philosophy and religion,
      chivalry, literature, and society in Canterbury Tales and Troilus
      and Criseyde. His manipulation of the conventions of dream
      vision highlights discussions of Book of the Duchess, House of
      Fame, and Parliament of Fowls.

58   COULTON, G.G. Chaucer and his England. 1908. 8th ed.
      London: Methuen & Co., 1963, 300 pp.
          A classic, impressionistic description of Chaucer's life,
      his works, and, most importantly, the social history of his age.
      Topical arrangement and copious quotation of contemporary sources
      provide a lively atmosphere and much information, although some
      of the material is ethnocentric or outdated. Topics include
      marriage, the poor, law, revelry, and attitudes toward the
      clergy.

59   DuBOULAY, F.R.H. "The Historical Chaucer." In Geoffrey
      Chaucer. Edited by Derek Brewer. Writers and Their Back-
      ground. London: G. Bell & Sons, 1974. Reprint. Athens:
      Ohio University Press, 1976, pp. 33-57.
          Eloquently surveys the important social conditions and
      public affairs of fourteenth-century England, noting where they
      touch Chaucer's poetry and how they relate to his life.

60   GALWAY, MARGARET. "The Troilus Frontispiece." Modern
      Language Review 44 (1949):161-77.
          Analyzes the portraits, details, and historical backgrounds
      of the depiction of Chaucer reading to the royal audience in MS
      61, Corpus Christi College, Cambridge, arguing that the illustra-
      tion celebrates the life and accomplishments of Joan of Kent,
      mother of Richard II, in particular her patronage of Chaucer.

61   HUSSEY, MAURICE. "Chaucer's England." In An Introduction to
      Chaucer. By Maurice Hussey, A.C. Spearing, and James Winny.
      Cambridge: Cambridge University Press, 1965, pp. 28-55.
          Introduces the political and social backgrounds to
      Chaucer's life and poetry, clarifying the relations among
      economics, demographics, the plague, the Peasant's Revolt, and
      shifts of political power. Chaucer's pilgrims reflect contempo-

rary society, but Chaucer does not depict the major events of his day.

62   _____. Chaucer's World: A Pictorial Companion. London: Cambridge University Press, 1967, 172 pp.
A black-and-white pictorial index to Chaucer's England, arranged by topics associated with the Canterbury pilgrims, and combining medieval maps, art, architecture, and manuscript illuminations. Explanatory comments accompany the depictions of intellectual, religious, domestic, and court life, reflecting Chaucer's breadth and poetic range.

63   RICKERT, EDITH, comp. Chaucer's World. Edited by Clair C. Olson and Martin M. Crow. New York: Columbia University Press, 1948, 477 pp.
Fourteenth-century social records--translated and modernized--arranged under ten subject categories: London life, the home, training and education, careers, entertainment, travel, war, the rich and the poor, religion, death and burial. Further subdividing, judicious selection, and occasional notes clarify the relation between Chaucer's social and political life and this background.

See also entries 4, 5, 11, 65. For court life: 93, 185, 357-58, 366, 370, 527, 553, 593, 623, 860; art and culture: 231, 287; religious life: 205, 207, 235, 456, 464, 469, 490, 578, 602, 609-10, 760; city life: 257, 508, 513, 568; class distinctions and the lower classes: 248, 250, 334, 338-39, 350-51, 382, 392, 431, 443, 549-50, 552.

Biography

64   BLAND, D.S. "Chaucer and the Inns of Court: A Re-
      examination." English Studies 33 (1952):145-55.
           Explores the question of Chaucer's possible education at
      the Inns of Court by assessing historical records that pertain to
      the nature and development of the Inns. That Chaucer was edu-
      cated in such an "embryo university" is "attractive" and
      "plausible," but not certain.

65   BREWER, DEREK S. Chaucer and His World. New York: Dodd,
      Mead & Co., 1978, 224 pp.
           A biography of Chaucer and a social history of his age that
      presents solid information and a remarkably rich atmosphere.
      Reconstructs Chaucer as a sensitive man at the vanguard of his
      culture, documenting his early life and civic career, reflecting
      on his poetic vocation through impressionistic criticism of his
      works and occasional psychoanalysis. Generous illustrations
      illuminate fourteenth-century England and the growing awareness
      of "inner life" captured by Chaucer's poetry.

66   _____. An Introduction to Chaucer. London: Longman, 1984,
      270 pp.
           An introduction to Chaucer and his poetry, sketching the
      poet's psychology as reflected in his life and art. Surveys
      Chaucer's schooling, his civic career, and the major literary and
      intellectual traditions of his time. Presents Chaucer as an
      "Expositor" of his own poetry—a contribution to the ongoing dis-
      cussion of narrative persona. Distinguishes various impersonated
      voices and a "general Chaucerian" voice even early in the poet's
      career, but rejects the notion of a consistent background narra-
      tor as a "novelistic" technique unknown to Chaucer and therefore
      inappropriate to Chaucer criticism. The narrator of Troilus and
      Criseyde changes from book to book and the voices of Canterbury
      Tales shift with "Gothic" multiplicity. The chronological survey
      of the poetry touches on many traditional issues of theme and
      technique.

67   BURROW, J.A. "The Poet as Petitioner." <u>Studies in the Age of
      Chaucer</u> 3 (1981):61-75.
          Surveys autobiographical petitions in English poetry from
      Cynewulf to Chaucer and Gower, contrasting the sincere requests
      for aid from God or patron in the early poems with the
      "playfulness . . . of the Ricardian poet in his role as peti-
      tioner." Examines Chaucer's petitionary role in <u>Lenvoy to
      Scogan</u>, <u>Legend of Good Women</u>, and <u>House of Fame</u>.

68   CROW, MARTIN M., and OLSON, CLAIR C., eds. <u>Chaucer Life-
      records</u>. Oxford: Clarendon Press, 1966, 755 pp.
          The 493 records of Chaucer's life collected by J.M. Manly
      and Edith Rickert from civil, ecclesiastical, and private
      sources, organized under thirty-one subject headings. Each
      section includes the appropriate records, textual description of
      these records, and discussion of the materials as they pertain to
      Chaucer's "career as a courtier, diplomat, and civil servant."
      The texts, with their marginalia, are printed in their original
      French and Latin (one in Spanish), edited moderately for modern
      use. The commentary explains the references in the records and
      provides historical and social context. The editors make no
      attempt to resolve controversial issues but they do identify
      controversies in the footnotes. The appendix lists the records
      chonologically and the index cites persons and places.

69   GALWAY, MARGARET. "Geoffrey Chaucer, J.P. and M.P." <u>Modern
      Language Review</u> 36 (1941):1-36.
          Examines in detail the political and social circumstances
      of Chaucer's commission as a justice of the peace, his appoint-
      ment as clerk of the king's works, and his election as knight of
      the shire, clarifying his late relations with the royal family
      and examining the conditions and status of his political
      appointments.

70   GARDNER, JOHN [CHAMPLIN]. <u>The Life and Times of Chaucer</u>. New
      York: Alfred A. Knopf, 1977, 347 pp.
          Speculatively reconstructs Chaucer's personal and profes-
      sional biography from fourteenth-century social and intellectual
      history, Chaucer's <u>Life-Records</u> (entry 68), and his poetry,
      presenting his life through imaginative, narrative episodes.
      Where possible, biographical fiction is grounded in historical
      fact; where not possible, admiration for the poet or interpreta-
      tion of his poetry underlie confident conjecture. A "novelistic"
      biography by a respected novelist and solid critic of Chaucer.

71   HULBERT, JAMES ROOT. <u>Chaucer's Official Life</u>. Menasha, Wis.:
      G. Banta Publishing Co., 1912. Reprint. New York: Phaeton
      Press, 1970, 96 pp.
          Documents Chaucer's intricate political life from
      historical records, identifying those who held appointments and
      annuities similar to his, and clarifying the nature of his
      offices. Challenges the traditional view that John of Gaunt was

Chaucer's patron, arguing that Chaucer's career reflects "no exceptional favors" and that he was at times politically aligned with factions that opposed Gaunt. Also challenges the assumption that Chaucer had financial problems late in life, arguing that all available evidence suggests that "Chaucer led a prosperous and important life."

72   KANE, GEORGE. The Autobiographical Fallacy in Chaucer and
      Langland Studies. London: H.K. Lewis & Co., 1965, 20 pp.
         Argues that the oral delivery, close-knit audiences, and
      dream-vision conventions of fourteenth-century verse encouraged
      poets to identify themselves with their narrators. But such
      identification is part of a literary game, especially in
      Chaucer's and Langland's poetry which is clearly ironic and
      therefore cannot help us establish the events of their lives.

73   KERN, ALFRED ALLAN. The Ancestry of Chaucer. Baltimore:
      Lord Baltimore Press, 1906, 178 pp.
         Explores historical records and early scholarship to trace
      the meaning and use of the name "Chaucer," establish the gene-
      alogy of the poet for four generations, and detail the lives of
      his parents and grandparents. Provides some information about
      more distant relatives and family connections, and appends forty
      previously unpublished documents pertinent to Chaucer family
      history.

74   KRAUSS, RUSSELL. "Chaucerian Problems: Especially the
      Petherton Forestership and the Question of Thomas Chaucer."
      In Three Chaucer Studies. Edited by Carleton Brown. New
      York: Oxford University Press, 1932, 182 pp.
         Basic biographical information that establishes the date of
      Chaucer's marriage to Phillipa "as early as 1366," clarifies the
      consanguinity of Philippa and Katherine Swynford, distinguishes
      between Geoffrey and Thomas Chaucer's foresterships in Somerset,
      and argues for the theory that Thomas was John of Gaunt's bastard
      son by Philippa. Derives evidence from contemporary heraldry,
      public records of Geoffrey's and Thomas's careers, and early
      biographies. Contrasts Ruud (entry 76).

75   LELAND, VIRGINIA E. "Chaucer as Commissioner of Dikes and
      Ditches, 1390." Michigan Academician 14 (1981):71-79.
         Details the nature of Chaucer's responsibilities as commis-
      sioner of dikes and ditches, discusses other men who held the
      position in his time, and suggests echoes of his experience as
      commissioner in the characters and details of Canterbury Tales.

76   RUUD, MARTIN B. "VII. Thomas Chaucer: Son of the Poet." In
      Thomas Chaucer. Studies in Language and Literature, no. 9.
      Minneapolis: University of Minnesota, 1926. Reprint. New
      York: AMS Press, 1972, pp. 68-86.
         Challenges interpretations of the evidence that suggest
      John of Gaunt was the father of Thomas Chaucer, concluding that

his mother was "a Roet . . . the sister of Katherine Swynford" and that there is no "single good reason" for believing Thomas was not the son of Geoffrey. Contrasts Krauss (entry 74).

77   WAGENKNECHT, EDWARD. <u>The Personality of Chaucer</u>. Norman: University of Oklahoma Press, 1968, 168 pp.
       Attempts to describe Chaucer's personality by gleaning from his poetry evidence of his sensibilities and attitudes, aligning them where possible with biographical background and scholarly opinion. Surveys Chaucer's sensitivity to nature, society, and the arts and sciences, typifying him as a man of enthusiasm and learning. Documents the poet's orthodox view of chivalry and his awareness of social change, paralleling these with his poetic conventionality and willingness to experiment. Considers Chaucer's attitudes toward love and sex by examining the characters of Criseyde and the Wife of Bath, evidence from Chaucer's life, and the decorum of the <u>fabliaux</u>. Confronts the issue of Chaucer's supposed religious skepticism, and finds him, as in all things, thoughtful but orthodox, capable of satire without losing sympathy.

       See also entries 4-7, 11-12, 26, 45, 47, 55, 58-60, 63, 83, 86, 257, 350, 688, 689. For occasional verse: 88, 357, 819, 825, 835, 839, 847-48, 873, 889, 907-8, 917, 920.

The Persona

78   BETHURUM, DOROTHY. "Chaucer's Point of View as Narrator in
      the Love Poems." PMLA 74 (1959):511-20. Reprinted in Chaucer
      Criticism, vol. 2, "Troilus and Criseyde" & The Minor Poems,
      ed. Richard J. Schoeck and Jerome Taylor (Notre Dame, Ind.:
      University of Notre Dame Press, 1961), pp. 211-31.
          Studies Chaucer's developing personas in his love poems in
      light of the Neoplatonic poetic tradition of Boethius, Macrobius,
      Alain de Lille, and Jean de Meun. Behind his comic masks,
      Chaucer's appreciation of love is clear in his contrasting its
      fragility with the stability of learning and belief in God.

79   BLOOMFIELD, MORTON W. "The Gloomy Chaucer." In Veins of
      Humor. Edited by Harry Levin. Harvard English Studies, no.
      3. Cambridge, Mass.: Harvard University Press, 1972, pp. 57-
      68.
          Explores one aspect of Chaucer's humor—his persona's
      replies to a "querulous objector," apostrophic responses to un-
      spoken challenges or questions. Apostrophes that defend, for
      example, Criseyde's quick falling in love or Arveragus's con-
      cession to Dorigen's promise humorously delay the inevitable and
      playfully underscore the unreality of Chaucer's pose. Yet the
      ploy also posits an external observer or judge and thereby mixes
      gravity with levity.

80   DONALDSON, E. TALBOT. "Chaucer the Pilgrim." PMLA 69
      (1954):928-36. Reprinted in Chaucer Criticism, vol. 1, The
      "Canterbury Tales," ed. Richard J. Schoeck and Jerome Taylor
      (Notre Dame, Ind.: University of Notre Dame Press, 1960), pp.
      1-13; Speaking of Chaucer (New York: W.W. Norton & Co.,
      1970), pp. 1-12; Chaucer—The "Canterbury Tales": A Casebook,
      ed. J.J. Andersen (London: Macmillan & Co., 1974), pp. 93-104.
          A seminal essay that first distinguished Chaucer the pil-
      grim from Chaucer the poet. As a "fallible first person singu-
      lar" narrator, the pilgrim compliments his social superiors,
      patronizes his equals, and assesses his inferiors, helping to
      establish the "moral realism" of Canterbury Tales and contribut-
      ing largely to its comic irony.

81   DONNER, MORTON. "Chaucer and His Narrators: The Poet's Place
      in His Poems." Western Humanities Review 27 (1973):189-95.
           Traces the development of Chaucer's narrative personas,
      describing his subjective participation in Book of the Duchess
      and House of Fame, and his role as objective observer in
      Parliament of Fowls and Troilus and Criseyde. In Canterbury
      Tales, the separation of poet and pilgrim includes both subjec-
      tive and objective vantages.

82   GARBÁTY, THOMAS J. "The Degradation of Chaucer's 'Geffrey.'"
      PMLA 89 (1974):97-104.
           Assesses the evolution of Chaucer's "pose" or persona, ex-
      ploring his manipulation of various levels of perception. In his
      early poems, Chaucer's "reasonable" but blase´ pose ironically
      evokes humor in the face of dream-vision wonders. The less per-
      ceptive Canterbury narrator functions more obliquely and there-
      fore more suggestively.

83   HOWARD, DONALD R. "Chaucer the Man." PMLA 80 (1965):337-43.
      Reprinted in Chaucer's Mind and Art, ed. A.C. Cawley, Essays
      Old and New, no. 3 (London: Oliver & Boyd, 1969), pp. 31-45.
           Correlates Chaucer the man and the naive persona developed
      from House of Fame to Canterbury Tales. Chaucer forces his
      readers to project themselves into the "role of the implied
      author" in the same way that he, as bourgeois statesman, success-
      fully disarmed and manipulated the aristocracy. The man, like
      the persona, refuses to criticize, thereby implying the goodness
      of all.

84   PAYNE, ROBERT O. "Late Medieval Images and Self-Images of the
      Poet: Chaucer, Gower, Lydgate, Henryson, Dunbar." In
      Vernacular Poetics in the Middle Ages. Edited by Lois Ebin.
      Studies in Medieval Culture, no. 16. Kalamazoo, Mich.:
      Medieval Institute Publications, 1984, pp. 249-61.
           Contrasts various kinds of personas evident in the works of
      Chaucer and his near contemporaries, suggesting that the variety
      reflects their varied poetic purposes more than their individual
      personalities or the strictures of convention. In House of Fame,
      Chaucer manipulates his persona to clarify the difficulty of con-
      fronting poetry.

85   WATTS, ANN CHALMERS. "Chaucerian Selves—Especially Two
      Serious Ones." Chaucer Review 4 (1970):229-41.
           Describes the relations between various Chaucerian personas
      and the poetic worlds in which they appear, noting the fluctua-
      tions in these relations and the dominant tendency for the narra-
      tors to seem less real than their imaginary settings. However,
      at the end of Troilus and Criseyde and during Geffrey's rejection
      of fame in House of Fame, the narrators become tangible, dissolv-
      ing authorial distance, adopting serious tones, and condemning
      the poetic worlds they inhabit.

86   WINNY, JAMES. "Chaucer Himself." In <u>An Introduction to</u>
      <u>Chaucer</u>, by Maurice Hussey, A.C. Spearing, and James Winney.
      Cambridge: Cambridge University Press, 1965, pp. 1–27.
         Summarizes the details of Chaucer's political life and
      assesses the deprecatory self-portraits found in his poetry,
      suggesting that the personas of the poems reflect his awareness
      of the disparity between himself as an inspired poet and as a
      "commonplace individual."

         See also entries 10, 66, 87, 154, 162, 167. In <u>Canterbury</u>
      <u>Tales</u>: 169, 298, 503; <u>Troilus and Criseyde</u>: 795–96, 798; <u>Book</u>
      <u>of the Duchess</u>: 815–16, 819, 827; <u>Legend of Good Women</u>: 900.

Audience and Oral Recitation

87   BRONSON, BERTRAND H. "Chaucer's Art in Relation to His
      Audience." In Five Studies in Literature, by Bertrand H.
      Bronson et al. University of California Publications in
      English, vol. 8, no. 1. Berkeley: University of California
      Press, 1940, pp. 1-53.
         Assesses Chaucer's sensitivity to his aural audience,
      summarizing the evidence that he read his poetry aloud and
      surveying the ways that oral performance affected his works.
      Oral performance influenced Chaucer's habits of dialogue and
      transition, and restricted his subject matter and his rhetoric.
      His personal relationship with his audience encouraged topical
      allusions and his modest narrative pose, perhaps leading to the
      dramatic technique of Canterbury Tales.

88   GIFFIN, MARY. Studies in Chaucer and His Audience. Quebec:
      Leclerc Printers, 1956, 127 pp.
         Explores the historical and aesthetic issues involved in
      reading four Chaucerian poems as occasional pieces, appropriate
      in style and tone. The tale of St. Cecilia was composed to
      recognize the appointment of Adam Easton as cardinal priest to
      Santa Cecilia in Trastavere; its elevated mood and conservatism
      reflect it religious audience. Parliament of Fowls, appropriate
      to its courtly audience and the occasion of St. Valentine's day,
      balances hierarchical orders but takes some liberties with
      courtly codes. The tale of Constance, originally addressed to
      Chaucer's merchant peers, attempts to foster support for Costanza
      of Castile and John of Gaunt's Spanish campaign. Complaint to
      His Purse is a personal address to Henry, apt in tone and sensi-
      tive to its quite narrow audience.

89   GREEN, RICHARD FIRTH. "Women in Chaucer's Audience." Chaucer
      Review 18 (1983):146-54.
         Argues by assessing contemporary records and the direct
      addresses to the "implied audience" in Chaucer's poetry that the
      number of women in Chaucer's audience was small.

90   MEHL, DIETER. "The Audience of Chaucer's <u>Troilus and Criseyde</u>." In <u>Chaucer and Middle English Studies, in Honour of Rossell Hope Robbins</u>. Edited by Beryl Rowland. London: George Allen & Unwin, 1974, pp. 173-89. Reprinted in <u>Chaucer's "Troilus": Essays in Criticism</u>, ed. Stephen A. Barney (Hamden, Conn.: Archon Books, 1980), pp. 211-29.

    Studies the relation between Chaucer and his audience in <u>Troilus and Criseyde</u>, exploring how he addresses a "fictional audience" to compel his readers to be a "self-conscious and critical audience," especially in their assessment of the poem's characters. Chaucer uses techniques similar to those of novelists Henry Fielding and Laurence Sterne, leaving ambiguous many "crucial questions raised by his story," thereby engaging his audience.

91   _____. "Chaucer's Audience." <u>Leeds Studies in English</u> 10 (1978):58-74.

    Studies Chaucer's creation and manipulation of "fictional audiences" that provoke the "active participation" of the reader, especially in <u>Canterbury Tales</u>. Examines various links between the tales, the interrupted tales, and the opinions of the Host to show how Chaucer encourages participation by the fictional audience and sensitivity to the variety of responses tale-telling can provoke.

92   REISS, EDMUND. "Chaucer and His Audience." <u>Chaucer Review</u> 14 (1980):390-402.

    Surveys critical attempts to define Chaucer's audience and theorizes about his engagement of audience expectations, especially his manipulation of familiar doctrines and plots to produce irony and humor, and his exploration of familiar notions in unfamiliar contexts to encourage serious intellectual analysis.

93   STROHM, PAUL. "Chaucer's Audience." <u>Literature and History</u> 5 (1977):26-41.

    Sketches the possible social range of Chaucer's original audience, suggesting that a specific group was at its center: "later fourteenth-century knights, esquires, civil servants, and women of equivalent station." Associates Chaucer's "poetics of juxtaposition" with the social mobility, attitudes toward tradition and hierarchy, and concomitant "complexity of response" of this group.

94   _____. "Chaucer's Fifteenth-Century Audience and the Narrowing of the Chaucer Tradition." <u>Studies in the Age of Chaucer</u> 4 (1982):3-32.

    Contrasts Chaucer's fourteenth- and fifteenth-century audiences. The earlier, more elite audience preferred and encouraged Chaucer's innovations, while his more conservative poetry appealed to the class consciousness of the later group. Manuscript evidence of the reception of the Prioress's Tale parallels modern reactions and indicates how different audiences can "esteem a single work" for different reasons.

95   WILSON, GEORGE P. "Chaucer and Oral Reading." South Atlantic Quarterly 25 (1926):283-99.
      Surveys the custom of oral reading in ancient Greece, medieval France, and fourteenth-century England, attributing the custom in Chaucer's day to contemporary educational, linguistic, and paleographic conditions. Cites several passages that indicate that Chaucer intended his poetry to be read aloud.

      See also entries 8, 10, 55, 141, 154, 396, 424, 806. For oral recitation: 60, 72, 96, 134, 152, 158, 435, 581, 772, 830, 863.

Language

96   BATESON, F.W. "Could Chaucer Spell?" <u>Essays in Criticism</u> 25
(1975):2-24.
       Attributes much of Chaucer's metrical richness and his
variant spellings to his oral delivery. Spelling and elision
indicate the poet's willingness to modify "superficial syllables"
with more natural stresses. The G text of Prologue to <u>Legend of
Good Women</u> seems to best record Chaucer's mature spelling habits.
Compare Samuels (entry 105).

97   BRADDY, HALDEEN. "Chaucer's Bilingual Idiom." <u>Southern
Folklore Quarterly</u> 32 (1968):1-6. Reprinted in <u>Geoffrey
Chaucer: Literary and Historical Studies</u> (Port Washington,
N.Y.: Kennikat Press, 1971), pp.140-45.
       Surveys Chaucer's idiomatic expressions, ribald language,
and oaths to show how his "earthy" tales "reproduce faithfully
the speech of fourteenth-century England" which combined English
and French elements.

98   BURNLEY, DAVID. <u>A Guide to Chaucer's Language</u>. Norman:
University of Oklahoma Press; London: Macmillan & Co., 1983,
279 pp.
       Introduces the complexity of reading Chaucer by describing
contemporary grammar and syntax and exploring his evocative use
of vocabulary in various registers and collocational sets. Part
1 describes the basics of Chaucer's language in some detail,
discussing such features as parts of speech and techniques of
negation and coherence. Part 2 defines the resources available
to Chaucer for representing diverse dialects and social registers
by explaining the place of his late Middle English in linguistic
history. Also demonstrates how Chaucer achieves rich poetic
effects by capitalizing upon the fluid state of English in his
day and by manipulating the lexical assumptions of his audience,
especially those triggered by specific terms or sets of terms.

99   _____. "Inflexion in Chaucer's Adjectives." <u>Neuphilologische</u>
      <u>Mitteilungen</u> 83 (1982):169-77.
      Demonstrates that the use of inflectional -e of mono-
syllabic adjectives in the Hengwrt manuscript is very regular,
even though extended into "environments where it is not
etymologically correct." The Ellesmere is much less regular,
evidence that it is later than the Hengwrt although by the same
scribe.

100   ELLIOTT, RALPH W.V. <u>Chaucer's English</u>. Language Library.
      London: Andre Deutsch, 1974, 447 pp.
      Surveys the significant aspects of Chaucer's language by
discussing his pronunciation, grammar, syntax, and especially his
lexicon, documenting his deviation from contemporary norms.
Demonstrates the flexibility of his grammar and syntax in the
service of rhyme and meter and identifies his broad range of
rhetorical ornament, including puns, plays on names, classical
tropes, alliteration, and use of synonyms. Analyzes how syntax
and vocabulary produce the "pedagogic tone" of <u>Treatise on the</u>
<u>Astrolabe</u> and Parson's Tale in contrast to the abstruseness of
<u>Boece</u> and the intentional irony of Tale of Melibee. Describes
Chaucer's colloquial language, oaths, and technical terminology
in individual chapters and closes with a valuable assessment of
how he manipulates speech and dialogue to suggest the individuality of characters.

101   KERKHOF, J. <u>Studies in the Language of Geoffrey Chaucer</u>.   2d
      ed. Leidse Germanistische en Anglistische Reeks van de
      Rijksuniversiteit te Leiden, no. 1. Leiden: E.J. Brill and
      Leiden University Press, 1982, 515 pp.
      A descriptive analysis of Chaucer's grammar and usage,
organized according to the traditional parts of speech with
examples from Chaucer's works. Describes in intelligible
linguistic terminology the nature and functions of Chaucer's
usage, noting the influence of prosody and rhetoric upon his
language and his place in the development of the history of
English. Provides bibliography for each category, including the
various tenses, aspects, and moods of verbs, and the functions of
nouns, pronouns, articles, adjectives, adverbs, numerals, inter-
jections and conjunctions, and functional shift from one part of
speech to another.

102   KÖKERITZ, HELGE. <u>A Guide to Chaucer's Pronunciation</u>.
      Stockholm: Almqvist & Wiksell; New Haven, Conn.: Whitlock's,
      1954. Reprint. Medieval Academy Reprints for Teaching, no.
      3. Toronto: University of Toronto Press, 1978, 32 pp.
      A lucid introduction to Chaucer's pronunciation, phonology,
word contraction, stress, and final -e. Includes selections from
<u>Canterbury Tales</u> in simple phonetic transcription.

103   ROSCOW, G.H. Syntax and Style in Chaucer's Poetry. Chaucer
       Studies, no. 6. Cambridge: D.S. Brewer; Totowa, N.J.:
       Rowman & Littlefield, 1981, 168 pp.
          Compares Chaucer's syntax with that of contemporary
       romances, observing variations from Old English and Modern
       English syntactical patterns, and suggesting ways in which his
       "loose syntax" effects immediacy or colloquial flavor. Considers
       word-order, idiomatic usage, pleonasm, ellipsis, relative
       clauses, coordination, and parataxis, drawing examples from a
       range of Chaucerian works.

104   SALTER, ELIZABETH. "Chaucer and Internationalism." Studies
       in the Age of Chaucer 2 (1980):71-79.
          Views Chaucer's use of English, not as a "triumph of
       English over French," but as a natural development of French
       models produced in the English court. The milieu of the court,
       its patronage, and the French models encouraged Chaucer's use of
       English.

105   SAMUELS, M.L. "Chaucer's Spelling." In Middle English
       Studies: Presented to Norman Davis in Honour of His
       Seventieth Birthday. Edited by Douglas Gray and E.G. Stanley.
       Oxford: Clarendon Press, 1983, pp. 17-37.
          Through comparison with the Gower manuscripts, demonstrates
       that the spelling of Chaucerian manuscripts Hengwrt and Ellesmere
       is scribal rather than authorial, and argues that the manuscript
       of Equatorie of the Planets reflects Chaucer's own spelling.
       Uses rhymes and dialectical evidence, corroborating them with
       parallels from manuscripts of Boece and Treatise on the
       Astrolabe. Compare Bateson (entry 96).

106   SPEARING, A.C. "Chaucer's Language." In An Introduction to
       Chaucer, by Maurice Hussey, A.C. Spearing, and James Winny.
       Cambridge: Cambridge University Press, 1965, pp. 89-114.
          A concise and specific introduction to Chaucer's language
       and verse that places his dialect historically, clarifies in
       traditional fashion the details of his grammar, pronunciation,
       and versification, and summarizes the importance of medieval
       rhetorical principles in his poetry.

          See also entries 123-24, 130, 181, 259, 692. For
       colloquial speech: 66, 114, 131, 149-50, 191, 290, 332, 445,
       379, 395, 399, 716, 793, 814, 892.

Language

LEXICON

107   BAUM PAULL F.   "Chaucer's Puns."   <u>PMLA</u> 71 (1956):225-46.
       One of the earliest recognitions of Chaucer's lexical
sophistication. Corrects the traditional assumption that Chaucer
did not pun by surveying the rhetorical tradition of puns and
listing alphabetically more than one hundred puns from Chaucer's
corpus. Supplemented in "Chaucer's Puns: A Supplemental List,"
<u>PMLA</u> 73 (1958):167-70.

108   BRADDY, HALDEEN.   "Chaucer's Bawdy Tongue."   <u>Southern Folklore
       Quarterly</u> 30 (1966):214-22. Reprinted in <u>Geoffrey Chaucer:
       Literary and Historical Studies</u> (Port Washington, N.Y.:
       Kennikat Press, 1971), pp. 131-39.
       Chaucer's sexual and scatological vocabulary is largely
Anglo-Saxon. He uses it in association with low-class characters, or, more fastidiously, with the bourgeoisie and thereby
achieves a "crude but basic humor."

109   DONNER, MORTON.   "Derived Words in Chaucer's Language."
       <u>Chaucer Review</u> 13 (1978):1-15.
       Surveys Chaucer's neologistic derived words--the words he
apparently coined by adding affixes to familiar roots. Argues
that such words consistently enrich imagery and meaning even when
prompted by syntax, meter, or rhyme.

110   ELLIOTT, R.W.V.   "When Chaucer Swears."   In <u>Proceedings of the
       Twelfth Congress of the Australasian Universities Language and
       Literature Association</u>. Edited by A.P. Treweek. Sydney:
       Australasian Universities Language and Literature Association,
       1970, pp. 417-34.
       Surveys the swearing by Chaucerian characters, identifying
different kinds of oaths and curses, and exploring their impact
upon characterization, situation, and mood. Focuses upon
<u>Canterbury Tales</u> and <u>Troilus and Criseyde</u> but includes earlier
works, concluding that Chaucer's use of swearing is prevalent and
artful.

111   MERSAND, JOSEPH.   <u>Chaucer's Romance Vocabulary</u>. 2d ed. New
       York: Comet Press, 1939. Reprint. Port Washington, N.Y.:
       Kennikat Press, 1968, 188 pp.
       Tabulates the words Chaucer derived from the Romance lan-
guages, comparing his usage to that of his contemporaries, and
generalizing about Chaucer's language, the chronology of his
works, and his contributions to the development of English.
Chaucer's vocabulary included about eight thousand words, about
half of which are of Romance origin, nearly twice the percentage
found in John Gower's English verse, and three times the
percentage in <u>Mandeville's Travels</u>. The evolution of Chaucer's
Romance vocabulary parallels the "accepted chronology of his

works": his use of such words increased steadily until late in
his career when he began to abandon them, perhaps because he fell
out of favor with the Gallic court. Appends various tables,
including a list of Romance words introduced by Chaucer into
English.

    See also entries 48, 51, 53, 55, 97-98, 100, 137, 290,
378, 475, 633, 765. For puns: 51, 384, 397, 436, 506, 592, 600,
666, 881, 912.

Prosody

112   ADAMS, PERCY. "Chaucer's Assonance." <u>JEGP: Journal of</u>
       <u>English and Germanic Philology</u> 71 (1972):527-39.
           Surveys Chaucer's use of assonance, its effects in his
       poetry, and possible models for his use of this poetic device.
       For modifications, see Bruce W. Finnie, "On Chaucer's Stressed
       Vowel Phonemes," <u>Chaucer Review</u> 3 (1975):337-41.

113   BAUM, PAULL F. <u>Chaucer's Verse</u>. Durham: Duke University
       Press, 1961, 145 pp.
           Describes Chaucer's meter and prosody, examines passages of
       his most intense poetic embellishment, and explores his place in
       poetic tradition. His meter reflects both native English forms
       and French models, although we cannot be certain of the influence
       of contemporary speech nor sure how his audience "heard" his
       rhythms. Primarily narrative, his poetry mutes the extravagances
       of prosody in favor of "naturalness," except in rare cases of en-
       hancement. Yet he commands alliteration easily, firmly controls
       rhyme, and employs a wide range of grammatical and syntactical
       variation in lines and stanzas.

114   EVERETT, DOROTHY. "Chaucer's Good Ear." <u>Review of English</u>
       <u>Studies</u> 23 (1947):201-8. Reprinted in <u>Essays on Middle</u>
       <u>English Literature by Dorothy Everett</u>, ed. Patricia Kean
       (Oxford: Clarendon Press, 1955), pp. 139-48.
           Establishes Chaucer's imitative facility with rhythm and
       sound by assessing passages where he uses alliteration to recall
       heroic and hagiographic verse, and examining the "idiosyncracies"
       of the speech of select characters, particularly the Wife of
       Bath.

115   FIFIELD, MERLE. <u>Theoretical Techniques for the Analysis of</u>
       <u>Variety in Chaucer's Metrical Stress</u>. Ball State Monographs,
       no. 23. Publications in English, no. 17. Muncie, Ind.: Ball
       State University, 1973, 47 pp.
           Employs techniques of "objective" linguistic analysis to
       corroborate traditional assumptions about Chaucer's meter and
       pronunciation of final -e, applying Trager-Smith analysis of word

stress and generative analysis of phrasal stress. Chaucer's
syntax normally coincides with an iambic pattern.

116   HALLE, MORRIS, and KEYSER, SAMUEL JAY. "Chaucer and the Study
       of Prosody." College English 28 (1966):187-219.
       Devises a system to analyze Chaucer's stress, built on
patterns of contrastive rather than absolute stress. Assumes his
basic line to be decasyllabic, and accepts the frequent
pronunciation of final -e and French influence on accent.

117   LYNN, KAREN. "Chaucer's Decasyllabic Line: The Myth of the
       Hundred-Year Hibernation." Chaucer Review 13 (1978):116-27.
       Applies Halle and Keyser's (entry 116) system of metrical
analysis, comparing Chaucer with Hoccleve, Lydgate, Dunbar, and
Skelton. Tallies the variations between the later poets and
Chaucer to help account for their lack of virtuosity.

118   MAYNARD, THEODORE. The Connection between the Ballade,
       Chaucer's Modification of It, Rime Royal, and the Spenserian
       Stanza. Washington, D.C.: Catholic University Press, 1934,
       139 pp.
       Establishes the literary history of the ballade verse form,
and assesses Chaucer's use, transformation, and transmission of
the form modified as the rhyme royal stanza. Chaucer wrote no
strict ballades, but he emulated the form as practiced by
Machaut, Froissart, and Deschamps. Influenced by Italian
prosody, he sophisticated the stanza form, experimenting with
caesural variation and applying the stanza to new subjects.
Documents the tradition of rhyme royal after Chaucer, noting its
confusion with the original ballade, and argues that Chaucer's
rhyme royal stanza is the direct ancestor of the Spenserian
stanza.

119   OWEN, CHARLES A., Jr. "'Thy Drasty Rhymyng. . . .'" Studies
       in Philology 63 (1966):533-64.
       Studies Chaucer's manipulation of rhyme and rhyme patterns.
In various lyrics and short poems, especially Anelida and Arcite,
he experiments successfully with patterns built on French models
to create "emotional intensity." In Tale of Sir Thopas, he exploits subtleties of parody and form through emphatic rhymes. In
the rhyme royal of Troilus and Criseyde, he provides rich
dialogue and psychological depth. The couplets of Canterbury
Tales reflect his freedom and dexterity with rhyme.

120   ROBINSON, IAN. Chaucer's Prosody: A Study of the Middle
       English Verse Tradition. London: Cambridge University Press,
       1971, 263 pp.
       Treats the vexed issues of Chaucer's prosody through
sensitive reading and compromise, describing his mature verse-
line as "balanced pentameter," a combination of metrical and
rhythmic patterns that dominate English verse from Chaucer to
Wyatt. Analysis of previous critical assumptions, discussion of

fourteeth- and fifteenth-century prosodic traditions, and interpretive readings of sample Chaucerian passages show that such
concerns as pronunciation of final -e and variable stress are
unimportant. The phrasal rhythms of Chaucer's verse and its rich
metrical variation coincide well with manuscript punctuation and
encourage unproblematic readings unless distorted by modern
prosodic models or editorial practice. Essentially English, the
verse of Chaucer shares similarities with Langland's and Gower's,
and was imitated with relative success by later poets: Hoccleve,
Lydgate, Hawes, Skelton, Barclay, and Wyatt.

121   SAMUELS, M.L. "Chaucerian Final '-e.'" Notes and Queries,
       n.s. 19 (1972):445-48.
           Adduces grammatical evidence for the pronunciation of final
       -e in Chaucer's works, documenting the regularity of pronunci-
       ation in patterns that follow Old English usage. Responds to
       specific challenges of Chaucer's decasyllabic line by Southworth
       (entry 124) and Robinson (entry 120).

122   SOUTHWORTH, JAMES G. "Chaucer: A Plea for a Reliable Text."
       College English 26 (1964):173-79. Revised as "Chaucer's
       Prosody: A Plea for a Reliable Text," in Chaucer's Mind and
       Art, ed. A.C. Cawley, Essays Old and New, no. 3 (London:
       Oliver & Boyd, 1969), pp. 86-96.
           Argues against assuming that Chaucer's poetry was
       metrically regular. Iambic scanning of the verse is impossible
       when scribal punctuation is considered and when final -e is not
       pronounced. Editions should not make the texts appear metrically
       regular.

123   _____. "Chaucer's Final e in Rhyme." PMLA 62 (1947):910-35.
           Challenges the traditional assumption that Chaucerian
       rhymes demand pronunciation of final -e, arguing that elsewhere
       in Chaucer's lines final -e is inorganic, pronounced only for
       special poetic effects, and indefensible on the grounds of
       historical grammar. Final -e should not be pronounced in rhymes.
       For reply by E. Talbot Donaldson and Southworth's counterreply,
       see PMLA 63 (1948):1101-24; 64 (1949):601-9.

124   _____. Verses of Cadence: An Introduction to the Prosody of
       Chaucer and His Followers. Oxford: Basil Blackwell, 1954, 94
       pp.
           Challenges the traditional theory that Chaucer wrote iambic
       pentameter, describing the erratic history of the theory, and
       assessing the evidence of Chaucer's manuscripts. The iambic
       pentameter "myth" assumes that the single line is Chaucer's basic
       unit of verse and that final -e should be pronounced. But
       manuscripts of Chaucer and his followers suggest that his verse
       depends upon time rather than stress, that he wrote in rhetorical
       rather than metrical units, and that final -e should be silent.
       Uses musical notation to record Chaucer's rhythms. Supplementary
       application of this theory to the poetry of Chaucer and his

followers is available in Southworth's <u>Prosody of Chaucer and</u>
<u>His Followers</u> (Oxford: Basil Blackwell, 1962).

125   STANLEY, E.G. "Stanza and Ictus: Chaucer's Emphasis in
       <u>Troilus and Criseyde</u>." In <u>Chaucer und seine Zeit: Symposion</u>
       <u>für Walter F. Schirmer</u>. Edited by Arno Esch. Buchreihe der
       Anglia: Zeitschrift für englische Philologie. Tübingen: Max
       Niemeyer, 1968, pp. 123–48.
           Documents several patterns of repetition, bridging, and
       emphasis within and among Chaucer's rhyme royal stanzas in
       <u>Troilus and Criseyde</u>, showing how Chaucer manipulated the stanza.
       Suggests that the last line of the stanza and the stressed
       syllable preceding the caesura in that line receive consistent
       special attention.

126   _____. "The Use of Bob-Lines in <u>Sir Thopas</u>."
       <u>Neuphilologische Mitteilungen</u> 73 (1972):417–26.
           Describes the stanzaic variety produced in Tale of Sir
       Thopas by the bob-lines, clarifying their metrical effects and
       the ways manuscript punctuation represents such variety.

127   STEVENS, MARTIN. "The Royal Stanza in Early English Litera-
       ture." <u>PMLA</u> 94 (1979):62–76.
           Traces the history of the name of the "rhyme royal" stanza
       and its associations with high ceremonial verse in Chaucer's
       time, challenging its traditional association with James I of
       Scotland. Surveys Chaucer's use of the stanza, especially in Man
       of Law's Tale, and justifies the application of the term "prose"
       to the stanza.

128   SUDO, JAN. "Some Specific Rime-Units in Chaucer." <u>Studies in</u>
       <u>English Literature</u> (Tokyo) 45 (1969):221–36.
           Describes the "conventional" rhymes and "specific rime-
       units" in Chaucer's poetry, documenting his habit of deriving his
       rhymes from earlier French and English occurrence, and his
       tendency to associate given pairs of words consistently through
       rhyme, often a proper name and an appropriate attribute or
       quality.

129   TARLINSKAJA, MARINA G. "Meter and Rhythm of Pre-Chaucerian
       Rhymed Verse." <u>Linguistics</u> 121 (1974):65–87. Revised
       slightly as "The Formation of English Syllabo-Tonic Poetry,"
       in <u>English Verse: Theory and History</u>. De Proprietatibus
       Litterraum, Series Practica, no. 117 (The Hague: Mouton,
       1976), pp. 84–99.
           Places Chaucer's metrical innovations in the ongoing
       development of English verse, statistically contrasting his
       poetry with earlier romances and contemporary practice. Docu-
       ments the "high precision" of Chaucer's syllabic lines, that is,
       "the uniform number of ictuses and the almost complete identity
       of syllabic intervals with ictuses."

130   WEISS, ALEXANDER. "Chaucer's Early Translations from French:
        The Art of Creative Transformation." In <u>Literary and</u>
        <u>Historical Perspectives of the Middle Ages: Proceedings of</u>
        <u>the 1981 SEMA Meeting</u>. Edited by Patricia W. Cummins, Patrick
        W. Conner, and Charles W. Connell. Morgantown: West Virginia
        University Press, 1982, pp. 174-82.
            Examines Chaucer's creative use of enjambment and stress in
        <u>Romaunt of the Rose</u> and <u>An A.B.C.</u>, showing how these translations
        benefit from his manipulations of sense, sound, and syntax.

            See also entries 47, 55, 96, 181, 616, 892. For final -e:
        99-100, 102, 892.

Style and Rhetoric,
Including Ironic Technique

131   BENSON, ROBERT G. <u>Medieval Body Language: A Study of the Use of Gesture in Chaucer's Poetry</u>. Anglistica, no. 21. Copenhagen: Rosenkilde & Bagger, 1980, 170 pp.

     Analyzes references to bodily movement, manner, bearing, posture, and expression in Chaucer's poetry, linking such gestures to colloquial style and showing how they vivify action, produce irony, and establish character. In his early poems, Chaucer reproduces conventional gestures of romance and hagiography, modifying them somewhat in <u>House of Fame</u>, <u>Parliament of Fowls</u>, and <u>Legend of Good Women</u>. In the <u>fabliaux</u> of the <u>Canterbury Tales</u>, colloquial style and a wider range of gestures enliven action and parody conventional gestures, producing irony. Pandarus is individualized by his gestures in <u>Troilus and Criseyde</u>, Chaucer's most sustained and sophisticated use of gesture. Includes an appendix of gestures explicit in Chaucer.

132   BIRNEY, EARLE. "Is Chaucer's Irony a Modern Discovery?" <u>JEGP: Journal of English and Germanic Philology</u> 41 (1942):303-19.

     Surveys sensitivity to Chaucer's humor from the Ellesmere illustrator through the nineteenth century, noting how readers and critics generally responded positively to Chaucer's ironic comedy, although their emphases reflect their particular assumptions and interests.

133   BISHOP, IAN. "Chaucer and the Rhetoric of Consolation." <u>Medium Ævum</u> 52 (1983):38-50.

     Chaucer obliquely and ironically exploits traditional methods of consolation. Failed consolation conveys inexpressible grief in <u>Book of the Duchess</u> and establishes Troilus's distance from Pandarus in <u>Troilus and Criseyde</u>. Theseus's expedient consolation in Knight's Tale is a "resolution rather than a solution." Aurelius's consolation of Dorigen's complaint against the rocks encourages illusion in Franklin's Tale. Through the hag's "amplified" consolatory discussion of <u>gentilesse</u> in Wife of Bath's Tale, Chaucer makes game of the traditional "remedies against Fortune."

134   CROSBY, RUTH. "Chaucer and the Custom of Oral Delivery."
       <u>Speculum</u> 13 (1938):413-32.
            Collects examples of Chaucer's direct address to his
       audience as evidence of his oral delivery and identifies his use
       of oral conventions—epithetic adjectives, stock phrases,
       asseverations, and "religious beginnings and endings"—to
       demonstrate the influence of popular romances on him.

135   EVERETT, DOROTHY. "Some Reflections on Chaucer's 'Art
       Poetical.'" <u>Proceedings of the British Academy</u> 36 (1950):132-
       54. Reprinted in <u>Essays on Middle English Literature by
       Dorothy Everett</u>, ed. Patricia Kean (Oxford: Clarendon Press,
       1955), pp. 149-74; <u>Chaucer's Mind and Art</u>, ed. A.C. Cawley,
       Essays Old and New, no. 3 (London: Oliver & Boyd, 1969), pp.
       99-124.
            Identifies patterns of verbal repetition and formal
       parallelism in <u>Book of the Duchess</u>, <u>Parliament of Fowls</u>, and
       elsewhere. These patterns and the arrangement of rhetorical
       devices in the tales of the Pardoner, Manciple, and Nun's Priest
       demonstrate that Chaucer learned more from rhetorical handbooks
       than simple colors and techniques of adornment.

136   KIERNAN, KEVIN S. "The Art of the Descending Catalogue, and a
       Fresh Look at Alison." <u>Chaucer Review</u> 10 (1975):1-16.
            Studies Chaucer's manipulation of the typical head-to-toe
       <u>effictio</u> of beauty. Chaucer's descriptions of Criseyde, Emily,
       the Prioress, the Wife of Bath, Sir Thopas, Malyne, and es-
       pecially Alisoun of Miller's Tale modify conventions of the
       <u>effictio</u> to produce special effects.

137   KNIGHT, STEPHEN. <u>Rymyng Craftily: Meaning in Chaucer's
       Poetry</u>. Sydney: Angus & Robertson, 1973, 265 pp.
            Examines Chaucer's poetic style, summarizing critical
       opinion and evaluating his rhetorical figures, levels of diction,
       syntax, prosody, stylistic consistency, variety, and range.
       Criticizes <u>Anelida and Arcite</u> for inconsistency and Manciple's
       Tale for deviation from its prologue. Praises <u>Parliament of
       Fowls</u>, <u>Troilus and Criseyde</u>, and the tales of the Knight,
       Franklin, and Nun's Priest for their "meaning-implying poetic
       modulation." Cadence and rhetorical density establish authorial
       tone and the attitudes of high and low characters. Chaucer's
       poetry draws upon medieval rhetorical tradition, especially
       Geoffrey of Vinsauf, but it also repays close, modern attention
       to sound and sense. Appendix defines thirty-five rhetorical
       figures.

138   MacDONALD, DONALD. "Proverbs, <u>Sententiae</u>, and <u>Exempla</u> in
       Chaucer's Comic Tales: The Function of Comic Misapplication."
       <u>Speculum</u> 41 (1966):453-65.
            Surveys Chaucer's comic abusers of such "monitory elements"
       as proverbs, <u>sententiae</u>, and <u>exempla</u>: the foolish, the calcu-
       latedly shrewd, and the would-be deceivers who fail. Such char-

acterizations derive from the context in which the characters use
admonitory material, often irrelevantly or in order to manipulate
others.

139   MANLY, JOHN MATTHEWS. "Chaucer and the Rhetoricians."
       Proceedings of the British Academy 12 (1926):95-113.
       Reprinted in Chaucer Criticism, vol. 1, "The Canterbury
       Tales," ed. Richard J. Schoeck and Jerome Taylor (Notre Dame,
       Ind.: University of Notre Dame Press, 1960), pp. 268-90.
          Initiated the study of Chaucer's knowledge and use of
       rhetoric and rhetorical theory by summarizing the tradition and
       exemplifying its impact on Chaucer's poetry: his methods of
       organization and techniques of amplification and abbreviation.
       Argues that Chaucer abandoned an early, serious use of rhetorical
       figures, later putting them in the mouths of characters for
       dramatic, ironic effect. Challenged by Murphy (entry 140).

140   MURPHY, JAMES J. "A New Look at Chaucer and the Rhetori-
       cians." Review of English Studies 15 (1964):1-20.
          Challenges Manly's assertion (entry 139) that Chaucer was
       directly influenced by the medieval rhetoricians, specifically
       Geoffrey of Vinsauf, demonstrating how Chaucer's scattered allu-
       sions to rhetoric, style, and Vinsauf reflect a "generalized con-
       cept of rhetoric" rather than expertise, and how the rhetorical
       figures Chaucer uses were available to him in grammatical
       handbooks and French models.

141   MUSCATINE, CHARLES. Chaucer and the French Tradition.
       Berkeley: University of California Press, 1957, 282 pp.
          An important study that examines the styles of French
       poetry as they contribute to Chaucer's style, tracing the ideal-
       izing, nonrepresentational conventions of court romances from the
       early twelfth century to their epitome in Guillaume de Lorris's
       portion of Roman de la rose, and surveying the bourgeois but no
       less conventional characteristics of fabliaux, beast epics, and
       fables as they influence Jean de Meun's portion of the Roman.
       Chaucer fused these traditions in his mature poetry through
       juxtaposition, blending, and parody. Book of the Duchess
       reflects a relatively pure courtly style; increasing use of
       bourgeois conventions enrich House of Fame and Parliament of
       Fowls. Troilus and Criseyde balances courtliness and bour-
       geoisie, contrasting both with Boethian sublimity to disclose
       their limits. Canterbury Tales displays the courtly (Knight's
       and Clerk's tales), the bourgeois (Reeve's, Wife of Bath's, and
       Canon's Yeoman's tales), and rich mixtures (Miller's, Merchant's,
       and Nun's Priest's tales). The various styles and tones accumu-
       late to produce a Gothic tension between the ideal and the
       phenomenal.

142   _____. "Chaucer: Irony and Its Alternatives." In Poetry and
       Crisis in the Age of Chaucer. University of Notre Dame Ward-
       Phillips Lectures in English Language and Literature, no. 4.

Notre Dame, Ind.: University of Notre Dame Press, 1972, pp. 111-45.

Grants that irony is Chaucer's "characteristic response to the fourteenth-century dilemma," but identifies other strains in his poetry: dramatic realism, courtly idealism, epic heroism, romance, and especially pathos. Locates these styles in Chaucer's works and links them to contemporary sensibilities.

143   NORTON-SMITH, J. "Chaucer's Epistolary Style." In <u>Essays on Style and Language: Linguistic and Critical Approaches to Literary Style</u>. Edited by Roger Fowler. London: Routledge & Kegan Paul, 1966, pp. 157-65.

Discusses Chaucer's innovative and influential verse epistles in <u>Troilus and Criseyde</u>. Argues also that Horace's <u>Satires</u> and <u>Odes</u> influenced the syntax, imagery, tone, and structure of <u>Envoy to Scogan</u>, and, less clearly, <u>Envoy to Bukton</u>.

144   PAYNE, ROBERT O. <u>The Key of Remembrance: A Study of Chaucer's Poetics</u>. New Haven: Yale University Press, 1963, 258 pp.

A seminal study of Chaucer's poetic self-consciousness that surveys the development of medieval poetic theory out of classical poetic and rhetorical traditions, documents Chaucer's rich sensitivity to poetic and rhetorical concerns, and reads the corpus of Chaucer's poetry as an ongoing exploration of and experimentation with his poetic assumptions. Chaucer's poems examine the relations among tradition, ethics, and language. The early love visions counterpose the demands of tradition and ethics with the limits of poetry and the poet. <u>Canterbury Tales</u> experiments with individual styles and genres to explore the potential value of poetry. <u>Troilus and Criseyde</u>, Chaucer's most traditionally rhetorical poem, leads its audience beyond aesthetic reaction to ethical discovery.

145   _____. "Rhetoric in Chaucer: Chaucer's Realization of Himself as Rhetor." In <u>Medieval Eloquence: Studies in the Theory and Practice of Medieval Rhetoric</u>. Edited by James J. Murphy. Berkeley: University of California Press, 1978, pp. 270-87.

Places Chaucer's narrative techniques in the context of classical and Christian rhetoric, arguing that his reintroduction of rhetorical <u>ethos</u> differs from dominant medieval rhetorical theory and reclaims a commonplace of classical tradition. Contrasts Parson and Pardoner as preachers who, respectively, do and do not reflect themselves in their rhetoric.

146   PRESSON, ROBERT K. "The Aesthetic of Chaucer's Art of Contrast." <u>English Miscellany</u> 15 (1964):9-23.

Surveys Chaucer's penchant for using meaningful oppositions, disjunctions, and juxtapositions, exemplifying various contrasts in diction, imagery, characterization, and levels of style from <u>Canterbury Tales</u>.

147   REISS, EDMUND. "Chaucer and Medieval Irony." <u>Studies in the</u>
       <u>Age of Chaucer</u> 1 (1979):67–82.
           Links Chaucer's irony to Augustinian theory of the inade-
       quacy of language, tracing the tentative relation between word
       and truth in select passages of <u>Canterbury Tales</u> and the conclu-
       sion to <u>Troilus and Criseyde</u>. The essence of Chaucer's irony
       lies in his awareness that poetry must be superseded in order to
       be fulfilled.

148   _____. "Chaucer's Thematic Particulars." In <u>Signs and</u>
       <u>Symbols in Chaucer's Poetry</u>. Edited by John P. Herman and
       John J. Burke, Jr. University: University of Alabama Press,
       1981, pp. 27–42.
           Surveys representative examples of Chaucer's "thematic par-
       ticulars," his details that signify on a thematic or symbolic
       level. Such details as the number of Canterbury pilgrims, re-
       peated words or phrases, or suggestive references blend symbol
       and irony to do more than merely advance plot.

149   SALMON, VIVIAN. "The Representation of Colloquial Speech in
       the <u>Canterbury Tales</u>." In <u>Style and Text: Studies Presented</u>
       <u>to Nils Erik Enkvist</u>. Edited by Håkan Ringbom. Stockholm:
       Skriptor, 1975, pp. 263–77.
           Illustrates Chaucer's representation of colloquial speech,
       analyzing the linguistic and performative features of such speech
       as they appear in the dialogues in Chaucer's works. Discusses
       features of colloquial speech in three categories: expression,
       exchange, and intention.

150   SCHLAUCH, MARGARET. "Chaucer's Colloquial English: Its
       Structural Traits." <u>PMLA</u> 67 (1952):1103–16.
           Examines Chaucer's syntax to demonstrate how he suggests
       colloquial idiom. Analyzes syntactical "looseness," repetition,
       ellipsis, and "overlapping and shifted constructions" to show how
       he creates character through dialogue and atmosphere through
       description.

151   WENZEL, SIEGFRIED. "Chaucer and the Language of Contemporary
       Preaching." <u>Studies in Philology</u> 73 (1976):138–61.
           Surveys a variety of echoes from contemporary sermons and
       sermon handbooks in Chaucer's poetry, identifying not specific
       sources but plots, images, and terminology common to the sermons.
       Chaucer's narratives do not emulate sermons structurally, but
       they reflect his sensitivity to the "idiom of contemporary
       preaching."

           See also entries 45, 47, 87, 100, 114, 176, 181, 189, 287–
       88, 292, 336, 381, 439, 453, 714, 716, 718, 749, 751, 806, 812,
       890. For rhetoric: 3, 106, 277, 279, 284, 313, 341, 418, 526,
       635, 713, 849. For rhetorical figures, irony, and realism, see
       index.

Poetic Self-Consciousness
and Narrative Technique

152   BOITANI, PIERO. <u>La narrativa del medioevo inglese</u>. Bari:
       Adriatica, 1980. Translated by Joan Krakover Hall. <u>English
       Medieval Narrative in the Thirteenth and Fourteenth Centuries</u>.
       Cambridge: Cambridge University Press, 1982, 318 pp.
          Discusses Chaucer's works as the culmination of the
       medieval English narrative tradition, examining the growing
       literary self-consciousness of pre-Chaucerian works and demon-
       strating the function of self-consciousness in Chaucer's corpus.
       Part 1 summarizes and describes various narrative forms—homily,
       romance, dream vision, and narrative collection—tracing a com-
       plex pattern of growth from oral, hortatory works to literary,
       intellectual ones. In Part 2, discussion of Chaucer's dream
       visions, <u>Troilus and Criseyde</u>, and <u>Canterbury Tales</u> (in particu-
       lar Pardoner's Tale and Nun's Priest's Tale) establishes that
       Chaucer wrote to be read (rather than heard) and often wrote
       about reading. He modified tradition and reflected contemporary
       Italian self-consciousness, producing works uniquely literate.

153   BREWER, DEREK [S]. "Towards a Chaucerian Poetic."
       <u>Proceedings of the British Academy</u> 60 (1974):219-52. Printed
       separately. London: Oxford University Press, 1974.
       Reprinted in <u>Chaucer: The Poet as Storyteller</u>. (London:
       Macmillan Press), 1984, pp. 54-79.
          Examines the ways in which Chaucer's narratives "mean"—the
       ways they compel an audience to make a "complex interrelated
       structure in the imagination." Assesses Chaucer's uses of
       allegory, fantasy, truth-claims, rhetoric, and neoclassical
       precision, and concentrates on the ways conventional structures
       create intelligibility and coherence.

154   BURLIN, ROBERT B. <u>Chaucerian Fiction</u>. Princeton: Princeton
       University Press, 1977, 302 pp.
          Considers Chaucer's major works against a background of
       contemporary epistemology. Studies the role or roles of his
       narrators, tracing a logical (not chronological) development in
       his exploration of what can be known through poetry and how it
       can be known. Chaucer's "Poetic Fictions" (<u>Legend of Good Women</u>,

House of Fame, Book of the Duchess) speculate on "the poet's
relation to his audience" and the epistemological value of
poetry. His "Philosophic Fictions" (Parliament of Fowls,
Knight's Tale, Troilus and Criseyde, Clerk's Tale) analyze the
narrative process, exploring poetry's philosophical range. His
"Psychological Fictions" (select Canterbury tales) examine
through various narrators the "unspoken motives for telling a
tale as well as the teller's pronounced intention."

155   DAVID, ALFRED. The Strumpet Muse: Art and Morals in
        Chaucer's Poetry. Bloomington: Indiana University Press,
        1976, 280 pp.
        Traces the development of Chaucer's idea of the value of
poetry, describing his early works as his attempts to be an ideal
conventional poet, observing his increasingly self-conscious
dexterity with the art of illusion in Troilus and Criseyde and
Legend of Good Women, and analyzing his distrust of poetry's
"potential for expressing moral truths" evident in Canterbury
Tales. Explores the ambivalent opposition between Chaucer's
desire to be a didactic poet and his emotional commitment to
human vitality, reading his works as poems about poetry or reflections of personal struggle with the poet's role. Early chapters survey the growth of this ambivalence, while the bulk of the
work assesses the "ironic images of the poet embodied in the
various tellers of the Canterbury tales," especially the Miller,
the Man of Law, the Wife of Bath, and the Prioress.

156   DIEKSTRA, F. "Chaucer's Way with His Sources: Accident into
        Substance and Substance into Accident." English Studies 62
        (1981):215-36.
        Discusses the ways in which Chaucer modifies traditional
materials to produce original effects: his welding of disparate
traditions, his manipulation of genre conventions, and his
juxtaposing idealism and realism.

157   FICHTE, JOERG O. Chaucer's "Art Poetical": A Study of
        Chaucerian Poetics. Studies and Texts in English, no. 1.
        Tübingen: Narr, 1980, 137 pp.
        Describes a Chaucerian poetics by examining the thematic
interaction of courtly love, morality, order, and poetry in
several Chaucerian narratives, observing development from his
"limited awareness of the power of poetry to the recognition that
the poetic art equals the paradigmatic act of creation in a world
characterized by confusion." Since grief overwhelms love, the
only "positive resolution" of Book of the Duchess is the consolation the narrator receives from writing the poem (compare
Robinson, entry 133). Similarly, poetry seeks to mitigate the
destabiliizing effects of love in Parliament of Fowls. House of
Fame subordinates morality to poetic exploration and challenges
authority. Artistic ordering imposes control on "dissonant
thematic material" in Knight's Tale, one of the many investiga-
tions of poetry as a partial solution to the disorder of life.

158   FRANCIS, W. NELSON. "Chaucer Shortens a Tale." PMLA 68
       (1953):1126-41.
           Surveys Chaucer's narrative "self-conscious abbreviation"--
       his techniques for signaling omitted details, accelerated pace,
       summarizing, and shortening. Attributes such abbreviation to
       three causes: lengthy source material, Chaucer's recognition of
       his "tendency to prolixity," and, most significantly, his ability
       to maintain audience attention and create humor in ways derived
       from oral delivery.

159   JORDAN, ROBERT M. Chaucer and the Shape of Creation: The
       Aesthetic Possibilities of Inorganic Structure. Cambridge,
       Mass.: Harvard University Press, 1967, 264 pp.
           Defines the inorganic, associative system of medieval
       aesthetics grounded in Pythagorean number theory and Platonic
       ideas of rational order, and carried into the Middle Ages by
       Augustine, Boethius, and Macrobius. Analogous to the rigorously
       structured and clearly divisible Ptolemaic finite universe, this
       aesthetic system is evident in Gothic architecture and Dante's
       Commedia as well as in Chaucer's major works. Troilus and
       Criseyde is best understood in terms of a hierarchy of
       perspectives wherein narrative intrusions clearly separate the
       work into discrete, cumulative parts. Troilus, Pandarus, the
       narrator, and finally the poet in the Epilogue offer distinct
       perspectives on love. Structurally, Canterbury Tales is better
       understood as an additive collocation than as a unified,
       realistic drama. Dramatic unity is a modern concern. The tales
       offer a medieval structure of prefabricated units in a controlled
       outline, as exemplified by the Wife of Bath's Prologue and the
       tales of the Merchant, Knight, Miller, Clerk, and Parson.

160   RENOIR, ALAIN. "Tradition and Moral Realism: Chaucer's
       Conception of the Poet." Studia Neophilologica 35 (1963):199-
       210.
           Discusses Chaucer's Retraction and his comments about his
       own poetry, exploring apparent inconsistencies and concluding
       that Chaucer conceived of the poet as a "moral realist," familiar
       with rhetorical tradition but sensitive enough to record his own
       age and convey morality.

161   SCHAAR, CLAES. Some Types of Narrative in Chaucer's Poetry.
       Lund Studies in English, no. 25. Lund: Gleerup; Copenhagen:
       Ejnar Munkgaard, 1954, 193 pp.
           A theoretical exploration of narrative technique in
       Chaucer's poetry and its tradition, attempting to describe
       Chaucer's dependencies and innovations. Defines three kinds of
       narrative, their syntactic and stylistic characteristics, and
       their occurrences in the classical and medieval works known to
       Chaucer. Chaucer's "summary narrative" with its corollary
       "contrasting summary" is his most innovative technique, his means
       to appropriate sources succinctly and create associative echoes.
       He uses "close chronology" in his later, realistic tales and puts

it to unusual "preparatory" use in his early poems. The more digressive "loose chronological narrative" is rare in Chaucer's poetry, indicating his economy and talent for drama. Chaucer achieves his most striking effects by juxtaposing rambling and condensed styles.

162   SKLUTE, LARRY. <u>Virtue of Necessity: Inconclusiveness and Narrative Form in Chaucer's Poetry</u>. Columbus: Ohio State University Press, 1984, 167 pp.

    Addresses the "inconclusive form" of Chaucer's major poetry, that is, incompleteness, failure to answer questions raised, or offering of obviously partial answers. Loose, associative form typifies Chaucer's early dream visions, leading the reader to conceptual inconclusiveness that matches the discomfiture of the personas. The narrator's personal involvement in <u>Troilus and Criseyde</u> qualifies the historicity of the story, raising unanswered questions about the subjectivity of any narrated action. <u>Legend of Good Women</u> combines vision and history, freeing Chaucer from authority and enabling him to capitalize upon extreme subjectivity. Unlike his other works, Chaucer's <u>Canterbury Tales</u> is intentionally inconclusive; it exploits various subjective narrators to express a pluralistic view of reality, a view with precedent in late-medieval epistemology.

    See also entries 3, 8, 10, 47. For poetic self-consciousness: 84, 144, 192, 277A, 300, 303, 702, 812, 826, 867-68, 890-91, 894, 900; narrative technique: 93, 294, 725, 728, 806-7, 824, 855, 883.

Prose Technique

163 SCHLAUCH, MARGARET. "The Art of Chaucer's Prose." In Chaucer
and Chaucerians: Critical Studies in Middle English
Literature. Edited by D.S. Brewer. London: Thomas Nelson &
Sons; University: University of Alabama Press, 1966.
Reprint. Norwich: Nelson's University Paperbacks, 1970, pp.
140-63.
  Argues that all of Chaucer's prose includes a certain
amount of repetition and verbal echo for clarity, but that use of
vocatives, apostrophes, and pronouns of direct address distinguish Treatise on the Astrolabe. Parson's Tale includes a fair
range of rhetorical devices. Cadenced art-prose characterizes
the more eloquent Tale of Melibee and Boece without becoming
mannered.

164 _____. "Chaucer's Prose Rhythms." PMLA 55 (1950):568-89.
  Surveys critical assessments of Chaucer's prose and
establishes the influence upon him of classical tradition of
cadenced cursus, demonstrating his modifications of typical
patterns by crossing word boundaries and introducing metrical
variety. Analyzes the appearance of cursus patterns in Boece,
Tale of Melibee, Parson's Tale, and Treatise on the Astrolabe.

  See also entries 100, 618.

Classical and Late-Classical
Literary Relations

165   DEAN, NANCY. "Chaucer's Complaint: A Genre Descended from
       the Heroides." Comparative Literature 19 (1967):1-27.
          Surveys the complaint genre and suggests that Ovid's
       Heroides influenced Chaucer's Complaint of Mars. Chaucer's
       complaints to Pity, His Lady, and of Venus are conventional, but
       dramatic context enriches the complaint of the Black Knight in
       Book of the Duchess as Ovidian irony does the Complaint of Mars.

166   _____. "Ovid's Elegies from Exile and Chaucer's House of
       Fame." Hunter College Studies, no. 3 (1966):75-90.
          Suggests that Ovid's Tristia and Ex Ponto "may have been an
       important influence" on book 3 of House of Fame, both for spe-
       cific details and for the conceptions of Fame, Fortune, Rumor,
       and their relation to men.

167   FYLER, JOHN M. Chaucer and Ovid. New Haven: Yale University
       Press, 1979, 216 pp.
          Compares Chaucer to Ovid, identifying their mutual expres-
       sion of the "comic pathos of human frailty," and tracing how each
       explores this pathos through manipulation of biased or reduction-
       istic personae. Offers Ovidian precedent for Chaucer's narra-
       tors, assessing their comic value and their relation to Chaucer's
       world view. In House of Fame, the narrator tries unsuccessfully
       to understand "structures that immediately fall apart." In Book
       of the Duchess and Parliament of Fowls, the narrators fail to
       understand the facts of nature. The narrator of Legend of Good
       Women retells stories, but Alceste forces him to omit much of the
       traditional material. Identification with their characters
       limits the narrators of Troilus and Criseyde and Knight's Tale.
       Canterbury Tales portrays several unresolved perspectives, in-
       cluding the Manciple's banality and the Nun's Priest's wry
       rhetoric.

168   HARBERT, BRUCE. "Chaucer and the Latin Classics." In
       Geoffrey Chaucer. Edited by Derek Brewer. Writers and Their
       Background. London: G. Bell & Sons, 1974. Reprint. Athens:
       Ohio University Press, 1976, pp. 137-53.

Describes medieval access to classical Latin literature through manuscripts of miscellanea and florilegia (collections of excerpts). Suggests what Chaucer probably knew of classical authors, and surveys Chaucer's use of this literature--his adjustments through mistranslation and change of context, and his reshaping to fit medieval conventions.

169   HOFFMAN, RICHARD L. Ovid and the "Canterbury Tales."
      Philadelphia: University of Pennsylvania Press, 1966, 229 pp.
      Surveys Chaucer's relations to Ovid in Canterbury Tales,
suggesting that the Roman poet may have inspired the frame, the
unifying theme of love, and the sophisticated manipulation of
narrators. Catalogs Chaucer's direct allusions to Ovid, comparing Chaucer's derivative passages with Ovidian originals and with
medieval analogues and commentaries. Treats at length General
Prologue, Knight's Tale, Wife of Bath's Prologue, and Franklin's
Tale, and somewhat more briefly, Man of Law's Prologue, the
Monk's account of Hercules, Tale of Melibee, and the tales of the
Miller, Wife of Bath, Summoner, Merchant, Squire, Physician, and
Manciple.

170   JEFFERSON, BERNARD L. Chaucer and the "Consolation of
      Philosophy." Princeton: Princeton University Press, 1917.
      Reprint. New York: Gordian Press, 1968, 173 pp.
      A seminal investigation that catalogs Chaucer's borrowings
from Boethius, examines the relation of Chaucer's Boece to
Boethius's Consolation of Philosophy, gauges the influence on
Chaucer of Boethian concepts of fortune, Providence, happiness,
and gentilesse, and discusses Chaucer's use of the Consolation in
Troilus and Criseyde, Knight's Tale, and Truth. Chaucer knew the
Consolation through the Latin original, Jean de Meun's translation, and Nicholas Trivet's commentary. He absorbed its thought
and imagery so thoroughly that his poetry reflects intense and
consistent concern with the same fundamental questions.

171   MINNIS, A.J. Chaucer and Pagan Antiquity. Chaucer Studies,
      no. 8. Woodbridge, Suffolk: Boydell & Brewer; Totowa, N.J.:
      Rowman & Littlefield, 1982, 208 pp.
      Assesses Chaucer's Troilus and Criseyde and Knight's Tale
as romans d'antiquite. Anachronistic only in their social conventions, these works reflect Chaucer's conscious and sophisticated attempt to represent the philosophy and faith of the pagan
past, primarily its fatalism, polytheism, and idolatry. Surveys
the sources of Chaucer's understanding of the pre-Christians and
examines his characters in the context of their analogues to show
that the poet emphasized not only the limitations of the pagans
but their "shadowy perfection." Particularly wise characters
like Theseus anticipate Christianity. Fatalism mars Troilus's
love. Other characters considered include Calkas, Cassandra,
Criseyde, the narrator of Troilus and Criseyde, and the "young
fatalists" of Knight's Tale: Emelye, Arcite, and Palamon.

172   PAYNE, F. ANNE. <u>Chaucer and Menippean Satire</u>. Madison:
      University of Wisconsin Press, 1981, 302 pp.
         Traces the history of Menippean satire and demonstrates its
      impact on Chaucer's irony, diversity, and disjunctions. The
      Menippean tradition in Lucan, Petronius, Apuleius, Martianus
      Capella, and especially Boethius provide context for discussion
      of three Chaucerian narratives. In <u>Troilus and Criseyde</u>, follow-
      ing Boethius's unresolved conflation of Cynical, Platonic,
      Aristotelian, and Augustinian thought, Chaucer poses a tragedy of
      disjunction between event and character. His Nun's Priest's Tale
      is a "gleeful attack" on theoretical explanations that disguise
      the Priest's sense of empty commitment. Knight's Tale parodies
      Boethius's <u>Consolation of Philosophy</u> and, in Menippean fashion,
      undercuts the Menippean acceptance of conflict.

173   SARNO, RONALD A. "Chaucer and the Satirical Tradition."
      <u>Classical Folia</u> 21 (1967):41–61.
         Summarizes Chaucer's place in satirical tradition, suggest-
      ing that he may have known Horace's <u>Satires</u>, and arguing that if
      he did not, he combines moral censure with amused acceptence in
      Horatian fashion. Far from Juvenalian invective or the Christian
      complaint tradition of Jerome that most of his contemporaries
      follow, Chaucer's spirit is Horatian, especially his use of
      double entendre.

174   SHANNON, EDGAR F. <u>Chaucer and the Roman Poets</u>. Harvard
      Studies in Comparative Literature, no. 7. Cambridge, Mass.:
      Harvard University Press, 1929, 423 pp.
         Catalogs Chaucer's references and allusions to classical
      authors, including Statius, Lucan, Valerius Flaccus, Claudian,
      Horace, Juvenal, Persius, Catullus, Vergil, and especially Ovid.
      Examines the references to determine Chaucer's knowledge of these
      authors at firsthand or through <u>florilegia</u>. Investigates
      Chaucer's use of Ovid most extensively, considering the Ovidian
      influence on each of Chaucer's major poems and concluding that he
      followed Ovid in technique, realism, attitudes toward women, and
      use of allusions. The Ovidian works Chaucer knew most intimately
      were <u>Heroides</u> and <u>Metamorphoses</u>. Suggests that Chaucer's con-
      tact with Italian poetry contributed to his familiarity with
      classical literature, and notes where he may have borrowed clas-
      sical references from French and Italian sources.

         See also entries 8, 47, 144–45, 164, 182, 252, 308, 418,
      702, 811, 826, 846, 868–69, 894. For individual classical and
      late-classical authors and works, see index.

Medieval Latin Literary Relations

175   Chaucer Library. General editor Robert E. Lewis. Athens:
       University of Georgia Press, 1978-.
       A series of publications intended to present texts that
       Chaucer knew in the form in which he probably knew them. Three
       volumes have been published so far: Robert E. Lewis, ed., De
       miseria conditionis, by Lotario dei Segni (Pope Innocent III)
       (1978); Sigmund Eisner, Jr., ed., The Kalendarium of Nicholas of
       Lynn, trans. Gary MacEoin and Sigmund Eisner (1980); Siegfried
       Wenzel, ed., Summa virtutem de remediis anime (1984). In prepa-
       ration are: alchemical treatises, edited by E.H. Duncan and John
       Reidy; "Book of Wikked Wives," edited by R.A. Pratt, Ralph Hanna
       III, and Traugott Lawler; St. Jerome, "Epistola Adversus
       Jovinium," edited by John P. Brennan, Jr.; Nicholas Trevet, "Les
       Cronicles," edited by William G. Provost; Boccaccio, "Il
       Teseida," edited by William E. and Edvige A. Coleman; Fray Juan
       Garcia de Castrojeriz, "Regimento de Principes," edited by Martha
       S. Waller; "Summa de viciis abbreviata," edited by Siegfried
       Wenzel; Marie de France, Pierre de St. Cloud, and le Clerc de
       Troyes, Cock and Fox Episodes, edited by Margaret E. Winters.

176   DRONKE, PETER, and MANN, JILL. "Chaucer and the Medieval
       Latin Poets." In Geoffrey Chaucer. Edited by Derek Brewer.
       Writers and Their Background. London: G. Bell & Sons, 1974.
       Reprint. Athens: Ohio University Press, 1976, pp. 154-83.
       Part A (by Dronke) surveys Chaucer's use of Latin cosmo-
       logical poetry (Bernard Silvestris, Alain de Lille), Trojan
       poetry (Joseph of Exeter, Frigii Daretis Ylias), and poetic
       rhetoric (Geoffrey of Vinsauf). Part B (by Mann) demonstrates
       how Latin satirical tradition (Goliards, Speculum Stultorum,
       Walter of Châtillon) influenced Chaucer's satiric technique in
       Wife of Bath's Prologue, that is, the use of orthodox arguments
       and rhetoric to support unorthodox thought.

177   FLEMING, JOHN V. "Gospel Asceticism: Some Chaucerian Images
       of Perfection." In Chaucer and Scriptural Tradition. Edited
       by David Lyle Jeffrey. Ottawa: University of Ottawa Press,
       1984, pp. 183-95.

Argues for the pervasive influence of the literature of
ascetic ideals on Chaucer's characterizations, citing the impact
of works by, respectively, William of Saint-Amour, Bonaventure,
Peter Damian, and Jerome on details of the portraits of the
Summoner, Pardoner, Monk, and Absolon of Miller's Tale.

178   PRATT, ROBERT A. "Chaucer and the Hand That Fed Him."
       Speculum 41 (1966):619-42.
          Demonstrates Chaucer's use of a preacher's manual like John
       of Wales's Communiloquium sive summa collationem as a source for
       sententiae and exempla in Wife of Bath's Prologue and Tale,
       Summoner's Tale, Pardoner's Tale, and elsewhere, comparing
       passages from Chaucer, John, and their progenitors to show how
       Chaucer's text follows John's more closely than the originals,
       even when the Ellesmere manuscript glosses cite the originals.
       Chaucer used the friarly text to help characterize his insincere
       preachers, expecting his audience to recognize the nature of the
       materials.

          See also 140, 144-45, 151, 182, 229, 338, 252, 403, 569,
       626, 651, 694-96, 698, 702, 705, 751, 846. For individual
       medieval Latin authors and works, see index.

Continental Literary Relations

179   BOITANI, PIERO. <u>Chaucer and Boccaccio</u>. Medium Ævum
       Monographs, no. 8. Oxford: Society for the Study of Medieval
       Languages and Literature, 1977, 210 pp.
           Documents Chaucer's use of Boccaccio's <u>Teseida</u> in Knight's
       Tale and explores the impact of the Italian poem upon his intel-
       lectual and poetic career. Knight's Tale differs in style and
       characterization from its source, but it is firmly rooted in its
       iconography and culture. <u>Teseida</u> inspired Chaucer to reinterpret
       the poetry of Ovid, Statius, and the <u>Roman de la rose</u>; it intro-
       duced Chaucer to early humanism and helped shape his poetic
       technique.

180   CUMMINGS, HUBERTIS M. <u>The Indebtedness of Chaucer's Works to
       the Italian Works of Boccaccio</u>. Menasha, Wis.: George Banta
       Publishing Co., 1916. Reprint. New York: Haskell House,
       1965, 202 pp.
           A collection of essays that examines Chaucer's use of
       Boccaccio's vernacular works and concludes that he was familar
       with only <u>Filostrato</u> and <u>Teseida</u>, that he neither knew Boccaccio
       personally nor sought to emulate him, and that his debt was
       merely "that of a borrower." Somewhat dated, the discussion of
       <u>Filostrato</u> and <u>Troilus and Criseyde</u> places the two within a
       single romance tradition rather than emphasizing Chaucer's alter-
       ations. Chaucer's use of <u>Teseida</u> suggests that he wrote his
       version with the Knight clearly in mind as narrator. Other
       discussions deny attempts to establish influence on Chaucer of
       Boccaccio's <u>Filocolo</u>, <u>Amorosa Visione</u>, <u>Ameto</u>, <u>Corbaccio</u>,
       <u>Decameron</u>, and others.

181   FISHER, JOHN H. "Chaucer and the French Influence." In <u>New
       Perspectives in Chaucer Criticism</u>. Edited by Donald M. Rose.
       Norman, Okla.: Pilgrim Books, 1981, pp. 177-91.
           Surveys the influence of French and English traditions on
       Chaucer's poetic style, focusing on stress and meter, and con-
       cluding that "Chaucer's idiom and music" are based on French
       models from which he fashioned "a completely harmonious and
       idiomatic equivalent in English."

182   MILLER, ROBERT P., ed. Chaucer: Sources and Backgrounds.
       New York: Oxford University Press, 1977, 522 pp.
          Selected translations from forty-eight works: biblical,
       medieval, and classical. Each selection accompanied is by a
       brief introduction discussing its place in medieval culture and
       its relation to Chaucer. Intended for classroom use, materials
       are arranged topically and cross-referenced. Categories include:
       Creation and Fall, medieval literary theory, selected narrative
       sources, the three estates, antifraternal texts, modes of love,
       marriage and good women, antifeminist tradition, and end of the
       world and last judgment.

183   OLSON, GLENDING. "Deschamps' Art de dictier and Chaucer's
       Literary Environment." Speculum 48 (1973):714-23.
          Summarizes the theory of poetry expressed in Deschamps's
       L'art de dictier et de fere chancons, balades, virelais et
       rondeaulx and suggests that Chaucer's lyrics reflect its non-
       didactic and pleasure-oriented aesthetic rather than the more
       often discussed tradition of medieval moralism.

184   PRATT, ROBERT A. "Chaucer and Les Cronicles of Nicholas
       Trevet." In Studies in Language, Literature, and Culture of
       the Middle Ages and Later. Edited by E. Bagby Atwood and
       Archibald A. Hill. Austin: University of Texas Press, 1969,
       pp. 303-12.
          Establishes the likelihood that Chaucer knew more of
       Nicholas Trivet's Les cronicles than simply the tale of
       Constance, identifying several other echoes of Trivet's accounts
       and attitudes in Chaucer's narratives and suggesting that Trivet
       may have influenced Chaucer's sense of history.

185   SCHLESS, HOWARD. "Transformations: Chaucer's Use of
       Italian." In Geoffrey Chaucer. Edited by Derek Brewer.
       Writers and Their Background. London: G. Bell & Sons, 1974.
       Reprint. Athens: Ohio University Press, 1976, pp. 184-223.
          Sketches a method for assessing literary influence and
       demonstrates how Chaucer emulates his Italian sources.
       Boccaccio's temple of Venus in Teseida becomes a temple of
       luxuria in Parliament of Fowls; the static characters of
       Filostrato become dynamic in Troilus and Criseyde; Dante's
       terrifying Ugolino episode becomes pathetic in Monk's Tale.
       Includes a survey of fourteenth-century Italian presence at the
       English court and Chaucer's likely contact with it.

186   WIMSATT, JAMES I. "Chaucer and French Poetry." In Geoffrey
       Chaucer. Edited by Derek Brewer. Writers and Their Back-
       ground. London: G. Bell & Sons, 1974. Reprint. Athens:
       Ohio University Press, 1976, pp. 109-36.
          Demonstrates the pervasive influence of French poetry on
       Chaucer by describing how the poetry of Guillaume de Lorris,
       Guillaume de Machaut, and Jean de Meun affected the ambience and
       many details of Chaucer's works. Chaucer borrowed substantially

from each poet. From de Lorris he learned the conventions of love and the dream vision. From Machaut he derived his style and his comic narrators. From Jean de Meun he learned diversity.

187 _____. "Chaucer, Fortune, and Machaut's Il m'est avis." In Chaucer Problems and Perspectives: Essays Presented to Paul E. Beichner, C.S.C. Edited by Edward Vasta and Zacharias P. Thundy. Notre Dame, Ind.: University of Notre Dame Press, 1979, pp. 119-31.
Establishes the substantial influence of Guillaume de Machaut throughout Chaucer's career by following the "meaningful employment" of a single Machaut poem, Il m'est avis, through a range of Chaucer's works, early and late: imagery in Book of the Duchess and Merchant's Tale, philosophical language and social comment in Boece and Lak of Stedfastness, and both aspects in Fortune.

188 _____. "Guillaume de Machaut and Chaucer's Love Lyrics." Medium Ævum 47 (1978):66-87.
Demonstrates that Guillaume de Machaut's lyrics are sources for nearly all of Chaucer's short poems, adducing parallels of detail and expression in individual poems. Both poets follow convention, but the nature and variety of the similarities clarify Chaucer's debt to "his great French master."

See also entries 6, 8, 47, 191, 252, 308, 811. For French influences: 7, 41, 141, 229, 233, 309, 337, 452, 701, 703, 705, 806, 922; for Italian: 174, 201, 224, 295, 696-701, 704-5, 757, 915; for Spanish: 569, 698; for Arabic: 220, 297. For individual continental authors and works, see index.

Contemporary English
Literary Relations

189   BREWER, D[EREK] S., ed. "The Relationship of Chaucer to the
        English and European Traditions." In Chaucer and Chaucerians:
        Critical Studies in Middle English Literature. London:
        Thomas Nelson & Sons; University: University of Alabama
        Press, 1966. Reprint. Norwich: Nelson's University
        Paperbacks, 1970, pp. 1-38. Reprinted in Chaucer: The Poet
        as Storyteller (London: Macmillan & Co., 1984), pp. 8-36.
            Surveys the sociolinguistic conditions that fostered
        Chaucer's poetic style and language, concentrating upon the
        influence of English lyrics and metrical romances and the
        development of a learned English style. Discusses Chaucer's
        innovative vocabulary in relation to current French and English
        usage.

190   FISHER, JOHN H. John Gower: Moral Philosopher and Friend of
        Chaucer. New York: New York University Press, 1964, 388 pp.
            Explores the significant parallels between Chaucer's and
        John Gower's poetic careers, first describing Gower's career and
        art, and then demonstrating the influence Gower had on Chaucer.
        As a "sort of a conscience" to the younger poet, Gower encouraged
        Chaucer's shift from courtly poetry to social criticism. The
        eagle of Chaucer's House of Fame represents Gower, Troilus and
        Criseyde is dedicated to him and Ralph Strode, and Legend of Good
        Women and Gower's Confessio Amantis "appear to stem from the same
        royal command." But Chaucer's debt and the moral proximity of
        the two men is most evident in Canterbury Tales, where Chaucer's
        use of estates satire recalls Gower's Vox Clamantis and Miroir de
        l'omme, particularly in the General Prologue and in the figures
        of the Man of Law and the Wife of Bath.

191   KIRK, ELIZABETH D. "Chaucer and His English Contemporaries."
        In Geoffrey Chaucer: A Collection of Original Essays. Edited
        by George Economou. New York: McGraw-Hill, 1975, pp. 111-27.
            Assesses Chaucer's style in light of his contemporaries.
        Gower's "plain style" and formal precision, the intense social
        consciousness of Langland's Piers Plowman, and the poetic density
        of Pearl-poet help us recognize Chaucer's balance of allegory,

mimesis, and poetic compression. Contemporary "bad" poetry indicates, by contrast, Chaucer's successful fashioning of a common language to characterize his speakers.

192   SALTER, ELIZABETH. "Chaucer and Medieval English Tradition." In Fourteenth-Century Poetry: Contexts and Readings. Oxford: Clarendon Press, 1983, pp. 117-40.
       Places Chaucer in the context of "late Gothic" Middle English verse and distinguishes him from his contemporaries by his self-conscious use of the vernacular, his experimentation in House of Fame, and his appropriation of diverse Continental sources in Parliament of Fowls.

       See also entries 8, 55, 104, 117-18, 120, 129, 134, 151-52, 182, 201, 312, 337, 807. For individual works by Chaucer's contemporaries, see index.

Literary Influence and Reputation

193 ALDERSON, WILLIAM L., and HENDERSON, ARNOLD C. Chaucer and Augustan Scholarship. University of California Publications, English Studies Series, no. 35. Berkeley: University of California Press, 1970, 284 pp.

Describes the reception of Chaucer between 1660 and 1750 by examining the editions of his works published during this time: the "Edition of 1687" (a reissue of Speght), Dryden's Fables, Urry's, and Morrel's. These editions of the Augustan era are "pivotal" in several respects: they comprise the first attempts to collate identifiable manuscripts, record variant readings, "annotate" Chaucer's details, and understand Chaucer's language in light of contemporary usage. These endeavors reflect much about Augustan social, aesthetic, and lexicographic assumptions, and anticipate the more scholarly techniques of Tyrwhitt's edition (1775). Includes an important collection of Chaucer allusions that supplements Spurgeon (entry 202); the chapter on Urry is excerpted in Ruggiers's Editing Chaucer (entry 21).

194 BREWER, D[EREK] S., ed. "Images of Chaucer 1386-1900." In Chaucer and Chaucerians: Critical Studies in Middle English Literature. London: Thomas Nelson & Sons; University: University of Alabama Press, 1966. Reprint. Norwich: Nelson's University Paperbacks, 1970, pp. 240-70.

Surveys Chaucer's reputation as a poet among English literary figures from his contemporaries to 1900, noting the effect on his reputation of such factors as the increasing obscurity of his language, changing literary taste, and rising literary scholarship.

195 FOX, DENTON. "The Scottish Chaucerians." In Chaucer and Chaucerians: Critical Studies in Middle English Literature. Edited by D.S. Brewer. London: Thomas Nelson & Sons; University: University of Alabama Press, 1966. Reprint. Norwich: Nelson's University Paperbacks, 1970, pp. 164-200.

Describes the literary tradition of the fifteenth-century Scottish Chaucerians, concentrating on Robert Henryson, William Dunbar, and Gavin Douglas to clarify the appropriateness of the

62

term "Chaucerian" and to assess their poetic achievements. What Henryson lacks of Chaucer's poetic voice he makes up in earnestness. Dunbar's range and the musical quality of his works perhaps owe their inspiration to Chaucer. Douglas's rhetorical virtuosity and narrative dexterity reflect a profound understanding of Chaucer's works.

196   HIEATT, A. KENT. Chaucer, Spenser, Milton: Mythopoeic
      Continuities and Transformations. Montreal: McGill-Queen's
      University Press, 1975, 306 pp.
      Examines the Chaucerian narratives that most directly influenced Spenser and identifies the poets' mutual concern with Neoplatonic love, friendship, and political harmony. Influenced by the sixteenth-century editions of Chaucer, Spenser finished Squire's Tale in book 4 of Faerie Queene, modeling his plot and themes on Knight's Tale and emulating the "mythic" concern with "unconstrained sexual choice" and "charitable self-control" he found in the Marriage Group. Spenser's Mutability Cantos, considering Neoplatonic issues against a "moralized landscape," owes much to Chaucer's Parliament of Fowls and reflects Spenser's philosophical and narrative dependence upon Chaucer. Examines Milton's similar appropriation of Spenser.

197   LOOMIS, DOROTHY BETHURUM. "Chaucer and Shakespeare." In
      Chaucer's Mind and Art. Edited by A.C. Cawley. Essays Old
      and New, no. 3. London: Oliver & Boyd, 1969, pp. 166-90.
      Surveys points of similarity and contrast between the two great writers, including biography, relation to contemporary traditions, and taste for bawdry. Assesses Shakespeare's use of Troilus and Criseyde and Knight's Tale, and compares the comic techniques of these "supreme masters of comedy in English literature."

198   MISKIMIN, ALICE S. "The Illustrated Eighteenth-Century
      Chaucer." Modern Philology 77 (1979):26-55.
      Analyzes the popular understanding of Chaucer as reflected in eighteenth-century editions, book illustration, and painting, noticing the disregard for his wit and the concentration on the shallowly perceived romantic elements of gentilesse, sentiment, and the supernatural. Focuses principally on Urry's edition and Stothard's depictions.

199   _____. The Renaissance Chaucer. New Haven: Yale University
      Press, 1975, 375 pp.
      Investigates the critical perception of Chaucer and his works in the Renaissance by tracing understanding of his language, canon, and persona—his development into "England's Homer." Early chapters treat Chaucer's works as precursors of Sidney's, Spenser's, and Shakespeare's, that is, as self-conscious pieces that explore the relations among authority, the poet, the audience, and the value of art. Later chapters trace the decline of the Troilus story from Chaucer to Dryden, examine

the Renaissance Chaucer canon and editions of Chaucer, and assess
Spenser's lionization of him in Shepherd's Calendar.

200 PEARSALL, DEREK. "The English Chaucerians." In Chaucer and
     Chaucerians: Critical Studies in Middle English Literature.
     Edited by D.S. Brewer. London: Thomas Nelson & Sons;
     University: University of Alabama Press, 1966. Reprint.
     Norwich: Nelson's University Paperbacks, 1970, pp. 201-39.
          Surveys Chaucer's influence on fifteenth-century English
     poetry. Only Thomas Hoccleve tries to emulate Chaucer's natural
     language and ironic persona. Others, including John Clanvowe,
     Stephen Hawes, John Skelton, Alexander Barclay, etc., all reflect
     John Lydgate's ponderous imitations of Chaucerian moral vision,
     rhetoric, and courtly allegory.

201 ROBINSON, IAN. Chaucer and the English Tradition. Cambridge:
     Cambridge University Press, 1972, 307 pp.
          Studies Chaucer's place at the head of the English tradi-
     tion of poetry, analyzing his individual works for their progress
     toward "pure poetry," comparing him to his Italian predecessors,
     his English contemporaries, and his Scottish successors, and
     commenting upon the directions of Chaucer criticism. Treats the
     relations between literature and language and the interaction of
     convention and context, arguing that Chaucer created a particu-
     larly English poetry that combines comic effect and serious
     intent. Chaucer's most successful works—Parliament of Fowls,
     General Prologue, Miller's Tale, Nun's Priest's Tale, and Wife of
     Bath's Prologue—fulfill the potential of English letters in such
     a way as to establish the meaning of poet, poem, and tale, and
     give to English literature the form it has today.

202 SPURGEON, CAROLINE F.E. Five Hundred Years of Chaucer
     Criticism and Allusion, 1357-1900. 7 vols. Chaucer Society
     Publications, 2nd ser., nos. 48-50, 52-56. London: K. Paul,
     Trench, Trübner, & Co., and Oxford University Press, 1908-17.
     Reprint. 3 vols. Cambridge: Cambridge University Press,
     1925; New York: Russell & Russell, 1960, 1437 pp.
          The most extensive collection of references to Chaucer and
     his works, documenting Chaucer's literary reputation and record-
     ing the development of Chaucer studies to the twentieth century.
     Drawn from literature, histories, criticism, and popular works,
     the references are "fairly" complete to 1800, selective from 1800
     to 1868, and restricted to "chief editions" and "notable or typi-
     cal criticism" from 1869 to 1900. Arranges individual entries
     chronologically and presents original-language quotation of
     commentary on Chaucer, complete with bibliographic information.
     The bulk of the main list is English, with some Latin entries
     included; French and German references (and addenda) appear in
     appendixes. The extensive introduction outlines Chaucer's
     literary reputation and the evolution of his biography, classi-
     fies the quotations by content, and theorizes about the develop-
     ment of literary criticism and scholarship. The author and

subject index includes an analysis of the quoted material under the entry "Chaucer, Geoffrey." Updated in entry 44.

203   SWART, FELIX. "Chaucer and the English Reformation." Neophilologus 62 (1978):616–19.
    Explains the importance of the apocryphal Pilgrim's Tale and Plowman's Tale to the sixteenth-century view of Chaucer as a proto-Reformer.

204   THOMPSON, ANN. Shakespeare's Chaucer: A Study in Literary Origins. Liverpool: Liverpool University Press; New York: Barnes & Noble, 1978, 249 pp.
    Summarizes Chaucer's reputation in the English Renaissance and surveys the use of his poetry by Renaissance dramatists as background to discussing Shakespeare's considerable debt to him. In A Midsummer Night's Dream, Shakespeare borrowed elements from Legend of Good Women, Merchant's Tale, Knight's Tale, and perhaps Parliament of Fowls. The latter two had influence on other Shakespearean works, especially Knight's Tale on Two Noble Kinsmen. Chaucer's Troilus and Criseyde, modified for dark effect, stands behind Shakespeare's Troilus and Cressida and is a subsidiary source for Romeo and Juliet.

    See also entries 5, 8, 26, 34, 36, 55, 117–18, 120, 143, 359, 614, 635, 695, 726, 768, 771, 864. For individual authors or works influenced by Chaucer, see index.

Philosophy and Religion

205   BOYD, BEVERLY. <u>Chaucer and the Liturgy</u>. Philadelphia:
        Dorrance & Co., 1967, 95 pp.
          Surveys Chaucer's treatment of the sacraments, the canoni-
        cal hours, saints, and holy days to discover his attitudes toward
        church ritual. Chaucer very often uses saints' names as oaths to
        serve rhyme, and holy days in his works are most often occasions
        of merrymaking. His treatment of sacramental and canonical
        liturgies reveal his familiarity with and essential lack of
        interest in both. In his liturgical references, Chaucer is
        neither Wycliffite zealot nor "orthodox ascetic." He criticizes
        clerical abuses and ritualism, but his criticism is witty and
        secular rather than acerbic.

206   HOLLEY, LINDA TARTE. "Chaucer. T.S. Eliot, and the Regenera-
        tive Pilgrimage." <u>Studies in Medievalism</u> 2 (1982):19-33.
          Parallels Chaucer's awareness and valuation of language
        with T.S. Eliot's, arguing that for both poets language mediates
        between past and present, faith and experience, idea and reality.
        Chaucer's self-conscious use of books in his dream visions and
        his awareness of the "social dimension of rhetoric" in <u>Canterbury
        Tales</u> indicates his conviction that discovery and regeneration
        come through words, analogous to the Christian notion of Word.

207   HUSSEY, MAURICE. "The Church." In <u>An Introduction to
        Chaucer</u>, by Maurice Hussey, A.C. Spearing, and James Winny.
        Cambridge: Cambridge University Press, 1965, pp. 56-88.
          Describes the religious officers of Chaucer's day from pope
        to parish priest, and clarifies contemporary theological issues
        and terminology. A guide to the fourteenth-century church,
        sensitive to Chaucer's religious attitudes.

208   MADELEVA, Sister M. "A Lost Language." In <u>A Lost Language
        and Other Essays on Chaucer</u>. New York: Sheed & Ward, 1951,
        pp. 11-26.
          Discusses the prayers in Chaucer's works, concentrating on
        <u>An A.B.C.</u> as his first work, and assessing prayer as evidence of
        Chaucer's religious sincerity and devotion. Other prayers in-

clude Dorigen's address to God, the prayers of Griselda and the
little clergeon's mother, the Retraction, and various other
references to God and the saints.

209   MOGAN, JOSEPH J., Jr. <u>Chaucer and the Theme of Mutability</u>.
       De Proprietatibus Litterarum, Series Practica, no.8. The
       Hague: Mouton, 1969, 190 pp.
            Demonstrates the pervasiveness of the theme of mutability
       in Chaucer's works, describing the Christian and classical back-
       grounds of the theme and investigating its functions in his
       works. Mutability may be the most important common feature in
       the works Chaucer translated--Boethius's <u>Consolation of
       Philosophy</u>, Innocent III's <u>De contemptu mundi</u>, and Jean de Meun's
       <u>Roman de la rose</u>--perhaps the reason he selected them. His short
       poems and love visions explore various aspects of mutability:
       fortune, fame, life's transitoriness, lack of stability, and
       <u>contemptus mundi</u>. <u>Troilus and Criseyde</u> exposes the antithesis of
       the spiritual and earthly realms in terms of mutability.
       Knight's Tale reflects Chaucer's progress toward resolution of
       this antithesis, but much of <u>Canterbury Tales</u> attests to his
       acceptence of the world "in all its transitoriness."

210   OWEN, CHARLES A., Jr. "The Problem of Free Will in Chaucer's
       Narratives." <u>Philological Quarterly</u> 46 (1967):433-56.
            Traces a developing pattern in Chaucer's portrayal of
       character, observing a philosphical and aesthetic contrast
       between determinism and free will. As Chaucer sophisticates his
       techniques from <u>Complaint of Mars</u> to the early Knight's Tale,
       <u>Troilus and Criseyde</u>, and <u>Canterbury Tales</u>, his characters become
       increasingly free from external influence and control by the
       narrator.

211   PECK, RUSSELL A. "Chaucer and the Nominalist Questions."
       <u>Speculum</u> 53 (1978):745-60.
            Suggests that Chaucer's dream visions reflect nominalistic
       inquiry through their concern with the narrators' efforts to know
       or understand. Timidity of will adversely affects the narrators'
       abilities to know, paralleling the cognition theory of William of
       Ockham as modified by Robert Holcot.

212   RUGGIERS, PAUL G. "Notes Towards a Theory of Tragedy in
       Chaucer." <u>Chaucer Review</u> 8 (1973):89-99.
            Suggests that Chaucer's idea of tragedy must be understood
       in terms of fortune and providence, whether manifested in the
       rare, elevated concern of Monk's Tale or the more familiar, more
       emotional pathos of <u>Legend of Good Women</u>. In either case,
       Chaucer's intellectual context encouraged the view that tragedy
       is "merely one episode in the larger pattern of reconciliation of
       man to God."

213   SHEPHERD, GEOFFREY T. "Religion and Philosophy in Chaucer."
       In <u>Geoffrey Chaucer</u>. Edited by Derek Brewer. Writers and

Their Background. London: G. Bell & Sons, 1974. Reprint. Athens: Ohio University Press, 1976, pp. 262-89.

Surveys the religious and philosophical polemics of the late fourteenth century, summarizing the attitudes of the major thinkers (Ockham, Bradwardine, Wyclif), and noting where Chaucer responds to such concerns. Religious issues in Chaucer's works are moral rather than doctrinal, "questions of doubt and conscience." Philosophically, his works reflect epistemological doubt and a strong concern with the issue of determinism.

214   WETHERBEE, WINTHROP. "Some Intellectual Themes in Chaucer's Poetry." In Geoffrey Chaucer: A Collection of Original Essays. Edited by George Economou. New York: McGraw-Hill, 1975, pp. 75-91.

Explores the influence of Boethian, Neoplatonic idealism in representative works by Chaucer. Parliament of Fowls leaves unresolved a tension between idealized love and resistence to this ideal. Troilus and Criseyde transcends a similar opposition. Knight's Tale synthesizes various philosophical ideals which the rest of the Canterbury tales test, suggesting that certainty cannot "be achieved in its own terms."

See also entries 3, 57, 171. For philosophy: 154, 159, 162, 170, 172, 196, 223, 259, 283, 336, 340, 493-95, 736, 846, 854, 864, 872, 880; religion: 12, 47, 77, 177, 288, 293, 317, 387, 573, 585, 594, 603, 820, 842.

Science, Including Astrology

215   CLARK, GEORGE. "Chaucer's Third and Fourth of May." Revue de l'Université d'Ottawa 52 (1982):257-65.

Surveys the criticism of Chaucer's three uses of May 3 or 4 (Nun's Priest's Tale, Knight's Tale, Troilus and Criseyde), clarifying astrological contexts and their ambiguities. Argues that Chaucer's use of the date in Troilus is based on contemporary "collective moon-books" (lunaria) and is an appropriate day for Pandarus to select for his matchmaking.

216   CURRY, WALTER CLYDE. Chaucer and the Mediaeval Sciences. 2d ed. New York: Barnes & Noble, 1960, 392 pp.

Eleven essays comprise a seminal study of Chaucer's poetic use of medieval medicine, physiognomy, astrology, and dream psychology. Five essays demonstrate and explain the rich characterization inherent in the references to physiognomy, medical humors, and planetary influence in Canterbury Tales: the Physician's erudition, the skin infections of the Summoner and Cook, the Pardoner's eunuchry, the contention between the Miller and Reeve, and the Wife of Bath's sexual aggressiveness. Four essays explore the interplay between astrological determinism and traditional plot in Troilus and Criseyde, Knight's Tale, Man of Law's Tale, and the Hypermnestra section of Legend of Good Women, focusing on tragic inevitability in Troilus, Arcite's death, and the providential care of Constance. Two essays investigate the dream psychology that helps characterize Chauntecleer and Pertelote in Nun's Priest's Tale and explain the nature and function of the kinds of dreams in Chaucer's love-visions.

217   EADE, J.C. "'We Ben to Lewed or to Slowe': Chaucer's Astronomy and Audience Participation." Studies in the Age of Chaucer 4 (1982):53-85.

Explains in clear detail three of Chaucer's thorniest astronomical passages (the clerk's casting in Franklin's Tale, the narrative section of Complaint of Mars, the apostrophe to the firmament in Man of Law's Tale), substantiating the thesis that Chaucer's astronomical references assume of their audience only moderate alertness and expertise.

218   KELLOGG, ALFRED L., and COX, ROBERT C. "Chaucer's May 3 and
       Its Contexts." In Chaucer, Langland, Arthur: Essays in
       Middle English Literature. By Alfred L. Kellogg. New
       Brunswick, N.J.: Rutgers University Press, 1972, pp. 155–98.
           Explores the traditional associations of May 3 with the
       malevolent workings of fortune in Chaucer's three uses of the
       date, suggesting that the determinism associated with 3 May in
       Troilus and Criseyde diminishes to a kind of humanism in Knight's
       Tale and to parody in Nun's Priest's Tale.

219   MANZALAOUI, MAHMOUD. "Chaucer and Science." In Geoffrey
       Chaucer. Edited by Derek Brewer. Writers and Their Back-
       ground. London: G. Bell & Sons, 1974. Reprint. Athens:
       Ohio University Press, 1976, pp. 224–61.
           Surveys the likely sources of Chaucer's scientific knowl-
       edge and illustrates the variety of uses to which he puts
       empirical science, pseudoscience, and the occult. Attempts to
       define the limits of Chaucer's acceptence of astrology, alchemy,
       magic, and physiognomy.

220   METLITZKI, DOROTHEE. "Scientific Imagery in Chaucer." In The
       Matter of Araby in Medieval England. New Haven: Yale
       University Press, 1977, pp. 73–92.
           Demonstrates Chaucer's indirect debt to Arabic science,
       tracing the names "Algarsyf" and "Elpheta" of Squire's Tale to
       Arabic star catalogs and the Canon's Yeoman's alchemical
       knowledge, especially his knowledge of alchemical mysteries, to
       Arabic sources.

221   NORTH, J.D. "Kalenderes Enlumyned Ben They: Some Astrologi-
       cal Terms in Chaucer." Review of English Studies, n.s. 20
       (1969):129–54, 257–83, 418–44.
           Analyzes the astrological and astronomical allusions in
       Chaucer's works, seeking to date the works and explain the
       allegorical significance of days and dates covertly embedded in
       his poetry. Discusses the scientific aspects of Chaucer's astro-
       logical knowledge, including his use of technical calendars, the
       information evident in Treatise on the Astrolabe, and the possi-
       bility that he wrote Equatorie of the Planets. Analyzes allu-
       sions in Complaint of Mars, Troilus and Criseyde, Parliament of
       Fowls, Legend of Hypermnestra, and the tales of the Knight,
       Squire, Franklin, Merchant, Nun's Priest, and Man of Law, and the
       prologues of the Wife of Bath, Man of Law, and Parson.

222   SMYSER, HAMILTON M. "A View of Chaucer's Astronomy."
       Speculum 45 (1970):359–73.
           Attempts to establish the evolution of Chaucer's interest
       in astronomy and astrology, identifying 1380 as a turning point,
       contrasting Chaucer's stellar references to John Gower's, chal-
       lenging North's astronomical dating of Parliament of Fowls (entry
       221), and assessing the cosmological imagery of Complaint of

Mars, Troilus and Criseyde, and Canterbury Tales, especially Man of Law's Tale.

223   WINNY, JAMES. "Chaucer's Science." In An Introduction to Chaucer, by Maurice Hussey, A.C. Spearing, and James Winny. Cambridge: Cambridge University Press, 1965, pp. 153-84.
       Discusses the nature of medieval science, emphasizing its philosophical underpinnings and demonstrating Chaucer's poetic use of astrology, physiognomy, medicine, and alchemy.

224   WOOD, CHAUNCEY. Chaucer and the Country of the Stars: Poetic Uses of Astrological Imagery. Princeton: Princeton University Press, 1970, 337 pp.
       Surveys medieval attitudes toward the study of the stars, their relation to determinism, and the confusion of astrology and astronomy. Describes Chaucer as "high among the skeptics on the medieval scale of belief in astrology," identifies Dante and Boccaccio as the sources of much of his astrological imagery, and interprets the value of such imagery in the Chaucerian works that it dominates. Complaint of Mars, Chaucer's only "astrological poem," conflates the mythography and iconography of Mars and Venus and traces the astrological motion of these planets to comment on the nature of love. Elsewhere, Chaucer manipulates astrological imagery to characterize his speakers or lend depth to his narratives. Discusses the opening of Canterbury Tales, Troilus's ascent through the spheres, the Wife of Bath's horo-scope, and, at greater length, the Parson's Prologue and the tales and characters of the Franklin and Man of Law.

       See also entries 47, 57, 355, 557, 565, 661, 878. For astrology, see index.

Imagery, Iconography,
and Mythography

225   BOITANI, PIERO. "Chaucer's Temples of Venus." <u>Studi Inglesi</u>
        2 (1975):9-31.
            Surveys classical and medieval depictions of Venus's temple
        and documents the relation between Boccaccio's and Chaucer's uses
        of the tradition. Chaucer borrows from <u>Teseida</u> in <u>Parliament of
        Fowls</u> and Knight's Tale, yet in these and in <u>House of Fame</u> his
        Venus is, unlike Boccaccio's, typically medieval in her ambiva-
        lence (love and lust) and in the way she is modified by other
        figures like Nature, Fame, Mars, and Diana.

226   CHAMBERLAIN, DAVID. "Musical Signs and Symbols in Chaucer:
        Convention and Originality." In <u>Signs and Symbols in
        Chaucer's Poetry</u>. Edited by John P. Hermann and John J.
        Burke, Jr. University: University of Alabama Press, 1981,
        pp. 43-80.
            Surveys Chaucer's use of musical images and references,
        organizing them according to four medieval musical traditions:
        philosophical, scriptural, poetic, and social. Within these,
        Chaucer employs a full range of musical signs, both convention-
        ally and ironically. Discusses three elaborate uses of music in
        detail: the description of Chauntecleer before Russell seizes
        him, the prevalence of "melodye" in <u>Canterbury Tales</u>, and the
        framing of the tales with opening images of earthly music and
        closing spiritual ones.

227   NEUSS, PAULA. "Images of Writing and the Book in Chaucer's
        Poetry." <u>Review of English Studies</u>, n.s. 32 (1981):385-97.
            Surveys Chaucer's poetic references to writing and to
        books, discovering that such references appear consistently in
        contexts that directly correlate writing with loving.

228   ORUCH, JACK B. "St. Valentine, Chaucer, and Spring in
        February." <u>Speculum</u> 56 (1981):534-65.
            Surveys the medieval tradition of St. Valentine in order to
        establish the "probable state" of the understanding of the saint
        before Chaucer and Chaucer's associating of him with love poetry
        and springtime. Since no coherent tradition preceded Chaucer and

72

since his contemporaries followed his lead, it seems likely that
Chaucer is "the original mythmaker in this instance," inaugurat-
ing the Valentine-day tradition as we know it.

229   ROBERTSON, D.W., Jr. A Preface to Chaucer: Studies in
       Medieval Perspective. Princeton: Princeton University Press,
       1962, 536 pp.
          A source book for theory and practice of patristic or
       exegetical criticism. Confronts issues such as medieval notions
       of beauty, nature, and love, and distinguishes them from post-
       romantic modern attitudes. Argues that medieval aesthetic
       standards are hierarchical in that all good art leads to God.
       Sketches the principles of biblical allegoresis common to Paul,
       Augustine, and other church fathers, and argues for its influence
       on poetry throughout the Middle Ages. Extended discussion of
       medieval iconography provides a handbook to medieval allegorical
       imagery—graphic and literary alike. Examines Chaucer's poetry
       in light of the traditions of Jean de Meun, Andreas Capellanus,
       Alain de Lille, Boethius, and others. Reads each poet, Chaucer
       included, as ironic and allegorical, as purveyors of Christian
       truth, however secular their poetry appears to the twentieth-
       century reader. Assesses by these standards all of Chaucer's
       major works, but Troilus and Criseyde and the tales of the
       Knight, Miller, and Wife of Bath receive the most extended
       treatment. Includes 118 black and white illustrations of
       sculpture, architecture, and manuscript illumination that
       exemplify the allegorical and ironic aspects of medieval art.

230   ROWLAND, BERYL. Blind Beasts: Chaucer's Animal World. Kent,
       Ohio: Kent State University Press, 1971, 223 pp.
          Argues that animal imagery emblematically represents human
       foibles in Chaucer's poetry and that such imagery depends upon
       the medieval conception of man as the only rational animal.
       Documents the vices that individual beasts traditionally por-
       trayed, surveying bestiaries and other iconographic collections
       to establish their representational value. Particularly in his
       mature works, Chaucer employs sophisticated networks of animal
       imagery to create thematic density and rich characterization.
       Considers all of Chaucer's references to animals, particularly
       the boar, hare, wolf, horse, sheep, and dog.

231   WILKINS, NIGEL. Music in the Age of Chaucer. Chaucer
       Studies, no. 1. Cambridge: D.S. Brewer; Totowa, N.J.:
       Rowman & Littlefield, 1979, 188 pp.
          Identifies Chaucer's images of music, singing, and musical
       instruments, considering their relations to contemporary prac-
       tices and describing the English and continental styles of
       fourteenth-century music. Includes individual chapters on the
       practice of minstrelsy and on contemporary musical instruments.
       Instruments are illustrated and sample compositions scored.

See also entries 47, 51, 224, 281, 313, 333, 359, 364, 380, 394, 487, 583, 594, 665, 676–77, 707, 709, 717, 719, 722, 820, 822, 830, 835–36, 840, 869, 881. For exegesis, iconography, and mythography, see index.

Love, Courtly and Otherwise

232   COLLINS, MARIE.   "Love, Nature and Law in the Poetry of Gower
       and Chaucer." In <u>Court and Poet: Selected Proceedings of the</u>
       <u>Third Congress of the International Courtly Literature Society</u>
       <u>(Liverpool 1980)</u>. Edited by Glyn S. Burgess. ARCA:
       Classical and Medieval Texts, Papers and Monographs, no. 5.
       Liverpool: Francis Cairns, 1981, pp. 113-28.
            Investigates Chaucer's and Gower's depictions of the
       morality of love, evident in their association of love with legal
       terminology. Bases the investigation upon Thomistic theory of
       the hierarchical relations among eternal, natural, and positive
       law and the necessity for law--like love--to be rational and for
       the common good.

233   DODD, WILLIAM G. <u>Courtly Love in Chaucer and Gower</u>. Boston:
       Ginn & Co., 1913. Reprint. Gloucester, Mass.: Peter Smith,
       1959, 265 pp.
            Dated but useful summary of the genesis and conventions of
       courtly love and its presence in late-medieval French works,
       especially Guillaume de Lorris's portion of <u>Roman de la rose</u>.
       Displays Chaucer's transformations of courtly love conventions by
       comparing his treatments to parallels in French models and John
       Gower. Only a few of Chaucer's lyrics are wholly conventional;
       his other poems adjust the conventions of love through complica-
       tions of character (<u>Book of the Duchess</u>), philosophy (<u>Troilus and</u>
       <u>Criseyde</u>), or context (<u>Canterbury Tales</u>). Discusses numerous
       lyrics, the General Prologue and four of the Canterbury tales,
       and Chaucer's other major poems.

234   KANE, GEORGE. "Chaucer, Love Poetry, and Romantic Love." In
       <u>Acts of Interpretation: The Text and Its Contexts, 700-1600:</u>
       <u>Essays on Medieval and Renaissance Literature in Honor of E.</u>
       <u>Talbot Donaldson</u>. Edited by Mary J. Carruthers and Elizabeth
       D. Kirk. Norman, Okla.: Pilgrim Books, 1982, pp. 237-55.
            Investigates what courtly love meant to Chaucer, exploring
       its dominant characteristics in earlier literature (troubadors,
       trouvères, Italian, fourteenth-century French) and demonstrating
       Chaucer's cautious use of these strains. While the conventions

of courtly love strongly influenced Chaucer's early poetry, later he dramatized the "effects of sexuality" in richer variety.

235   KELLY, HENRY ANSGAR. <u>Love and Marriage in the Age of Chaucer</u>. Ithaca: Cornell University Press, 1975, 359 pp.
    Studies the literary, theological, and legal conditions of love and marriage in the medieval tradition as background to Chaucer's and Gower's works, concentrating upon <u>Legend of Good Women</u>, <u>Confessio Amantis</u>, and especially <u>Troilus and Criseyde</u>. Challenges the notion that courtly love is adulterous, documents the importance of Ovid to medieval amorous tradition, demonstrates the legal and theological validity of "clandestine" marriage, and explores the moral aspects of passion. Chaucer follows Ovid in celebrating marital fidelity, and, except when satiric, emphasizing the compatibility of love and marriage. <u>Legend of Good Women</u>, influenced by Ovid's <u>Heroides</u>, endorses fidelity and encourages us to read <u>Troilus</u> as the account of a valid clandestine marriage (compare Maguire, entry 760) that goes awry because Criseyde is unfaithful. Her weakness highlights Troilus's constancy and noble passion.

236   LEWIS, C.S. "Chaucer." In <u>The Allegory of Love: A Study in Medieval Tradition</u>. Oxford: Oxford University Press, 1936, pp. 157-97.
    Part of the seminal, although dated, study of courtly love and allegory, demonstrating Chaucer's dependence upon <u>Roman de la rose</u>, his relatively spare use of allegorical conventions, and his development of a rich conceptualization of love. Surveys the impact of <u>Roman</u> upon Chaucer's lyrics, <u>Book of the Duchess</u>, and <u>Parliament of Fowls</u>, and examines <u>Troilus and Criseyde</u> as "the consummation . . . of his labours as a poet of courtly love," describing how his realization of the major characters in <u>Troilus</u> vitalizes the poem's courtly sentiment Sharrock (entry 716) challenges this analysis of <u>Troilus</u>.

237   REISS, EDMUND. "Chaucer's Courtly Love." In <u>The Learned and the Lewd: Studies in Chaucer and Medieval Literature</u>. Edited by Larry Benson. Harvard English Series, no. 5. Cambridge, Mass.: Harvard University Press, 1974, pp. 95-111.
    Examines Chaucer's portrayals of lovers and love, concluding that his works express "the ultimate destructiveness and folly" of love. In <u>Book of the Duchess</u>, love is "excoriated rather than celebrated," Knight's Tale renders it "ridiculous," and in <u>Troilus and Criseyde</u> it brings temporary joy and ultimate woe. Elsewhere Chaucer parodies, undercuts, or criticizes love even more directly.

238   SLAUGHTER, EUGENE EDWARD. <u>Virtue According to Love--in Chaucer</u>. New York: Bookman, 1957. Reprint. New York: AMS Press, 1972, 282 pp.
    Categorizes Chaucer's works according to the kind or "system" of love that dominates each work, listing them under

broad classes of "religio-philosophical" love, courtly love, heroic love, and syncretistic combinations. Describes how the action or sentiment of each work reflects its system and identifies the amorous virtues and vices appropriate to the given class. Prefaces this analysis with an extensive introduction to the backgrounds and development of the systems of love, ranging widely among Latin and vernacular authors, and defining the systems of love and their interactions with such Chaucerian concerns as marriage, mastery, the libido, and the place of love in nature.

See also entries 6, 77, 169, 227, 229, 286, 321, 364, 697, 700, 828, 880, 890, 895, 921. For love in Troilus and Criseyde, see 712, 754-61, 778, 799-802; in Parliament of Fowls: 846, 849-52, 856, 859, 862, 864, 866.

Feminism and Antifeminism

239   DIAMOND, ARLYN. "Chaucer's Women and Women's Chaucer." In
       The Authority of Experience: Essays in Feminist Criticism.
       Edited by Arlyn Diamond and Lee R. Edwards. Amherst:
       University of Massachusetts Press, 1977, pp. 60-84.
            Analyzes the women of the Marriage Group to demonstrate how
       Chaucer's "fundamental conservatism" limits his sympathy for
       women. Although he does not accept the "formulas of his age,"
       Chaucer's females are either "bloodless abstractions" or flawed
       individuals.

240   FRIES, MAUREEN. "The 'Other' Voice: Woman's Song, Its Satire
       and Its Transcendence in Late Medieval British Literature."
       In Vox Feminae: Studies in Medieval Woman's Songs. Edited by
       John F. Plummer. Studies in Medieval Culture, no. 15.
       Kalamazoo, Mich.: Western Michigan University, Medieval
       Institute, 1981, pp. 155-78.
            Considers Chaucer's lyrical female voices in contrast to
       the voices of other English medieval lyrics, noting his satirical
       mastery of the conventions of the alba in Reeve's Tale,
       Merchant's Tale, and Troilus and Criseyde. Assesses the unusual
       treatment of female voice in Antigone's song in Troilus where she
       questions the nature of love in abstract terms.

241   WEISSMAN, PHYLLIS HOPE. "Antifeminism and Chaucer's
       Characterization of Women." In Geoffrey Chaucer: A
       Collection of Original Essays. Edited by George Economou.
       New York: McGraw-Hill, 1975, pp. 93-110.
            Describes Chaucer's antifeminism in Canterbury Tales. The
       Knight's Emelye and the Miller's Alison are his "definitive
       statements on courtly and bourgeois images" of women. His
       portraits of the Prioress and Wife of Bath "focus attention on
       the difficulty of self-realization" in a restrictive environment.
       The Prioress mistakes her environment, and the Wife tries
       unsuccessfully to defeat hers.

            See also entries 89, 294, 324, 326, 383, 404, 425-27, 437,
       440-42, 501, 503, 541, 639, 641, 656, 765-66, 768, 773, 775, 893.

Honor, Chivalry, and Gentilesse

242   BAKER, DONALD C. "Chaucer's Clerk and the Wife of Bath on the Subject of Gentilesse." Studies in Philology 59 (1962):631-40.

     Demonstrates how the theme of gentilesse in Clerk's Tale tightens its relationship with Wife of Bath's Prologue, provides a "motive of a sort" for Walter, and indicates how the envoy fits the wry Clerk as teller. Through his presentation, the Clerk "neatly demonstrated the central fallacy of the Wife's interpretation" of sovereignty.

243   BLAMIRE, ALCUIN. "Chaucer's Revaluation of Chivalric Honor." Mediaevalia 5 (1979):245-69.

     Defines the "fundamentally belligerent style of honor" in late medieval literature and society, and identifies Chaucer's "profound misgivings" about this ideal of prowesss as expressed in Balade of Bon Conseyl, Complaint of Mars, Sir Thopas, Knight's Tale, and especially Tale of Melibee.

244   BREWER, D[EREK] S. "Honour in Chaucer." Essays and Studies 26 (1973):1-19. Reprinted in Tradition and Innovation in Chaucer (London: Macmillan & Co. 1982), pp. 89-109.

     Surveys many of Chaucer's references to honor to define his use of the term and demonstrate its importance in his poetry, especially Troilus and Criseyde and Franklin's Tale. Honor is both inner goodness and social reputation; it is a passive state of virtue or inheritance and an active meriting of honor or honoring of others. Both masculine heroic honor and feminine chaste honor are transcended by the spiritual honor of "trouthe."

245   COGHILL, NEVILL. Chaucer's Idea of What is Noble. Presidential Address, 1971. London: English Association, 1971, 18 pp.

     Considers Chaucer's understanding of gentilesse in Knight's portrait and tale and the tales of the Franklin and the Wife of Bath as part of Christian poetic tradition. In Chaucer, Dante, and Langland, gentilesse is associated with imitation of Christ.

246   HATTON, THOMAS J. "Thematic Relationships between Chaucer's
       Squire's Portrait and Tale and the Knight's Portrait and
       Tale." <u>Studies in Medieval Culture</u> 4 (1974):452-58.
          Contrasts Chaucer's sketches and tales of the Squire and
       Knight, emphasizing the disparity between their attitudes toward
       chivalry and arguing that Chaucer undercuts the Squire in order
       to encourage his court audience to return to the values of the
       past.

          See also entries 133, 170, 328, 353, 364-65, 425, 427, 430,
       476, 484, 530, 533, 537, 540, 549, 552, 749.

Thematic Studies

247   BREWER, DEREK [S]. "Children in Chaucer." <u>Review of English
Literature</u> 5 (1964):52-60. Reprinted in <u>Tradition and
Innovation in Chaucer</u> (London: Macmillan & Co., 1982), pp.
46-53.
      Surveys Chaucer's poetical treatment of children from pass-
ing references to his "great success in writing about children,"
especially the <u>Prioress's Tale</u>, isolating realistic callousness
and idealized sentimentality as examples of the poet's "amazing
juxtapositions."

248   _____. "Class Distinction in Chaucer." <u>Speculum</u> 43
(1968):290-305. Reprinted in <u>Tradition and Innovation in
Chaucer</u> (London: Macmillan & Co., 1982), pp. 54-72.
      Chaucer's works reflect three separate systems of class
distinction: the essentially social "ladder of degree" that distinguishes rank and nobility; the "socio-moral" distinction of
gentility concerned with propriety and virtue more than rank; and
the division of society in warriors, clergy, and laborers that
allows assessment of people according to how well they fulfill
their functions.

249   ELLIOTT, R.W.V. "Chaucer's Reading." In <u>Chaucer's Mind and
Art</u>. Edited by A.C. Cawley. Essays Old and New, no. 3.
London: Oliver & Boyd, 1969, pp. 46-68.
      Surveys the scholarship concerned with Chaucer's reading
and assesses the themes of books and reading in his poetry. The
genre of dream vision and the theme of dreaming complement and
comment upon Chaucer's use of written sources, especially in
<u>House of Fame</u>, <u>Parliament of Fowls</u>, and Nun's Priest's Tale.

250   PATCH, HOWARD R. "Chaucer and the Common People." <u>JEGP:
Journal of English and Germanic Philology</u> 29 (1930):376-84.
      Studies the attitudes toward the lower classes in Chaucer's
works, demonstrating his Boethian "kindly view" of human nature
as it extends down the social ladder, his concern for "common
profit," and the social range of his poetry.

See also entries 209, 543, 776. For individual themes, see index.

Canterbury Tales

GENERAL

251 BALDWIN, RALPH. The Unity of the Canterbury Tales.
Anglistica, no. 5. Copenhagen: Rosenkilde & Bagger, 1955.
Reprint. New York: AMS Press, 1971, 112 pp. Excerpted in
Chaucer Criticism, vol. 1, "The Canterbury Tales," ed. Richard
J. Schoeck and Jerome Taylor (Notre Dame, Ind.: University of
Notre Dame Press, 1960), pp. 14-51.
   A seminal study pointing to pilgrimage as the unifying idea
and central theme of the Canterbury collection, and concentrating
on the rhetoric of the beginning and end of the Canterbury Tales,
the only completed portions. The images of springtime and rebirth
in the General Prologue announce the pilgrimage and rhetorically
emphasize its social and religious implications. Chaucer creates
lifelike yet representational pilgrims and establishes a fictional chronology both immediate and timeless. The Parson's
Tale, a sermon on penance, is a fitting conclusion to this multi-
valenced journey, the only possible way to achieve the "Celestial
City" that Canterbury represents. The Parson's catalog of sins
reflects backward on the sins of the pilgrims and forward to
Chaucer's own confession in his Retraction.

252 BRYAN, W.F., and DEMPSTER, GERMAINE, eds. Sources and
Analogues of Chaucer's "Canterbury Tales." Chicago:
University of Chicago Press, 1941. Reprint. New York:
Humanities Press, 1958, 781 pp.
   Individual chapters by major scholars present the major
sources and analogues of each of the Canterbury tales, the Wife
of Bath's and Pardoner's prologues, and the storytelling frame.
Prints these sources and analogues in their original languages
with marginal English annotations that provide continuity and key
them to Chaucer's poetry by line number. Where no complete version is known, the composite sources or analogues of Chaucer's
works are provided. Individual essays introduce the materials,
discussing each tale or section generically and genetically,
clarifying Chaucer's originality and his debt to tradition. The
primary purpose of the volume is to present the texts for com-

parative study, yet several of the essays offer substantial
criticism, especially Laura Hibbard Loomis's on <u>Sir Thopas</u>. See
also Benson and Andersson (entry 308).

253   HOWARD, DONALD R. The Idea of the "<u>Canterbury Tales</u>."
       Berkeley: University of California Press, 1976, 419 pp.
           An important reading of <u>Canterbury Tales</u> as "unfinished but
       complete" in form (remembered pilgrimage) and structure
       (accumulation of paired opposites). The General Prologue compels
       the reader to share a sense of "obsolescence" with the pilgrim
       narrator whose memory of the pilgrims and their tales leads us to
       reconcile oppositions. Like remembering, reading <u>Canterbury</u>
       <u>Tales</u> leads us to understand our attitudes in terms of the varied
       points of view. Close reading elucidates the characters of the
       pilgrims, the structure of opposition among the tales, and their
       "unimpersonated" artistry, that is, the qualities attributable to
       the poet rather than the characters. Historical background pro-
       vides useful information about medieval memory theory, interlaced
       narrative structure, and visual models for the work such as rose
       windows and pavement labyrinths.

254   LAWRENCE, WILLIAM WITHERLE. <u>Chaucer and the "Canterbury</u>
       <u>Tales</u>." New York: Columbia University Press, 1950, 193 pp.
           Addresses many of the issues that result from approaching
       <u>Canterbury Tales</u> as a dramatic pilgrimage, employing
       "appreciative and historical criticism" to explain these issues
       to a nonspecialist audience. Emphasizes the verisimilitude of
       the pilgrimage while denying that it reflects an actual journey.
       Assesses the place and importance of the <u>fabliaux</u> as experiments
       in realism. Discusses the problem of the order of the tales,
       preferring the Chaucer Society order, and relates this problem to
       the drama of the pilgrimage, especially as represented by the
       Marriage Group, Chaucer's changing plans for the number of tales,
       and the pious conclusion in Parson's Tale and Retraction.

255   LUMIANSKY, R.M. <u>Of Sondry Folk: The Dramatic Principle in</u>
       the "<u>Canterbury Tales</u>." Austin: University of Texas Press,
       1955. Reprinted with additional bibliography, 1980, 297 pp.
           Presents the <u>Canterbury Tales</u> as an ongoing drama among the
       pilgrims, considering General Prologue, the tales, and especially
       the links among the tales as scenes or acts. Follows the Chaucer
       Society order of the tales, characterizing the pilgrims and iden-
       tifying their motives for telling their tales: conflicting
       ideals, professional antagonism, and one-upsmanship. The Host
       figures prominently as an actor, notable for his provocative
       tongue and questionable acumen. The tales suit the tellers in
       varying degrees since "upon occasion Chaucer sacrifices absolute
       literary criteria in favor of dramatic decorum."

256   McGRADY, DONALD. "Chaucer and the <u>Decameron</u> Reconsidered."
       <u>Chaucer Review</u> 12 (1977):1-26.

Challenges the traditional opinion that Boccaccio's
Decameron had no influence on Chaucer's Canterbury Tales, cri-
tiquing previous discussions and marshaling parallels between
Chaucer's and Boccaccio's tales, especially between Miller's Tale
and several tales of Decameron.

257　MANLY, JOHN M[ATTHEWS]. Some New Light on Chaucer. Lectures
delivered at the Lowell Institute. New York: Henry Holt &
Co., 1926. Reprint. New York: Peter Smith, 1952, 315 pp.
Attempts to identify real-life models for Chaucer's
Canterbury pilgrims, comparing the details in the General
Prologue and tales with historical documents. Admittedly specula-
tive, the discussions focus on historical individuals as models
especially for the Host, the Reeve, and the Man of Law. If no
individual can be so identified, other examinations collect typical records appropriate to a given pilgrim or tale, documenting
St. Michael's near Bath, for example, and alchemists at the court
of Richard. These discussions provide social context for
Canterbury Tales.

258　RUGGIERS, PAUL G. The Art of the "Canterbury Tales."
Madison: University of Wisconsin Press, 1965, 253 pp.
Explores the form of Canterbury Tales, especially the range
of the "great middle" of the pilgrimage. Defines the "ironic
detachment" of the narrator and his engagement only in matters
critical and prudential. Correlates this role, reflected in
Retraction, with the poet's genuine Christian endeavor to both
represent and appraise the world poetically. Analyzes individual
tales under the broad headings of romance and comedy, describing
how they depict aspects of the human condition, and how they
combine various literary forms. As parts of a greater whole, the
tales suggest more within the frame than they can in isolation,
reflecting not only the individuality and variety of their
tellers, but also their typicality. Includes analysis of all
tales except those of the Physician, Monk, Manciple, and Parson,
but discusses the importance of the Parson's theme of penance to
the work as a whole.

259　TAYLOR, P.B. "Chaucer's Cosyn to the Dede." Speculum 57
(1982):315-27.
Explores the relations among words, intents, and deeds in
Canterbury Tales, explaining contemporary realistic and nominalistic theories of language in the tradition of Platonic linguistic theory. Argues that Chaucer's apologies for rude language
reveal his complex attitude toward language, and that he privileges the Parson's linguistic realism over the Pardoner's
nominalism.

260　TRAVERSI, DEREK. The "Canterbury Tales": A Reading. Newark:
University of Delaware Press, 1983, 251 pp.
Examines the unfinished Canterbury Tales as it stands
between the "twin pillars" of the narrative: the departure from

General

the Tabard Inn and the arrival at "thropes ende." Three major
themes control the poem: contrasting loves in Fragment I, the
marriage argument, and from Pardoner's tale to Nun's Priest's a
somewhat less coherent notion concerned with the nature and function of art. All three concerns interact with the dominant
pilgrimage motif to communicate the richness of art and experience and their final spiritual insufficiency. Most valuable for
insights into nine tales: Knight, Miller, Reeve, Wife of Bath,
Clerk, Merchant, Pardoner, Nun's Priest, and Canon's Yeoman.

261   WHITTOCK, TREVOR. A Reading of the "Canterbury Tales."
       Cambridge: Cambridge University Press, 1968, 315 pp.
          Interpretive, tale-by-tale reading of Canterbury Tales,
       emphasizing the variety of world views represented in the work
       and noting how the recurrence of certain themes sustains a moral
       focus. Follows the Ellesmere order of the tales and argues for
       unity based on diversity, that is, argues that Chaucer's "mixed
       styles and tones" reflect his range and acceptence of diversity.
       Through genre and style, individual tales characterize their
       tellers and "depict the world as these people see and understand
       it." Through juxtaposition, diversity, and the recurrence of
       theme, Chaucer makes evident the comic and moral limitations of
       any one point of view.

          See also entries 2-3, 5, 7-9, 29-31, 33-35, 221, 284,
       300-301.

EVOLUTION AND ORDER

262   ALLEN, JUDSON BOYCE, and MORITZ, THERESA ANNE. A Distinction
       of Stories: The Medieval Unity of Chaucer's Fair Chain of
       Narratives for Canterbury. Columbus: Ohio State University
       Press, 1981, 269 pp.
          Proposes a new order for the Canterbury Tales as a collec-
       tion of exemplary narratives based on medieval precedent, espe-
       cially commentaries on Ovid's Metamorphoses, the quintessential
       collection of tales in the Middle Ages. Four categories derived
       from the commentaries structure the arrangement of Chaucer's
       tales, each category reflecting a kind of transformation and each
       including a descending order of tales: "natural" changes in
       human society (Knight's to Cook's tales), illusory changes of
       magic (Second Nun's to Pardoner's), moral transformations (Man of
       Law's to Shipman's), and spiritual change (Prioress's to
       Parson's). The arrangement prompts a cogent reading of each
       tale. In particular, the four-part structure of the Knight's
       Tale anticipates the four-part structure of the whole, and its
       resolution in marriage anticipates the predominance of marriage
       as an image of harmony throughout.

263   BENSON, LARRY D. "The Order of the Canterbury Tales."
       Studies in the Age of Chaucer 3 (1981):77-120.

Argues from manuscript evidence that only two orders of the
Canterbury Tales circulated early, perhaps before Chaucer's
death, and that the Ellesmere order "represents Chaucer's own
final arrangement." Directly addresses Manly and Rickert's
contention (entry 31) that manuscript evidence does not suggest a
satisfactory order, and challenges Blake's argument (entry 265)
for the primacy of the Hengwrt arrangement.

264   BLAKE, N.F. "Critics, Criticism and the Order of The
       Canterbury Tales." Archiv für das Studium der neueren
       Sprachen und Literaturen 218 (1981):47-58.
       Challenges critical attempts to find a logical structure
for the Canterbury Tales on the grounds that the poem is a
disorganized series of fragments. Manuscript evidence and
internal clues suggest that Chaucer had no overall, complete
design at the time of his death.

265   _____. "The Relationship between the Hengwrt and the
       Ellesmere Manuscripts of the Canterbury Tales." Essays and
       Studies, n.s. 32 (1979):1-18.
       Reconstructs the likely method of composition of the
Hengwrt and Ellesmere manuscripts of Canterbury Tales to argue
for the primacy of the Hengwrt and, therefore, for the inauthen-
ticity of the Ellesmere order of the tales. The Hengwrt was
probably compiled from disordered fragments left by Chaucer at
his death, and the apparent cogency of the descendent Ellesmere
is due to an editor who added the Canon's Yeoman's Tale and
clarified the role of the Wife of Bath.

266   COX, LEE SHERIDAN. "A Question of Order in the Canterbury
       Tales." Chaucer Review 1 (1967):228-52.
       Defends the Ellesmere manuscript's ordering of the Man of
Law's and Wife of Bath's tales on thematic and stylistic grounds
and argues for the authenticity of the Man of Law's endlink,
emending "scribal error" so that the Wife of Bath interrupts the
Host.

267   DEMPSTER, GERMAINE. "The Fifteenth-Century Editors of the
       Canterbury Tales and the Problem of Tale Order." PMLA 64
       (1949):1123-42.
       Attempts to establish the development of the various order-
ings of the Canterbury Tales as recorded in the manuscripts by
examining the relations among the orderings and suggesting
reasons for their influence on one another.

268   DONALDSON, E. T[ALBOT]. "The Ordering of the Canterbury
       Tales." In Medieval Literature and Folklore Studies: Essays
       in Honor of Francis Lee Utley. Edited by Jerome Mandel and
       Bruce A. Rosenberg. New Brunswick, N.J.: Rutgers University
       Press, 1970, pp. 193-204.
       Prefers the order of the Canterbury tales found in the
Ellesmere manuscript to emended orderings or those of other

Evolution and Order

manuscripts, even with the Ellesmere's apparent reversal of
Sittingbourne and Rochester and the textual uncertainty of Man of
Law's Epilogue. The geographical confusion is minor and the
epilogue was probably canceled by Chaucer. Includes an important
survey of related criticism.

269   HAMMOND, ELEANOR P. "On the Order of the Canterbury Tales:
      Caxton's Two Editons." Modern Philology 3 (1905):159-78.
         An important early plea for caution when discussing the
      issue of order of the Canterbury tales. Demonstrates the com-
      plexity of the issue by contrasting Caxton's editions of the
      tales, and suggests that the fragments may never be resolved into
      "organic unity."

270   KEISER, GEORGE. "In Defense of the Bradshaw Shift." Chaucer
      Review 12 (1978):191-201.
         Challenges the criticism leveled against the Bradshaw shift
      in the order of Canterbury Tales (moving Fragment VII to follow
      II), focusing on the relation of Man of Law's endlink to the Man
      of Law's Tale, the geographical justification for the shift, and
      the textual issues involved.

271   OWEN, CHARLES A., Jr. "The Alternative Reading of the
      Canterbury Tales: Chaucer's Text and the Early Manuscripts."
      PMLA 97 (1982):237-50.
         Studies the relations among the six earliest surviving
      manuscripts of Canterbury Tales to argue that, at his death,
      Chaucer left a group of fragments that reflect the stages in a
      developing plan rather than a unified work. The glosses, layout,
      rubrics, and spurious additions to these manuscripts indicate an
      ongoing attempt by an editor or the scribes to resolve the incon-
      sistencies Chaucer left.

272   _____. Pilgrimage and Storytelling in the "Canterbury Tales":
      The Dialectics of "Ernest" and "Game." Norman: University of
      Oklahoma Press, 1977, 262 pp.
         Hypothesizes the developmental stages in Chaucer's growing
      but unrevised scheme for Canterbury Tales, explaining inconsis-
      tencies in the text as the result of a shift in emphasis from
      "ernest" to "game," that is, from an emphasis on pilgrimage to an
      emphasis on the drama of the storytelling contest. The Wife of
      Bath's character and the chronology and geography of the Pil-
      grims' Way indicate the final plan for a six-day journey, three
      days to Canterbury and three returning, concluding with Parson's
      Prologue and an "unwritten final tale," a dramatic confrontation
      between the Host and his wife, and the prize-awarding supper.
      Traces the "dynamics of character" and the thematic concerns of
      individual portions, especially General Prologue, and tales of
      the Knight, Miller, Shipman, Nun's Priest, Pardoner, Thopas,
      Melibee, and the Marriage Group.

273 _____. "The Transformation of a Frame Story: The Dynamics of Fiction." In Chaucer at Albany. Ed by Rossell Hope Robbins. New York: Burt Franklin & Co., 1975, pp. 125-46.

Attempts to establish from internal evidence the changes in Chaucer's plan for the Canterbury tales. The contrasting prologues of the Man of Law and the Parson, the vitality of the Wife of Bath, and the polished completeness of Fragment I indicate stages in Chaucer's plan that was to end in a feast of celebration rather than the penance of the Parson's Tale.

274 PRATT, ROBERT A. "The Order of the Canterbury Tales." PMLA 66 (1951):1141-67.

Defends and the so-called "Bradshaw shift" in the Ellesmere order of Canterbury Tales, moving Fragment VII to follow Fragment II. Disagrees with the further shift involving Fragment VI entailed in the Chaucer Society order. Surveys the histories of the various orders and assesses internal and textual evidence to argue for the following order: I, II, VII, III, IV, V, VI, VIII, IX, X.

275 RUTLEDGE, SHERYL P. "Chaucer's Zodiac of Tales." Costerus 9 (1973):117-43.

Suggests that the sequence of the Canterbury tales follows the cycle of the zodiac, describing echoes of the iconography and symbolism of the zodiacical signs and their associated planets in General Prologue and the first ten tales of the Ellesmere order.

See also entries 35, 47, 251, 254, 295.

STYLE, RHETORIC, AND IMAGERY

276 BLOOMFIELD, MORTON W. "Authenticating Realism and the Realism of Chaucer." Thought 39 (1964):335-58.

Discusses several kinds of realism in the frame of Chaucer's Canterbury Tales--satiric realism, "circumstantial" realism of details, and especially "authenticating" realism which lends an "air of truth." Chaucer's manipulation of tone, detail, point of view, and narrative time produces an original interplay among various "realisms and unrealisms," in particular between the "authenticating" frame and the idealizing tales.

277 BOYD, HEATHER. "Fragment A of the Canterbury Tales: Character, Figure and Trope." English Studies in Africa 26 (1983):77-97.

Assesses the rhetorical adornment of the first three Canterbury tales, showing how the ordering and balancing figures of occupatio and anaphora fit the Neoplatonic philosophy of Knight's Tale, how adnominatio enables the Miller to invert this order rhetorically as well as structurally, and how the imagery of Reeve's Tale reduces the grandeur of Knight's Tale even further.

Style, Rhetoric, Imagery

277A COGHILL, NEVILL. "Chaucer's Narrative Art in the Canterbury Tales." In Chaucer and Chaucerians: Critical Studies in Middle English Literature. Edited by D.S. Brewer. London: Thomas Nelson & Sons; University: University of Alabama Press, 1966. Reprint. Norwich: Nelson's University Paperbacks, 1970, pp. 114-39.

Demonstrates the self-consciousness of Chaucer's "principles of short-storytelling" and exemplifies his dexterity with them. Discusses pace, theme, detailing, verbal precision, climax, and verisimilitude, demonstrating Chaucer's command of these techniques.

278 COURTNEY, NEIL. "Chaucer's Poetic Vision." Critical Review (1965):129-40.

Investigates the relation between allegory and realism in the Canterbury Tales by assessing the function of the pilgrimage frame, explicating the opening lines of the General Prologue, and comparing the poetic modes of portrait and tale for four pilgrims: Knight, Miller, Pardoner, and Parson.

279 FISHER, JOHN H. "The Three Styles of Fragment I of the Canterbury Tales." Chaucer Review 8 (1973):119-27.

Parallels the styles of the first three Canterbury tales with three styles in John of Garland's Poetria, defined by social class and appropriate speech. The courtly style of Knight's Tale, the bourgeois style of Miller's Tale, and the peasant's style of Reeve's Tale match the styles Garland distinguishes in his rectangular scheme which precedes his more familiar "wheel of Virgil."

280 HASKELL, ANN S. Essays on Chaucer's Saints. Studies in English Literature, no. 107. The Hague: Mouton, 1976, 83 pp.

Ten essays address many of the "referential saints" of Canterbury Tales, that is., those direct or punning allusions by oath, name, or passing reference to individual saints that evoke the lore that surrounded the saint in Chaucer's day, and that carry ironic complement or contrast into Chaucer's context. The saints discussed include Madrian (Adrian) from the Monk's Prologue, Ronyon (Ronan) from the Pardoner's Prologue, Giles from the Canon's Yeoman's Tale, Loy from the Prioress's sketch, Thomas and Simon from the Summoner's Tale, Joce from the Wife of Bath's Prologue, and Nicholas as a character-name in the Miller's Tale and as an allusion in the Prioress's Tale.

281 _____. "The Golden Ambiguity of the Canterbury Tales." Erasmus Review 11, no. 1 (1971):1-9.

Exemplifies the variety of associations of gold and love in Canterbury Tales, suggesting that they constitute an "extended pun" that explores the earthly and spiritual significance of cupidity and charity.

Canterbury Tales

282   JOSEPH, GERHARD. "Chaucerian 'Game'--'Ernest' and the
       'Argument of Herbergage' in the Canterbury Tales." Chaucer
       Review 5 (1970):83-96.
           Investigates Chaucer's manipulation of space in Canterbury
       Tales, contrasting the Knight's idea of human space as a prison
       with the sexual games in the confined spaces of Miller's and
       Reeve's fabliaux. Nun's Priest's Tale presents similar views of
       the widow's cottage and the barnyard, while the same contrast
       underlies the opposition of the Tabard Inn and Becket's tomb, the
       two poles of the Canterbury pilgrimage.

283   JUSTMAN, STEWART. "Literal and Symbolic in the Canterbury
       Tales." Chaucer Review 14 (1980):199-214.
           Surveys examples of challenges to analogical thinking or
       philosophical realism in Canterbury Tales, isolating details and
       passages in which the literal overwhelms the figurative. Puns,
       irony, and impersonation counterfeit meaning, and fiction fails
       to transcend experience. The tales represent a "major break"
       with the dominant medieval view which is characterized by
       analogy, allegory, and symbol.

284   KNIGHT, STEPHEN. The Poetry of the "Canterbury Tales."
       Sydney: Angus & Robertson, 1973, 214 pp.
           Analyzes Chaucer's poetic achievement in Canterbury Tales,
       noting where his style serves simply to maintain varied, appeal-
       ing narrative movement, and where he "deliberately implies mean-
       ing in the shape and tone of his poetry." Considers the tales
       sequentially, discussing imagery, shifts in level of style,
       rhetorical embellishment, and the effects of sound, syntax, and
       meter.

285   KOLVE, V.A. Chaucer and the Imagery of Narrative: The First
       Five Canterbury Tales. Stanford: Stanford University Press,
       1984, 565 pp.
           An iconographic reading of Chaucer's first five Canterbury
       tales, General Prologue excluded, supported by many illustrations
       from contemporary art. Theorizes that medieval memory was
       pictorial and that though we have few visual renderings of
       Chaucer's tales, he built them around central "narrative images"
       that impress themselves upon the memory and direct response to
       the tales. Images of amphitheater and prison-and-garden embody
       order in Knight's Tale; parody of Noah's Flood and images of
       youth and nature as opponents of order reflect disorder in
       Miller's Tale. Death-as-tapster and the unbridled horse define
       the bleak, rebellious mood of Reeve's Tale. Images of the sea
       and the rudderless boat suggest Christian allegory in Man of
       Law's Tale, especially since it follows the "morality of trade"
       implied by Cook's Tale.

286   McCANN, GARTH A. "Chaucer's First Three Tales: Unity in
       Trinity." Bulletin of the Rocky Mountain Modern Language
       Association 27 (1973):10-16.

Canterbury Tales

Style Rhetoric, Imagery
        Compares the approaches to love presented in Knight's Tale,
Miller's Tale, and Reeve's Tale, arguing that the three comprise
a "careful symmetry" wherein the first depicts the idealism of
"pure love," and the last the realism of revenge and "utter
satiety." Miller's Tale mediates between the two, presenting a
variety of motives and qualified sexual satisfaction.

287   MIDDLETON, ANNE. "Chaucer's 'New Men' and the Good of Litera-
       ture in the Canterbury Tales." In Literature and Society.
       Edited by Edward W. Said. Selected papers from the English
       Institute. N.s., no. 3. Baltimore: Johns Hopkins University
       Press, 1980, pp. 15-56.
        Argues that the performances of the Franklin, Man of Law,
Monk, Clerk, and Squire reflect Chaucer's "ideal of vernacular
eloquence" and suggest that for them the value of literature is
its pleasure. Chaucer embodies his concern for a contemporary
poetic in the tales of the "new men," the rising entreprenurial
class, who explore the technical virtuosity of courtly "making"
and the noble counsel of ancient "poesye," producing an aesthetic
of "endityng."

288   REISS, EDMUND. "Biblical Parody: Chaucer's 'Distortions' of
       Scripture." In Chaucer and Scriptural Tradition. Edited by
       David Lyle Jeffrey. Ottawa: University of Ottawa Press,
       1984, pp. 47-61.
        Surveys Chaucer's manipulation of biblical reference and
allusion, focusing upon how distortions of biblical texts and
narratives negatively characterize the narrators in the Canterbury tales of the Friar, Physician, Prioress, Man of Law,
Merchant, Monk, and Summoner, and the prologues of the Wife of
Bath and Pardoner.

289   ROBERTSON, D.W., Jr. "Some Disputed Chaucerian Terminology."
       Speculum 52 (1977):571-81. Reprinted in Essays in Medieval
       Culture (Princeton: Princeton University Press, 1980), pp.
       291-301.
        Clarifies the social rank and function of several of
Chaucer's characters of humble class (Reeve, Plowman, Yeoman, and
widow of Nun's Priest's Tale), arguing that their individual
"moral qualities," not Chaucer's "class consciousness," characterize them in Canterbury Tales.

290   ROGERS, WILLIAM ELFORD. "Individualization of Language in the
       Canterbury Frame Story." Annuale Mediaevale 15 (1974):74-108.
        Assesses the speech patterns of the Canterbury pilgrims in
the links between the tales, generalizing about their romance
vocabulary, their syntax, and their figurative language, focusing
on the Reeve's imagery and the individuating "speech mannerisms"
of the Host, Wife of Bath, and Pardoner. Appends a list of
Romance words used in each link, analyzed by speaker and statis-
tically tabulated.

291   THOMPSON, CHARLOTTE. "Cosmic Allegory and Cosmic Error in the
       Frame of the Canterbury Tales." Pacific Coast Philology 18
       (1983):77-83.
           Assesses the allegorical implications of references to
       Aries and Libra at the beginning of the General Prologue and in
       the Parson's Prologue. Argues that they cannot be taken liter-
       ally but that they help establish an allegory of the world's
       movement from creation to destruction and the church's progress
       from establishment to fulfillment.

292   WOOD, CHAUNCEY. "Artistic Intention and Chaucer's Use of
       Scriptural Allusion." In Chaucer and Scriptural Tradition.
       Edited by David Lyle Jeffrey. Ottawa: University of Ottawa
       Press, 1984, pp. 35-46.
           Describes the range and variety of biblical quotation and
       allusion in Chaucer's works, discussing uses of biblical texts
       and narratives in the tales of the Parson, Reeve, Summoner, and
       Miller, and the portraits of the Summoner and Physician.

           See also entries 56, 131-42, 144-51, 153-56, 226, 229-31,
       251, 258, 261, 311, 313, 336, 341, 379, 381, 388, 390, 453, 480,
       640, 674, 686.

FRAME AND STRUCTURE

293   ANDERSEN, JENS KR. "An Analysis of the Framework of Chaucer's
       Canterbury Tales." Orbis Litterarum 27 (1972):179-201.
           Identifies five ways in which the tales of Canterbury are
       structurally connected to their frame and demonstrates how the
       poet Chaucer is separated from the pilgrim in time rather than
       point of view. Concludes by noting differences between Chaucer's
       use of frame and Boccaccio's in Decameron.

294   BREWER, DEREK [S]., ed. "Gothic Chaucer." In Geoffrey
       Chaucer. Writers and Their Background. London: G. Bell &
       Sons, 1974. Reprint. Athens: Ohio University Press, 1976,
       pp. 1-32. Reprinted in Tradition and Innovation in Chaucer
       (London: Macmillan & Co., 1982), pp. 110-36.
           Considers the "inconsistencies and discontinuities" of
       form, thought, and genre in Canterbury Tales as bases for under-
       standing the Gothic aesthetics of Chaucer's art. Correlative to
       fourteenth-century visual art and to the "complex cultural
       pluralism" of the day, contrast, juxtaposition, and paradox
       typify Chaucer's works: his humor, his feminism, his irony, and
       his irreverence toward his art.

295   CLAWSON, W.H. "The Framework of the Canterbury Tales."
       University of Toronto Quarterly 20 (1951):137-54. Reprinted
       in Chaucer: Essays in Modern Criticism, ed. Edward
       Wagenknecht (New York: Oxford University Press, 1959), pp. 3-
       22.

Canterbury Tales

Frame and Structure

Surveys various kinds of frame stories that antedate
Canterbury Tales, summarizing and describing in particular
Boccaccio's _Ameto_ and _Decameron_ and Sercambi's _Novelle_. Describes Chaucer's innovations of characterization and drama, and
the problems of ordering his tales.

296   DELIGIORGIS, STAVROS. "Poetics of Anagogy for Chaucer: The
Canterbury Tales." In _Geoffrey Chaucer: A Collection of_
Original Essays. Edited by George D. Economou. New York:
McGraw-Hill, 1975, pp. 129-41.

Deconstructs the Canterbury pilgrimage to suggest the
conceptual paths down which it leads. Presents Honorius of
Auten's ten cities on the journey to the Fatherland (_On the_
Banishment and Fatherland of the Soul; or, On the Arts) as the
major foci of the tales: the seven liberal arts, physical
science, mechanics, and economics.

297   GITTES, KATHERINE SLATER. "_The Canterbury Tales_ and the
Arabic Frame Tradition." _PMLA_ 98 (1983):237-51.

Correlates Chaucer's frame narrative in _Canterbury Tales_
with Arabic narrative tradition, arguing that Arabic principles
of open-endedness, eyewitness narration, thematic grouping, and
didactic organization reached Western tradition and Chaucer
through Petrus Alfonsi's _Disciplina Clericus_. Chaucer's frame
reflects these Eastern roots in detail and construction.

298   HANNING, ROBERT W. "The Theme of Art and Life in Chaucer's
Poetry." In _Geoffrey Chaucer: A Collection of Original_
Essays. Edited by George D. Economou. New York: McGraw-
Hill, 1975, pp. 15-36.

Traces the dialectical themes of art and experience in
Canterbury Tales. The narrator espouses a mimetic, experiential
view of life, while the Host tries to order experience artfully.
Irony subsumes both of these extremes in a variety of artistic
attempts to control experience: the Prioress's role-playing, the
Pardoner's deceit, the illusion of Franklin's Tale, and the self-
conscious manipulation in the tales of the Canon's Yeoman and
Manciple.

299   HARRINGTON, NORMAN T. "Experince, Art and the Framing of the
Canterbury Tales." _Chaucer Review_ 10 (1976):187-200.

Contrasts the "fundamental pragmatism" of the links between
the Canterbury tales with the more fictive, ordered views of
truth found in the tales themselves. The prologues and epilogues
"amend" their neighboring tales, thereby leading readers to
assess the relative validity of art and experience and engaging
us in a "genuine movement towards truth."

300   JOSIPOVICI, G.D. "Fiction and Game in the _Canterbury Tales_."
Critical Quarterly 7 (1965):185-97.

An important examination of how the narrative layers of
Canterbury Tales reinforce the fictionality of the work. As

readers of self-proclaimed fiction, we must recognize that irony
envelops all the tales, modifying the apparently straightforward
Parson's Tale, complicating the paradigmatically complex Pardoner's Tale, and forcing us to see our own folly.

301 LAWLER, TRAUGOTT. The One and the Many in the "Canterbury
Tales." Hamden, Conn.: Archon Books, 1980, 209 pp.
Reads Canterbury Tales as a single work, unified by the
"complementary relationship" between "unity and diversity, one-
ness and multiplicity," concluding that this focus constitutes an
affirmation of unity. The poem mediates between one and many by
stereotyping the professions represented, focusing upon marriage
as an image of unity, and balancing the tension between experience and authority. Resolution of oppositions dominates the work
as it moves through fulfillment of expectations to closure.

302 STROHM, PAUL. "Form and Statement in Confessio Amantis and the
Canterbury Tales." Studies in the Age of Chaucer 1 (1979):17-
40.
Contrasts the formal structures of John Gower's Confessio
Amantis and Chaucer's Canterbury Tales, exploring how the
authors' different social and economic situations affected the
political attitudes "mediated" in these poems. Gower's hierar-
chial view of human relations emphasizes "acceptence of estate,
degree, and natural limits" as a solution to social diversity;
Chaucer's more democratic view presents factionalism and diversity as necessary conditions of life.

See also entries 91, 153, 156, 158-59, 162, 169, 253, 255,
261-62, 276-79, 286, 291, 304, 365, 374, 464, 664, 673.

PILGRIMAGE

303 HOWARD, DONALD R. "Chaucer." In Writers and Pilgrims:
Medieval Pilgrimage Narratives and Their Posterity. Berkeley:
University of California Press, 1980, pp. 77-105.
Compares Chaucer's Canterbury Tales to other medieval
travel literature. With the exception of Mandeville's Travels,
Chaucer's work is unique in this literature in its fictional
character, its self-consciousness, and its manipulation of first-
person point of view. Yet Chaucer "inherited" from travel
literature a form that invites "vicarious participation and
personal reaction from the reader."

304 KNAPP, DANIEL. "The Relyk of a Saint: A Gloss on Chaucer's
Pilgrimage." ELH: A Journal of English Literary History 39
(1972):1-26.
Erasmus's Peregrinatio Religionis Ergo (ca. 1514) and other
near-contemporary accounts describe the Canterbury shrine before
the Reformation, including such unsavory objects of veneration as
Becket's hair breeches. In the Host's brutal rejection of the

Pilgrimage

Pardoner, Chaucer alludes to such relics, suggesting the difference between religious and worldly pilgrimage, and supporting
conjecture about the function of oppositions in the pilgrimage
frame.

305   REISS, EDMUND. "The Pilgrimage Narrative and the Canterbury
      Tales." Studies in Philology 67 (1970):295-305.
          Studies the tradition of pilgrimage as it encourages us to
      view Chaucer's pilgrimage as a search for understanding. The
      tale-tellers represent the "usual allegorical figures" of the
      tradition and the reader is the central Everyman-figure in
      pursuit of knowledge and spiritual transformation.

306   ZACHER, CHRISTIAN K. Curiosity and Pilgrimage: The
      Literature of Discovery in Fourteenth-Century England.
      Baltimore: Johns Hopkins University Press, 1976, 206 pp.
          Defines the fourteenth-century moral status of curiositas
      and the social status of pilgrimage, describing their interrela-
      tion in Chaucer's Canterbury Tales, Richard de Bury's
      Philobiblon, and Mandeville's Travels. In each, pilgrimage in
      associated with instability and inquisitiveness rather than with
      spiritual rejection of the world, even though the pilgrimage
      theme is less adventuresome in Canterbury Tales than the others.
      The Canterbury fellowship is based upon a "spiritually imperti-
      nent kind of sworn pact" rather than Christian fellowship, mirth-
      ful disorder rather than order. The theme of social stability
      recurs, manifested in marriage, friendship, and tale-telling. By
      the end of Manciple's Tale, however, all pacts are broken.
      Parson's Tale reasserts order by rejecting fables, suppressing
      contentious noise, and replacing social disorder with moral
      order.

          See also entries 251, 254, 291, 320-21, 330, 338, 590, 677.

GENRES, INCLUDING FABLIAUX

307   ANDREAS, JAMES R. "The Rhetoric of Chaucerian Comedy: The
      Aristotelian Legacy." Comparatist 8 (1984):56-66.
          Surveys the comic elements of Canterbury Tales, identifying
      them in light of the comic theories of Aristotle, Bergson, Freud,
      and Bakhtin, and discussing such features as comedy's persuasive
      value, its realism and generality, and its associations with
      grotesquery, carnival, and sexuality.

308   BENSON, LARRY D., and ANDERSSON, THEODORE M., eds. The
      Literary Context of Chaucer's Fabliaux: Text and Translation.
      Library of Literature. Indianapolis: Bobbs-Merrill, 1971,
      410 pp.
          Anthologizes analogues to Chaucer's fabliaux and parallel
      materials from related genres that pertain to them, modernizing
      Middle English texts and printing foreign ones in both original

language and translation. Dates of materials range from the
second to the eighteenth centuries, but the majority come from
1300-1600, ennabling the reader to assess Chaucer's originality
and influence. Brief headnotes introduce each text and its
relation to Chaucer's work. Considerable attention given to the
tales of the Miller, Reeve, Merchant, and Shipman; less to Friar,
Summoner, and Manciple. See also Bryan and Dempster (entry 252).

309   COOKE, THOMAS D. "Chaucer's Fabliaux." In The Old French and
       Chaucerian Fabliaux: A Study of Their Comic Climax.
       Columbia: University of Missouri Press, 1978, pp. 170-94.
       Evaluates three Chaucerian fabliaux in the context of a
study of the French fabliaux tradition: Shipman's Tale as similar to the French in its "economy and symmetry," Miller's Tale
as the apex of the genre's development in its characterization of
comic types and its fusion of sacred and profane, and Merchant's
Tale as an ironic exploration beyond traditional fabliau conventions.

310   JORDAN, ROBERT M. "Chaucerian Romance?" Yale French Studies
       51 (1974):223-34.
       Considers the structural similarities of Chaucer's so-
called romances, noting their variety and diversity, and concentrating on Wife of Bath's Tale. Such narratives share no identifiable subject matter and are additive rather than organic.
Since most of Chaucer's narratives are so structured, the term
"romance" has limited value.

311   KNOX, NORMAN. "The Satiric Pattern of the Canterbury Tales."
       In Six Satirists, by A. Fred Sochatoff et al. Carnegie
       Series in English, no. 9. Pittsburgh: Carnegie Institute of
       Technology, 1965, pp. 17-34.
       Examines Canterbury Tales as a kind of "militant irony"
with clear moral norms, suggesting that its satiric quality
derives largely from its unfinished state. Documents the verbal
and situational irony in the work, perceiving Chaucer's basic
generosity of spirit in his variety and his willingness to accept
contradiction as an aspect of the transcendence of his worldly
perspective.

312   LEWIS, ROBERT ENZER. "The English Fabliau and Chaucer's the
       Miller's Tale." Modern Philology 79 (1982):241-55.
       Sketches the tradition of the fabliau in England and
examines parallels in style between Chaucer's Miller's Tale and
early English fabliaux and fabliau-like poetry. Finds precedent
for Chaucer's dextrous use of direct discourse to define character, his juxtaposing of courtly and colloquial language, and his
parody of the language of the romances in Dame Sirith,
Interludium de Clerico et Puella, and the Harley lyric, De
Clerico et Puella.

Genres, including Fabliaux

313   RICHARDSON, JANETTE. Blameth Nat Me: A Study of Imagery in
       Chaucer's Fabliaux. Studies in English Literature, no. 58.
       The Hague: Mouton, 1970, 186 pp.
           Defines imagery and traces its presence in medieval rhetor-
       ical theory, providing background to Chaucer's transformation of
       rhetoric in the imagery of his fabliaux. Analyzes the fabliaux
       individually to show how imagery reacts with significant details
       to produce irony in Reeve's Tale, Shipman's Tale, and Merchant's
       Tale, and how it ironically foreshadows events in the tales of
       the Friar, Summoner, and Miller. In each case, imagery helps to
       unify the individual tale and signal deviation from moral norms.
       Such sophisticated effects go well beyond the prescriptions of
       the rhetorical handbooks and testify to Chaucer's "deliberate,
       conscious artistry."

314   ROWLAND, BERYL. "What Chaucer Did to the Fabliau." Studia
       Neophilologica 51 (1979):205-13.
           Investigates Chaucer's modifications of the fabliau genre,
       suggesting that the "Gothic" juxtapositionings and intrusions in
       his fabliaux produce ironies and subtle sequences of associations
       not evident elsewhere in the genre.

315   RUGGIERS, PAUL G. "A Vocabulary for Chaucerian Comedy: A
       Preliminary Sketch." In Medieval Studies in Honor of Lillian
       Herlands Hornstein. Edited by Jess B. Bessinger and Robert R.
       Raymo. New York: New York University Press, 1976, pp. 193-
       225.
           Anatomizes the comedy of plot and character in Chaucer's
       comic tales of Canterbury, following Aristotelian principles and
       dividing the tales into two groups: sexual comedies and
       "unmasking" comedies. Gauges the effect of various comedic
       elements like laughter and deception, and assesses the function
       of seriousness, implied value systems, character types, and the
       relative probability of action.

316   STROHM, PAUL. "Some Generic Distinctions in the Canterbury
       Tales." Modern Philology 68 (1971):321-28.
           Explores the connotations of generic literary terminology
       applied by Chaucer to his literature. The broad term "tale"
       indicates a degree of fictionality, while "story" implies
       historicity. "Fable," like "tale," suggests fiction, while
       "tretys" implies nonfiction.

           See also entries 6, 10, 47, 212, 258, 261, 337, 402, 405,
       415, 439, 450, 492, 497, 524, 540, 546, 559, 563, 604, 654, 679,
       727. For fabliaux, see index.

MORAL VISION

317   AMES, RUTH M. "Corn and Shrimps: Chaucer's Mockery of
       Religious Controversy." In The Late Middle Ages. Edited by

Moral Vision

Peter Cocozzella. Acta, no. 8. Binghamton: State University
of New York at Binghamton, Center for Medieval & Early
Renaissance Studies, 1984, pp. 71-88.
   Reads Chaucer's presentation of topics associated with
Lollards—swearing, clerical celibacy, and predestination—as
burlesque of contemporary disputes. Through the Host, Shipman,
and Parson, and through Troilus's determinism, Chaucer "digs at
the orthodox, parodies the heretics, and laughs at both."

318   ____. "Prototype and Parody in Chaucerian Exegesis." In The
       Fourteenth Century. Edited by Paul Z. Szarmach and Bernard S.
       Levy. Acta, no. 4. Binghamton: State University of New York
       at Binghamton, Center for Medieval and Early Renaissance
       Studies, 1978, pp. 87-105.
          Surveys Chaucer's use of Old Testament materials in the
       Canterbury Tales to assess his opinion of exegetical interpreta-
       tion. He balances "popular vulgarization and learned allegoriza-
       tion," sanctioning neither wholeheartedly, and he consistently
       uses Old Testament "platitudes and stereotypes" for moral
       teaching.

319   BARTHOLOMEW, BARBARA. Fortuna and Natura: A Reading of Three
       Chaucerian Narratives. Studies in English Literature, no. 16.
       The Hague: Mouton & Co., 1966, 112 pp.
          Studies Chaucer's use of Fortuna and Natura as "dynamic
       opposities," a backdrop for the actions of his characters.
       Narratives with "strong Christian backgrounds" (Physician's and
       Clerk's tales) require that their characters transcend the
       malevolence of Fortuna and the "limited benevolence" of Natura
       through godlike love. In the dominantly Boethian Knight's Tale,
       the goddesses function as "the alternatives for human resolu-
       tion," representing nature as life, proper love, and rationality,
       and fortune as death, courtly love, and passion.

320   PECK, RUSSELL A. "St. Paul and the Canterbury Tales."
       Mediaevalia 7 (1981):91-131. Revised slightly in Chaucer and
       Scriptural Tradition, ed. David Lyle Jeffrey (Ottawa: Univer-
       sity of Ottawa Press, 1984), pp. 143-70.
          Suggests that Pauline imagery and allusion in Canterbury
       Tales help to structure and unify the work. Identifies Pauline
       concern with language, with proper use of time, and with the
       vetus homo, arguing that these sustain a consistent focus on
       spiritual pilgrimage.

321   WOO, CONSTANCE, and MATTHEWS, WILLIAM. "The Spiritual Purpose
       of the Canterbury Tales." Comitatus 1 (1970):85-109.
          Surveys the overt and covert "religious elements" of
       Chaucer's Canterbury Tales, exploring its image of pilgrimage,
       the interrelations among the portraits and tales of the
       ecclesiastical pilgrims (especially Pardoner and Parson), and
       investigating its rich presentation of spiritual and secular
       love.

Moral Vision

322   WOOLF, ROSEMARY. "Moral Chaucer and Kindly Gower." In <u>J.R.R.</u>
<u>Tolkien, Scholar and Storyteller: Essays in Memorium</u>. Edited
by Mary Salu and Robert T. Farrell. Ithaca: Cornell University Press, 1979, pp. 221-45.
    Appraises Chaucer's "very fine analytical moral imagination" in comparison to John Gower's, demonstrating the moral complexity and subtlety of the tales of the Merchant, the Franklin, and the Wife of Bath. Where Gower's morality in <u>Confessio</u> <u>Amantis</u> is "flat" and "uncontroversial," Chaucer's complicates his works with ironic subtexts and sympathy "for the sinner."

    See also entries 1-3, 80, 155, 160, 190, 206, 253, 258, 289, 311. For morality and individual tales: 209, 261, 313, 394, 407, 507, 560, 590, 621, 644, 674, 676-78, 686, 688; for morality and the pilgrimage frame: 251, 291, 305-6, 337.

THE MARRIAGE ARGUMENT

323   HODGE, JAMES L. "The Marriage Group: Precarious Equilibrium." <u>English Studies</u> 46 (1965):289-300.
    Argues for the "inconclusiveness" of the Marriage Group by extending it to include the Squire's and Shipman's tales as commentaries on the Merchant's, by assessing the importance of illusion in the Franklin's Tale, and by identifying the tendencies of the involved tales to cancel one another. No one tale embodies Chaucer's "answer" to the question of marriage.

324   KASKE, R.E. "Chaucer's Marriage Group." In <u>Chaucer the Love</u> <u>Poet</u>. Edited by Jerome Mitchell and William Provost. Athens: University of Georgia Press, 1973, pp. 45-66.
    Reads the Marriage Group as a cogent sequence within the <u>Canterbury Tales</u> that addresses two issues: male versus female sovereignty in marriage and the place of sex in marriage. Wife of Bath's Prologue introduces the themes and her tale presents them in an "archetypal" women's view. Clerk's Tale presents a "clerk's-eye view." The Merchant addressess both issues ironically, and the Franklin idealistically.

325   KITTREDGE, GEORGE LYMAN. "Chaucer's Discussion of Marriage." <u>Modern Philology</u> 9 (1912):435-67. Reprinted in <u>Chaucer:</u> <u>Modern Essays in Criticism</u>, ed. Edward Wagenknecht (New York Oxford University Press, 1959), pp. 188-215; <u>Chaucer</u> <u>Criticism</u>, vol. 1, <u>"The Canterbury Tales</u>," ed. Richard J. Schoeck and Jerome Taylor (Notre Dame, Ind.: University of Notre Dame Press, 1960), pp. 139-59; <u>Chaucer--"The Canterbury</u> <u>Tales</u>": A Casebook, ed. J.J. Anderson (London: Macmillan & Co., 1974), pp. 61-92.
    Establishes the outlines of the Marriage Argument of <u>Canterbury Tales</u>, first suggested by Hammond (entry 45), by demonstrating the dramatic and thematic interrelations among the prologues and tales of the Wife of Bath, Clerk, Merchant, and

Franklin. Verbal echoes, direct references, and thematic opposition indicate an ongoing argument among the pilgrims about the nature of marriage: the Wife's heretical assertion of female sovereignty, the Clerk's studied, orthodox response, the Merchant's personal bitterness, and the Franklin's idealized solution—mutual freedom of the spouses.

326   MURTAUGH, DANIEL M. "Women and Geoffrey Chaucer." ELH: A
       Journal of English Literary History 38 (1971):473-92.
           Compares Chaucer's Marriage Group to patristic antifeminist
       traditions, arguing that fantasy, marriage, and the patristic
       view of women coalesce into a noble ideal. The Clerk's and Mer-
       chant's tales present contrasting, one-sided views of the battle
       of the sexes, while two different "patristic dilemmas" are re-
       jected in the tales of the Wife and the Franklin respectively:
       the opposition of beauty and chastity, and the conflict between
       truth and chastity.

327   RICHMOND, VELMA BOURGEOIS. "Pacience in Adversitee:
       Chaucer's Presentation of Marriage." Viator 10 (1979):323-54.
           Argues that the Marriage Group teaches concord as well as
       competition. The Wife's prologue and tale suggest that she has
       learned that selflessness is necessary to a successful marriage.
       In Clerk's Tale, Griselda's patience overcomes Walter's
       chauvinism. January and May are resolved at the end of Mer-
       chant's Tale, and the Franklin's focus on freedom embodies this
       persistent theme.

328   SILVIA, D[ANIEL] S. "Geoffrey Chaucer on the Subject of Men,
       Women, and Gentilesse." Revue des langues vivantes 33
       (1967):228-36.
           Accepts the "Bradshaw shift" and considers the Marriage
       Group as a sequence of tales from Tale of Melibee to Franklin's
       Tale, arguing that Melibee poses a marital ideal, that the
       following tales (excepting the "interludes" of the Monk and
       Friar/Summoner) take exception to the ideal. Franklin's Tale
       accounts for these exceptions and reasserts the ideal based on
       gentilesse.

           See also entries 10, 54, 239, 254, 260, 262, 272, 345, 422,
       488, 518-19, 523, 541, 554, 622.

GENERAL PROLOGUE

329   BADENDYCK, J. LAWRENCE. "Chaucer's Portrait Technique and the
       Dream Vison Tradition." English Record 21, no. 1 (1970):113-
       25.
           Describes Chaucer's descriptive technique in the General
       Prologue as an art that derives not from a visual representation
       of contemporary reality, but from his ability to represent "a
       mode of existence similar to ours." He offers a sense of the

General Prologue

pilgrims' pasts as well as their present; he implies their social interactions, when not stated, in ways that help create the illusion of reality.

330   BOWDEN, MURIEL. A Commentary on the General Prologue to the "Canterbury Tales." 2d ed. New York: Macmillan, 1967, 341 pp.

An essential handbook to General Prologue that explains its many details through quotation of medieval sources and survey of modern scholarship. Defines dated terminology and provides context for references, allusions, and imagery. The format follows Chaucer's, moving from the images of springtime and pilgrimage through the details of each pilgrim's sketch, including the Host's. The heavily documented discussion clarifies the conventional quality of Chaucer's pilgrimage and pilgrims and establishes their individuating characteristics. Chaucer's idealization or criticism of the pilgrims is a recurrent concern. Does not consider the iconographic tradition of the sketches nor more recent work in estates satire, yet makes apparent much of the breadth of Chaucer's learning and social sensitivity.

331   CUNNINGHAM, J.V. "The Literary Form of the Prologue to the Canterbury Tales." Modern Philology 49 (1952):172-81.

Compares the techniques of description used in the General Prologue to those of the portraits on the wall of the garden in Roman de la rose, concluding that Chaucer modeled his Prologue on the French poem and was influenced by the tradition of dream vision.

332   EBERLE, PATRICIA J. "Commercial Language and the Commercial Outlook in the General Prologue." Chaucer Review 18 (1983):161-74.

Maintains that Chaucer combines and modifies the language and imagery of estates satire and courtly literature in his General Prologue, producing an innovative "common idiom" that assumes its audience's familiarity with the commercial world, regardless of their income or class.

333   HIGDON, DAVID L. "Diverse Melodies in Chaucer's General Prologue." Criticism 14 (1972):97-108.

Briefly summarizes medieval notions of the relation between music and morality, and explores the use of musical imagery as a technique of characterization in General Prologue. Groups the pilgrims according to their associations with pleasant music or sound, with cacaphony, and with silence or open hostility to music.

334   HIGGS, ELTON D. "The Old Order and the 'Newe World' in the General Prologue to the Canterbury Tales." Huntington Library Quarterly 45 (1982):155-73.

Follows Howard's analysis (entry 253) of the arrangement of the pilgrims in General Prologue and discusses it as evidence of

Chaucer's sensitivity to contemporary social change. The Knight's feudal fealty contrasts with the new social mobility and fashion evident in the sequence of pilgrims from the Squire to the Merchant. The Clerk's traditional learning opposes the entrepreneurial knowledge of the pilgrims who immediately follow him in the Prologue. The Parson and the Plowman represent "old rural service" in contrast to the "unprincipled manipulation" of the concluding "rogues of disorder."

335   HOFFMAN, ARTHUR W. "Chaucer's Prologue to Pilgrimage: The Two Voices." ELH: A Journal of English Literary History 21 (1954):1-16. Reprinted in Chaucer: Modern Essays in Criticism, ed. Edward Wagenknecht (New York: Oxford University Press, 1959), pp. 30-45; Chaucer: The "Canterbury Tales"--A Casebook, ed. J.J. Anderson (London: Macmillan & Co., 1974), pp. 105-20.
    Explores the dualism of the opening eighteen lines of General Prologue as it appears in representative sketches of the pilgrims. The relations between heaven and earth, spirit and body, health and sickness underlie the pairing of Knight and Squire, Parson and Plowman, and Summoner and Pardoner. The Prioress's sketch embodies a similar relation. This counterpoise unifies General Prologue.

336   KNIGHT, STEPHEN. "Chaucer--A Modern Writer?" Balcony 2 (1965):37-43.
    Approaches Chaucer's perceived modernity as an aspect of his portrayal of character, especially clear in those disreputable characters of General Prologue whose depictions reflect the modern nominalistic mode of perception that was just entering mainstream thought from the universities in Chaucer's day. Chaucer's ideal portaits reflect, on the other hand, traditional realist thought.

337   MANN, JILL. Chaucer and Medieval Estates Satire: The Literature of Social Classes and the General Prologue to the "Canterbury Tales." Cambridge: Cambridge University Press, 1973, 348 pp.
    Documents the fundamental importance of estates satire to the portraits in the General Prologue. Chaucer borrows from traditional complaints against the estates, but modifies our reaction to their details through "simple, attractive similes" and a shifting, often empathetic point of view. Surprising or ambiguous contexts remind us of the relative value of words, and the "omission of victims" directs our attention to the activities of the pilgrims rather than the effects of these actions upon others. The moral relativism that results is undercut by comic irony. Extensive notes and bibliography detail pertinent Chaucer criticism as well as primary estates material from Latin, French, and English traditions.

Canterbury Tales

338   MARTIN, LOY D. "History and Form in the General Prologue to
       the Canterbury Tales." ELH: A Journal of English Literary
       History 45 (1978):1-17.
           Identifies the form of General Prologue as a rhetorical
       catalog of types familiar in dream visions. The catalog of
       pilgrims consistently emphasizes the "disjunction between
       pilgrimage and ordinary life," enabling Chaucer to explore the
       "anxiety" of the late fourteenth-century shift from traditional
       social ranks to "materially motivated" economic classes.

339   MORGAN, GERALD. "The Design of the General Prologue to the
       Canterbury Tales." English Studies 59 (1978):481-98.
           Correlates the arrangement of the pilgrims in General
       Prologue with fourteenth-century social ranks, arguing from
       social history and lexical analysis. The portraits from Knight
       to Franklin constitute the gentles. The commoners follow, from
       the aspiring Guildsmen to the final group of churls. Irony and
       ambiguity derive from this social ordering.

340   _____. "The Universality of the Portraits in the General
       Prologue to the Canterbury Tales." English Studies 58
       (1977):481-93.
           Challenges the traditional descriptions of Chaucer's
       pilgrims as either "typical" or "individual" on the grounds that
       such distinctions are modern. Argues that the details of the
       portraits of Knight, Monk, and Wife of Bath reflect the medieval
       understanding of "concrete universals," a seminal notion in the
       Platonic and Aristotelian tradition of philosophical realism.

341   PARR, ROGER P. "Chaucer's Art of Portraiture." Studies in
       Medieval Culture 4 (1974):428-36.
           Explores Chaucer's use of rhetorical figures in the por-
       traits in the General Prologue, particularly the Knight, Pri-
       oress, and Monk, noting Chaucer's dominant concern with moral
       rather than physical description, with notatio rather than
       effictio.

342   SPENCER, WILLIAM. "Are Chaucer's Pilgrims Keyed to the
       Zodiac?" Chaucer Review 4 (1970):147-70.
           Tentatively suggests an astrological pattern in the ar-
       rangement of the pilgrims as they appear in General Prologue, an
       incomplete pattern based upon the planets that "rule" the signs
       of the zodiac. Identifies details of the sketches that corrobo-
       rate the association of each pilgrim with an individual sign and
       planet, and cites mythographic commentaries that clarify the
       relations.

           See also entries 6, 47, 169, 177, 201, 216, 251, 253, 255,
       257, 261, 272, 275, 678.

THE HOST

343   GAYLORD, ALAN T.   "Sentence and Solaas in Fragment VII of the
       Canterbury Tales: Harry Bailly as Horseback Editor." PMLA 82
       (1967):226-35.
           Describes the Host's aesthetic sense as an aesthetic of the
       obvious and demonstrates how Chaucer challenges us to supply a
       more valid counteraesthetic in Fragment VII, the "Literature
       Group," by focusing attention on tale-telling itself. The
       pilgrim Chaucer, his two tales, and their links are of central
       importance.

344   KEEN, WILLIAM.   "'To Doon Yow Ese': A Study of the Host in
       the General Prologue to the Canterbury Tales." Topic 9, no.
       19 (1969):5-18.
           Assesses the presentation of the Host in the General Pro-
       logue, observing the reactions of the narrator and the other
       pilgrims to him, and characterizing him by his physical appear-
       ance, his literary credentials, and his "solicitousness and the
       spontaneity of his imagination."

345   PAGE, BARBARA.   "Concerning the Host." Chaucer Review 4
       (1970):1-13.
           Surveys the character and the thematic and structural
       functions of the Host in Canterbury Tales, identifying him as a
       medieval type of pride and comparing him to the bourgeoisie in
       estates satires. Assesses his anti-Boethian discourse on time
       and his contribution to the Marriage Argument through his
       relations with Goodelief.

346   RICHARDSON, CYNTHIA C.   "The Function of the Host in the
       Canterbury Tales." Texas Studies in Literature and Language
       12 (1970):325-44.
           Studies the character of the Host in Canterbury Tales in
       his representative capacity as the "forces external to the artist
       that press him to create." The Host's aesthetic judgments, his
       demands as an audience, and his concern with time motivate the
       tale-telling contest and embody Chaucer's awareness of the
       demands society places upon the artist.

347   SCHEPS, WALTER.   "'Up roos oure Hoost, and was oure aller
       cok': Harry Bailly's Tale-Telling Competition." Chaucer
       Review 10 (1976):113-28.
           Summarizes the Host's character and his citeria of literary
       quality by surveying his responses to individual Canterbury tales
       and their tellers. Argues that Chaucer foreshadows the Host's
       selection of Nun's Priest's Tale as the winner of the tale-
       telling contest.

       See also entries 255, 257, 272, 290, 298, 535, 572, 575,
       577, 580, 582, 586, 590, 610, 617, 642.

NAMES AND NUMBER OF PILGRIMS, AND PILGRIMS WITHOUT TALES

348   ECKHARDT, CAROLINE D. "The Number of Chaucer's Pilgrims: A
       Review and Reappraisal." Yearbook of English Studies 5
       (1975):1-18.
           Challenges the critical attempts to resolve the discrepancy
       between Chaucer's stated number of Canterbury pilgrims (29) and
       the actual count (30), and argues that the discrepancy is inten-
       tional, ironically characterizing the narrator and lending sym-
       bolic, numerological value to the poem.

349   ELIASON, NORMAN E. "Personal Names in the Canterbury Tales."
       Names 21 (1973):137-52.
           Surveys the names of the pilgrims and characters of
       Canterbury Tales, noting Chaucer's use of his sources and his
       borrowing from contemporary naming practice. Chaucer's naming
       contributes stylistyically to the impression of nonchalance so
       important to his poetic effect.

350   GARBÁTY, THOMAS JAY. "Chaucer's Guildsmen and Their Frater-
       nity." JEGP: Journal of English and Germanic Philology 59
       (1960):691-709.
           Explores the possible political and religious affiliations
       of Chaucer's Guildsmen, surveying earlier criticism, and identi-
       fying their guild as the "pure parish fraternity" of Sts. Fabian
       and Sebastian of St. Botolph's church, Aldersgate.

351   HORRELL, JOSEPH. "Chaucer's Symbolic Plowman." Speculum 14
       (1939):89-92. Reprinted in Chaucer Criticism, vol. 1, "The
       Canterbury Tales", ed. Richard J. Schoeck and Jerome Taylor
       (Notre Dame, Ind.: University of Notre Dame Press, 1960), pp.
       84-97.
           Sketches the social and literary status of plowmen in
       Chaucer's day as background to his Plowman in the General Pro-
       logue. An ideal of worldly poverty and Christian charity, the
       Plowman symbolizes the "lower fringe of humanity seeking
       emancipation from economic and social servitude."

352   ROGERS, P. BURWELL. "The Names of the Canterbury Pilgrims."
       Names 16 (1968):339-46
           Analyzes the names Chaucer assigns to several of his
       Canterbury pilgrims (Eglantine, Hubert, John, daun Piers, Hodge,
       Harry Baily, Robyn, and Alice) and comments upon his more general
       use of generic terms for labels (e.g., the Knight, the Merchant,
       etc.).

THE KNIGHT AND HIS TALE

353   BLAKE, KATHLEEN A. "Order and the Noble Life in Chaucer's
       Knight's Tale." Modern Language Quarterly 34 (1973):3-19.

Canterbury Tales

The Knight

Argues that Theseus of Knight's Tale imposes his will upon
others to create order and control fate, reflecting both the
Knight's belief in the "ideal of a noble life" and the "shakiness
of the grounds for such faith." The tale reveals that "'noble
order' . . . is not the earthly embodiment of God's scheme."

354   BOHEEMEN, CHRISTEL VAN. "Chaucer's Knight's Tale and the
      Structure of Myth." Dutch Quarterly Review of Anglo-American
      Letters 9 (1979):176-90.
         Analyzes the structural opposition in Knight's Tale between
      Theseus and Palamon and Arcite. The two oppose the one in many
      ways in the poem (disorder vs. order, Thebes vs. Athens, passion
      vs. intellect, etc.) and the oppositions are resolved only
      through the dissolution of the pair through Arcite's death and
      resolution with Theseus in Palamon's marriage to Emelye.

355   BROOKS, DOUGLAS, and FOWLER, ALISTAIR. "The Meaning of
      Chaucer's Knight's Tale." Medium Ævum 39 (1970):123-46.
         Establishes the structural and thematic cogency of the
      Knight's Tale by analyzing physiognomic and iconographic details
      of the characters and the mythographic associations between the
      presiding planets and the Ages of Man. Psychology of humors
      distinguishes Palamon and Arcite (melancholy and cholera); their
      associations with Lygurge and Emetrius are consistent with this
      psychology; and their outcomes are reflected in the planets.
      Emelye is phlegmatic, and the jovial Theseus is colored by the
      Knight's own character.

356   BURROW, J.A. "Chaucer's Knight's Tale and the Three Ages of
      Man." In Essays on Medieval Literature. Oxford: Clarendon
      Press, 1984, pp. 27-48; Medieval and Pseudo-Medieval Litera-
      ture: The J.A.W. Bennett Memorial Lectures, Perugia, 1982-
      1983. Edited by Piero Boitani and Anna Torti. Tübinger
      Beiträge zur Anglistik, no. 6. Tübingen: Gunter Narr;
      Cambridge: D.S. Brewer, 1984, pp. 91-108.
         Studies the ages of the men and gods in Knight's Tale,
      discussing the youthful associations of Arcite and Mars, Palamon
      and Venus, and Emelye and Diana, the maturity of Theseus and
      Jupiter, and the old age of Egeus and Saturn. The Knight
      privileges middle age and Theseus, but pessimistically
      overshadows the action with Saturn rather than Jupiter.

357   COOK, ALBERT STANBURROUGH. "The Historical Background of
      Chaucer's Knight." Transactions of the Connecticut Academy of
      Arts and Sciences 20 (1916):161-240. Reprinted separately.
      New York: Haskell House, 1966, 80 pp.
         Reconstructs Chaucer's knowledge of and relations with
      Henry, earl of Derby, the future Henry IV, and examines Henry's
      military career, arguing that Chaucer derived much of the back-
      ground for the portrait of the Knight in Canterbury Tales from
      Henry and modeled the Knight, in part, on the future king.
      Matches several details of the Knight's sketch with Henry's

107

career, especially the northern locations in the catalog of
battles. Identifies the southern battles and attributes them to
the career of Henry of Lancaster, Derby's maternal grandfather.
Dates the Knight's sketch and part of Knight's Tale in 1393.

358   COWGILL, BRUCE KENT. "The Knight's Tale and the Hundred
       Years' War." Philological Quarterly 54 (1975):670-79.
          Argues that the "great tournament" of Knight's Tale is
       intentionally archaic, evident through comparison with other
       fourteenth-century accounts, and therefore indicative of
       Chaucer's criticism of the decline of contemporary "chivalric
       ideals in the debilitating antagonism of the Hundred Years' War."

359   CRAMPTON, GEORGIA R. The Conditions of Creatures: Suffering
       and Action in Chaucer and Spenser. New Haven: Yale Univer-
       sity Press, 1974, 217 pp.
          Contrasts the thematic interaction of action and suffering
       in Chaucer and Spenser, concentrating on Knight's Tale and The
       Faerie Queene, and observing Chaucer's preference for patience
       and forbearance, and Spenser's for action. Theseus is the active
       protagonist in Knight's Tale who comes to espouse sufferance.
       The tale's dominant imagery (cycle, prison, traps) enforces the
       advisability of such sufferance in the face of divine influence.
       Generally, the poets share the view of life as pilgrimage, but
       where Spenser's poetry emphasizes struggle as a means to success,
       Chaucer's works emphasize compromise: troth-plighting, bargain
       and treaty making, and game playing—all of which accept
       limitations on action.

360   EBNER, DEAN. "Chaucer's Precarious Knight." In Imagination
       and Spirit: Essays Presented to Clyde S. Kilby. Edited by
       C.A. Huttar. Grand Rapids, Mich.: William B. Eerdmans
       Publishing Co., 1971, pp. 87-100.
          Characterizes Chaucer's Knight by examining his sketch and
       tale in light of his interruption of the Monk's tragedies.
       Unlike the Monk, the Knight views Fortune as a positive, benefi-
       cial force—an attitude reflected in his personal success, the
       "happy ending" of his tale, and his rejection of the Monk's dour
       perspective.

361   ELBOW, PETER H. "How Chaucer Transcends Oppositions in the
       Knight's Tale." Chaucer Review 7 (1972):97-112. Revised
       slightly in Oppositions in Chaucer (Middletown, Conn.:
       Wesleyan University Press, 1975), pp. 73-94.
          Examines the Knight's Tale as a poem that transcends its
       own demande d'amour (which knight is more worthy?) by thoroughly
       developing Palamon and Arcite and revealing the "profound irrele-
       vancies" of courtly ways of judging worth. The examination of
       courtly ideals does not, however, deny their importance.

362   GAYLORD, ALAN T. "The Role of Saturn in the Knight's Tale."
       Chaucer Review 8 (1974):172-90.

Reads Saturn of Knight's Tale metaphorically, as an encap-
sulation of the effects of human folly, an "elaboration" of the
unfortunate aspects of Venus and Mars, and the representation of
the old order which is overwhelmed by the new order of "reason,
moderation, and pitee."

363   HANNING, ROBERT W. "'The Struggle between Noble Design and
       Chaos': The Literary Tradition of Chaucer's Knight's Tale."
       Literary Review 23 (1980):519-41.
            Traces the development of the thematic opposition between
       order and chaos from Statius's Thebaid through Boccaccio's
       Teseida to Chaucer's Knight's Tale. In Thebaid, epic
       "pessimistic vision" and horror overwhelm Theseus's attempt to
       civilize Thebes. Boccaccio imposes self-conscious, almost cyni-
       cal, poetic control on the narrative, suggesting the importance
       of manipulation to achieve order in either poetry or life.
       Attributed to a professional soldier, Chaucer's Knight's Tale
       exposes the tension within the chivalric code that "seeks to
       moralize and dignify aggression."

364   HELTERMAN, JEFFREY. "The Dehumanizing Metaphor of the
       Knight's Tale." ELH: A Journal of English Literary History
       38 (1971):199-211.
            Locates a disruptive subtext in Knight's Tale: a combina-
       tion of bestial imagery, the "rhetorical management" of the
       tournament, and the irony of occupatio. The subtext disturbs the
       order that the Knight seeks to express and reflects the
       fourteenth-century difficulty of resolving the ideals of chivalry
       and love.

365   HERZMAN, RONALD B. "The Paradox of Form: The Knight's Tale
       and Chaucerian Aesthetics." Papers in Language and Literature
       10 (1974):339-52.
            Assesses Knight's Tale thematically and formally, and as an
       aesthetic paradigm of Canterbury Tales. The structure of the
       tale dominates its romance form, and chivalric behavior--the
       structure of courtly life--dominates human action. Each
       structuring is overt and therefore reminiscent of a higher
       ordering, just as the tales themselves recall a higher
       pilgrimage.

366   KEEN, MAURICE. "Chaucer's Knight, the English Aristocracy,
       and the Crusade." In English Court Culture in the Later
       Middle Ages. Edited by V.J. Scattergood and J.W. Sherborne.
       London: Gerald Duckworth & Co.; New York: St. Martin's
       Press, 1983, pp. 45-61.
            Surveys the conditions of military crusading in Chaucer's
       time, illuminating the portrait of the Knight in Canterbury
       Tales. The crusading ideal was a "strong one" and the Knight's
       portrait reflects a "life-style and ideals much admired in the
       court of Richard II."

Canterbury Tales

The Knight

367 LOOMIS, DOROTHY BETHURUM. "Saturn in Chaucer's Knight's
Tale." In Chaucer und seine Zeit: Symposion für Walter F.
Schirmer. Edited by Arno Esch. Buchreihe der Anglia:
Zeitshrift für englische Philologie, no. 14. Tübingen: Max
Niemeyer, 1968, pp. 149–61.
    Assesses the figure of Saturn in Chaucer's Knight's Tale in
light of astrological and mythological tradition. Emphasizes the
importance of Bernard Silvestris in associating Saturn with determinism, his mythographic value as wisdom, and his malevolent
function in the zodiac.

368 MEIER, T.K. "Chaucer's Knight as 'Persona': Narration as
Control." English Miscellany 20 (1969):11–21.
    Characterizes the Knight of Canterbury Tales by assessing
the tone and details of his tale, observing the general, stoic
pessimism of his focus on the uncertainties of war, love, and
religion, and suggesting that he "counsels a lack of exuberance,"
reflects an "ironic tolerance" of others, and accepts the
"natural order of things."

369 MUSCATINE, CHARLES. "Form, Texture, and Meaning in Chaucer's
Knight's Tale." PMLA 65 (1950):911–29. Reprinted in Chaucer:
Modern Essays in Criticism, ed. Edward Wagenknecht (New York:
Oxford University Press, 1959), pp. 60–82.
    Examines the formal symmetry of Knight's Tale as it
conflicts with the "violent ups and downs of the surface
narrative," displaying an opposition between order and chaos
transcended in Theseus's faith in the "ultimate order of all
things." The actions and speeches of Palamon and Arcite define
the "struggle between noble designs and chaos."

370 OLSON, PAUL A. "Chaucer's Epic Statement and the Political
Milieu of the Late Fourteenth Century." Mediaevalia 5
(1979):61–87.
    Sets Knight's Tale in the tradition of political verse, and
argues that the tale encourages peace in the domestic and foreign
affairs of Chaucer's England. The hortatory, heroic style of the
tale presents Theseus as a peace-making ideal, pertinent to the
French wars of the time. The juxtaposition of the Miller's Tale
with the Knight's Tale encourages placid relations with the
peasant class.

371 REIDY, JOHN. "The Education of Chaucer's Duke Theseus." In
The Epic in Medieval Society: Asethetic and Moral Values.
Edited by Harald Scholler. Tübingen: Max Niemeyer, 1977, pp.
391–408.
    Traces the development of Theseus in Knight's Tale from
simply a "successful soldier" to a philosophical ruler, gauging
the propriety of his military actions against medieval law and
showing how he gains perspective through the death of Arcite and
recognizes the relation between human action and divine providence.

Canterbury Tales

372   SALTER, ELIZABETH. "Chaucer and Boccaccio: The Knight's
       Tale." In Fourteenth-Century English Poetry: Contexts and
       Readings. Oxford: Clarendon Press, 1983, pp. 141-81.
          Assesses Chaucer's modifications of Boccaccio's Teseida and
       his adaptation of Boethius's Consolation of Philosophy in
       Knight's Tale, highlighting his concern with "destinal forces"
       and challenging traditional interpretations by arguing that the
       poem presents a world that is "uncertain" and instable, heterodox
       in its emphasis upon the "stubborn truths of human experience."

373   SCHEPS, WALTER. "Chaucer's Theseus and the Knight's Tale."
       Leeds Studies in English 9 (1977):19-34.
          Sketches the classical and medieval backgrounds to Theseus
       as he appears in four Chaucerian narratives. In Anelida and
       Arcite, Chaucer depicts the positive, heroic Theseus derived from
       Statius's Thebaid; in House of Fame and Legend of Good Women, the
       negative, Ovidian deserter of Ariadne. In Knight's Tale, Chaucer
       either combines both views or follows a Petrarchan tradition,
       producing a "morally ambivalent" character who is "unable to
       impose his will upon events."

374   TURNER, FREDERICK. "A Structuralist Analysis of the Knight's
       Tale." Chaucer Review 8 (1974):279-96.
          Analyzes Knight's Tale as a "mythic" structure in which
       patterns of marriage and incest, kinship and rivalry, interact
       with the hierarchies and oppositions among the major characters
       and the gods that align with them. The tales of the the Miller
       and Reeve reflect "mock mythic" versions of the structure.

375   VAN, THOMAS A. "Theseus and the 'Right Way' of the Knight's
       Tale." Studies in the Literary Imagination 4 (1971):83-100.
          Assesses the development of Theseus in Knight's Tale from
       his early irascibleness to his philosophical resolve, identifying
       the "forgiveness scene" in the forest as his turning point and
       elucidating his "normative presence" in the second half of the
       poem.

          See also entries 137, 141, 159, 215, 229, 260, 272, 285,
       902. For theme and philosophy: 54, 154, 157, 209-10, 214, 216,
       218, 243, 245, 319, 719; sources and influence: 167, 170-72,
       179-80, 196, 225, 252; characters: 133, 136, 241, 237; relations
       to other tales: 246, 262, 277-79, 282, 376, 381, 527, 529, 531,
       534, 628, 638.

THE MILLER AND HIS TALE

376   BLOOMFIELD, MORTON W. "The Miller's Tale--An Un-Boethian
       Interpretation." In Medieval Literature and Folklore Studies:
       Essays in Honor of Francis Lee Utley. Edited by Jerome Mandel
       and Bruce A. Rosenberg. New Brunswick, N.J.: Rutgers
       University Press, 1970, pp. 205-11.

The Miller

      Asserts that Knight's Tale and Reeve's Tale assume a Boethian world view, in which order dominates and justice prevails. In Miller's Tale, however, the world is "deeply irrational and unjust" because Alison escapes punishment and "kind-hearted John" is overpunished. Nicholas's machinations create an illusion of man-made order that is hollow.

377   BRATCHER, JAMES T., and VON KREISLER, NICOLAI. "The Popularity of the Miller's Tale." Southern Folklore Quarterly 35 (1971):325-35.
      Compares Miller's Tale to three modern American analogues and suggests that the appeal of Chaucer's version results from his deft use of carpenter John in the plot. Our attention is distracted from the carpenter so that his abrupt reintroduction at the end creates much of the tale's humor.

378   COOPER, GEOFFREY. "'Sely John' in the 'Legende' of the Miller's Tale." JEGP: Journal of English and Germanic Philology 79 (1980):1-12.
      Identifies the medieval connotations of "sely" as Chaucer applied it to carpenter John in the Miller's Tale, demonstrating Chaucer's manipulation of meaning in context. Normally used in hagiographies or romances, "sely" carries the meanings of "pitiable" and "innocent"; in Chaucer's fabliau the meaning shifts to "pitiful" and ignorant.

379   DONALDSON, E. TALBOT. "Idiom of Popular Poetry in the Miller's Tale." English Institute Essays 1950. Edited by A.S. Downer. New York: Columbia University Press, 1951, pp. 116-40. Reprinted in Explication as Criticism: Selected Papers from the English Institute 1941-52, ed. W.K. Wimsatt, Jr. (New York: Columbia University Press, 1963), pp. 27-51; Chaucer and His Contemporaries: Essays on Medieval Literature and Thought, ed. Helaine Newstead (Greenwich, Conn.: Fawcett Publications, 1968), pp. 174-89; Speaking of Chaucer (New York: W.W. Norton & Co., 1970), pp. 13-29; Chaucer--The "Canterbury Tales": A Casebook, ed. J.J. Andersen (London: Macmillan & Co., 1974), pp. 143-60.
      Cites ironic examples of clichéd, courtly language that appear in Miller's Tale and characterize Nicholas, Alison, and Absolon. Usually found in metrical romances and love lyrics, such language indicates the parodic intent that operates in the "no man's land" between Chaucer and the Miller as teller. Similar language found in Tale of Sir Thopas.

380   GELLRICH, JESSE M. "The Parody of Music in the Miller's Tale." JEGP: Journal of English and Germanic Philology 73 (1974):176-88.
      Explores the musical imagery of the Miller's Tale, arguing that Nicholas's angelus, his psalter, Absolon's serenades, and the melody-making of Nicholas and Alison create poetic dis-

harmonies that are comic, ironic, and yet generously sensitive to human limitations.

381   JAMBECK, THOMAS J. "Characterization and Syntax in the Miller's Tale." Journal of Narrative Technique 5 (1975):73-85.
       Demonstrates how syntax helps characterize the Miller and the Knight. The heavily paratactic style of Miller's Tale contrasts the hypotactic style of Knight's Tale, idiomatically characterizing the Miller as a social inferior.

382   JONES, GEORGE F. "Chaucer and the Medieval Miller." Modern Language Quarterly 16 (1955):3-15.
       Surveys cultural and literary evidence to show that Chaucer's Miller "conforms to the accepted medieval idea of a miller." The social position of millers as newly emergent serfs, their economic positions as nouveau riche, and the history of their occupation contribute to the trenchancy of Chaucer's satire.

383   MILLER, ROBERT P. "The Miller's Tale as Complaint." Chaucer Review 5 (1970):147-60.
       Traditional complaints against each of the estates inform the characterizations of Miller's Tale: the aristocratic pretension of Absolom, the clergy's claims to divine knowledge in Nicholas, and the peasants' tendency to jeopardize their own interests in John. Alison reflects traditional antifeminist criticism.

384   NEUSS, PAULA. "Double Entendre in the Miller's Tale." Essays in Criticism 24 (1974):325-40.
       Traces the bawdy implications of "privetee," "queynt," and music-making in Miller's Tale, demonstrating how effectively Chaucer cultivates meaning through repetition and how the puns carry subtlety as well as mirth.

385   OLSON, PAUL A. "Poetic Justice in the Miller's Tale." Modern Language Quarterly 24 (1963):227-36.
       Examines Miller's Tale to show how the punishment of the three male figures constitutes a condemnation of the vices embodied in the characters: avarice in John, pride in Absolon, and lechery in Nicholas.

386   REISS, EDMUND. "Daun Gerveys in the Miller's Tale." Papers in Language and Literature 6 (1970):115-24.
       Identifies the demonic associations of Gerveys's smithy in Miller's Tale, exploring the tradition of Vulcan and other smiths, the implications of the coulter, and the meanings of "Neot" and "viritoot."

387   ROWLAND, BERYL. "Chaucer's Blasphemous Churl: A New Interpretation of the Miller's Tale." In Chaucer and Middle

The Miller

English Studies in Honour of Rossell Hope Robbins. Edited by
Beryl Rowland. London: George Allen & Unwin, 1974, pp. 43-
55.

Identifies a significant pattern of sacred allusions in
Miller's Tale, demonstrating that their accumulative effect parodies the Annunciation, Christ's family, Noah's flood, and the
Trinity. References to the cycle dramas, details of description,
and burlesque of biblical texts set "trivial lust and vulgar
jest" against the "cosmic and timeless background of divine
ordinance."

388   THRO, A. BOOKER. "Chaucer's Creative Comedy: A Study of the
       Miller's Tale and the Shipman's Tale." Chaucer Review 5
       (1970):97-111.
            Explores Chaucer's comic impulse to creativity, contrasting
       the creativeness of the characters in Miller's Tale with the more
       typical, farcical deflation of characters in the fabliaux, and
       examining the psychological creativity of Shipman's Tale. Sug-
       gests that these instances of creativity are both exemplary and
       mimetic, evidence of the "high Gothic" strain of Chaucer's
       comedy.

       See also entries 22, 56, 136, 141, 155, 159, 201, 216, 260, 272,
       285, 490. For sources and analogues: 169, 177, 252, 256, 308-
       09, 311-13; relations to other tales: 241, 277-79, 282, 370,
       374.

THE REEVE AND HIS TALE

389   BAIRD, JOSEPH L. "Law and the Reeve's Tale."
       Neuphilologische Mitteilungen 70 (1969):679-83.
            Identifies three legal references in Reeve's Tale through
       which Chaucer ironically plays the old Mosaic law against the new
       Christian law, private law against public law, and continental
       law against English law.

390   BREWER, DEREK S. "The Reeve's Tale and the King's Hall,
       Cambridge." Chaucer Review 5 (1971):311-17. Reprinted in
       Tradition and Innovation in Chaucer (London: Macmillan & Co.,
       1982), pp. 73-79.
            Argues that manuscript evidence does not negate the identi-
       fication of "S(c)oler Halle" of the Reeve's Tale with King's
       Hall, Cambridge. Correlations between details of the tale and
       fourteenth-century ideas of King's Hall exemplify how Chaucer
       permeates his fiction with "local supporting realism."

391   BURBRIDGE, ROGER T. "Chaucer's Reeve's Tale and the Fabliau
       Le meunier et les .II. clers." Annuale Medievale 12
       (1971):30-36.
            Compares Chaucer's Reeve's Tale to two analogues (versions
       of Le meunier et les .II. clers) to show how he improved the

drama and comedy of the plot by sharpening motive and detail and
how he shaped it to the Reeve's desire to "quit" the Miller.

392   DELANY, SHEILA. "Clerks and Quitting in the Reeve's Tale."
      Mediaeval Studies 29 (1967):351-56.
          Argues that the fluid social status of medieval clerks
      helps explain their frequent appearance and ironic function in
      fabliaux, especially Chaucer's Reeve's Tale. In the tale, the
      "almost-bourgeois Simkin" believes John and Aleyn are his social
      inferiors—a source of humorous irony to the aristocratic audi-
      ence who regarded them as his superiors.

393   FRANK, ROBERT W., Jr. "The Reeve's Tale and the Comedy of
      Limitation." In Directions in Literary Criticism: Contem-
      porary Appoaches to Literature. Edited by Stanley Weintraub
      and Philip Young. University Park: Pennsylvania State
      University, 1973, pp. 53-69.
          Analyzes the character, plot, and style of Reeve's Tale,
      identifying the nature of its comedy. Rich style and thematic
      focus on the notion of space combine with simple plot and direct
      characterization to produce an uproarious exposé of pretentions
      in conflict with simple necessities.

394   FRIEDMAN, JOHN BLOCK. "A Reading of Chaucer's Reeve's Tale."
      Chaucer Review 2 (1967):8-19.
          Identifies patterns of animal imagery in Reeve's Tale and
      sketches their exegetical backgrounds, describing how they set
      the "moral tone" of this tale of man's "ungoverned passions,"
      especially pride, wrath, and lust. Images of the runaway horse,
      peacock, magpie, and pig dominate the tale.

395   GARBÁTY, THOMAS J. "Satire and Regionalism: The Reeve and
      His Tale." Chaucer Review 8 (1973):1-18.
          Demonstrates through contemporary demographics and dialects
      that Chaucer's dialectical play in Reeve's Tale is a double-
      layered joke: the Reeve mimics "a provincial dialect in his own
      barbarous jargon." Compare Tolkien (entry 399) and Fisher (entry
      279).

396   GRENNEN, JOSEPH E. "The Calculating Reeve and His Camera
      obscura." Journal of Medieval and Renaissance Studies 14
      (1984):245-57.
          Suggests a variety of academic jokes in Reeve's Tale that
      heighten the gown's victory over the town in the main plot.
      Chaucer may have originally written the work for an academic
      audience who would have been knowledgeable enough to catch the
      jokes involving Symkyn's physiogomic snubnose, Scholastic
      distinctions, and optics.

397   LANCASHIRE, IAN. "Sexual Innuendo in the Reeve's Tale."
      Chaucer Review 6 (1972):159-70.

The Reeve

Discusses the complex network of puns of Reeve's Tale, not available in Chaucer's apparent sources. Sexual connotations of flour, milling or grinding, and horsemanship color the action of the narrative, contributing to the retributive punishment of Symkyn.

398 OLSON, GLENDING. "The Reeve's Tale as a Fabliau." Modern Language Quarterly 35 (1974):219-30.

Disagrees with readings of Reeve's Tale that emphasize the teller's vengeance, demonstrating the poem's similarity to French fabliaux. Since Chaucer is the first to present this genre from a lower-class perspective, we should not expect a complex tale-teller relationship; the tale's "craft, wit, satire . . . and morality" are enough.

399 TOLKIEN, J.R.R. "Chaucer as Philologist: The Reeve's Tale." Transactions of the Philological Society, 1934, pp. 1-70.

Examines the northern dialect features of Chaucer's Reeve's Tale, documenting the sensitivity with which Chaucer created a fictional dialect, its historical accuracy, and linguistic sophistication. Comments upon the phonological, morphological, and semantic particulars of each feature of the literary dialect. Compare Garbáty (entry 395).

See also entries 56, 141, 216, 240, 257, 260, 285, 290, 490. For sources and analogues: 252, 308-9, 313; relations to other tales: 277, 279, 282, 376, 394.

THE COOK AND HIS TALE

400 SCATTERGOOD, V.J. "Perkyn Revelour and the Cook's Tale." Chaucer Review 19 (1984):14-23.

Typifies Perkyn of Cook's Tale as a "dissipated urban wastrel," a precursor of the fifteenth-century tradition of the literary gallant. Compares Perkyn's characteristics with those of similar types found in complaint satires and morality plays, and from these comparisons hypothesizes what shape Cook's Tale might have taken.

See also entries 252, 285, 666, 668-69.

THE MAN OF LAW AND HIS TALE

401 BLOCK, EDWARD A. "Originality, Controlling Purpose, and Craftsmanship in Chaucer's Man of Law's Tale." PMLA 68 (1953):572-616.

Studies the differences between Chaucer's Man of Law's Tale and its source in Nicholas Trivet's Les chronicles, noting how Chaucer streamlined its details, added rhetorical flourishes, and "humanized" its characters. Chaucer did not alter the main out-

lines of the tale, yet his originality is evident in the two
thirds of the poem that he reworked.

402   BLOOMFIELD, MORTON W.   "The Man of Law's Tale: A Tragedy of
       Victimization and Christian Comedy." PMLA 87 (1972):384-90.
       Printed first in Italian in Strumenti Critici 9 (1969):195-
       207.
           Attributes modern unease with Chaucer's pathetic tales,
       especially Man of Law's Tale, to the distance "effected by the
       rhetoric of pathos." The narrator's apostrophes, the passivity
       of Constance, and the inevitable happy ending for the Christian
       victim encourage contemptus mundi rather than catharsis.
       Christian comedy and tragic victimization combine to create "the
       informed uneasiness all true believers must experience in the
       world."

403   CAIE, GRAHAM D.   "The Significance of Marginal Glosses in the
       Earliest Manuscripts of the Canterbury Tales." In Chaucer and
       Scriptural Tradition. Edited by David Lyle Jeffrey. Ottawa:
       University of Ottawa Press, 1984, pp. 75-88.
           Describes the medieval habit of making glosses in
       manuscripts that reveal the interaction between text and audi-
       ence. Discusses how the glosses to Man of Law's Tale from
       Bernard Silvestris's Cosmographia, Innocent III's De miseri
       conditionis humanae (De contemptu mundi) and Ptolemy's Almagest
       show how the Man of Law distorts his sources, undercutting his
       reliability.

404   CLARK, SUSAN L., and WASSERMAN, JULIAN N.   "Constance as
       Romance and Folk Heroine in Chaucer's Man of Law's Tale."
       Rice University Studies 64 (1978):13-24.
           Examines the romance and folktale elements of Chaucer's
       Constance in the Man of Law's Tale, showing how he emphasized
       these elements, exploring the paradoxical medieval view of woman
       and creating an unusually rich heroine who undergoes significant
       development.

405   CLOGAN, PAUL M.   "The Narrative Style of the Man of Law's
       Tale." Medievalia et Humanistica, n.s. 8 (1977):217-33.
           Describes the historical conflation of the genres of
       saint's life and romance and discusses Chaucer's Man of Law's
       Tale as a "hagiographical romance," notable for the clerkly
       persona of its narrator and the "heightened lyricism" of its
       apostrophes, moralizations, and verse form.

406   CULVER, T.D.   "The Imposition of Order: A Measure of Art in
       the Man of Law's Tale." Yearbook of English Studies 2
       (1972):13-20.
           Contrasts Nicolas Trivet's, John Gower's, and Chaucer's
       versions of the tale of Constance. Whereas Gower effectively
       reduces the details and introduces envy as a motive into Trivet's
       repetitious saint's life, Chaucer expands the exemplary value of

The Man of Law

the story, deepens the allegory, and sharpens the characterization of Constance.

407   DAVID, ALFRED. "The Man of Law vs. Chaucer: A Case in
       Poetics." PMLA 82 (1967):217-25.
           Reads Fragment II of the Canterbury Tales as a record of
       Chaucer's struggle with "his conscience" as an artist. Following
       the bawdiness of the Miller, Reeve, and Cook, the Man of Law's
       Prologue is Chaucer's "half-humorous" concession to morality
       which he quickly rescinds in the Man of Law's bombastic tale.
       Yet Chaucer finally chooses morality over aesthetics in Parson's
       Prologue.

408   DELASANTA, RODNEY. "And of Great Reverence: Chaucer's Man of
       Law." Chaucer Review 5 (1971):288-310.
           Traces the Man of Law's "pattern of errors about things
       literary," including his scriptural inaccuracies and his denigra-
       tion of Gower. Through these errors and through "rhetorical ex-
       cess" and "religious exhibitionism," Chaucer characterizes his
       Man of Law as a man too much taken with his own limited education
       and morality.

409   FARRELL, ROBERT T. "Chaucer's Use of the Theme of the Help of
       God in the Man of Law's Tale." Neuphilologische Mitteilungen
       71 (1970):239-43.
           Demonstrates that Constance is a type or figura of the Help
       of God in Man of Law's Tale by assessing the exegetical associa-
       tion and understanding of the scriptural precedents with which
       she is compared: Daniel, Jonah, the passing of the Red Sea, and
       the miracle of the loaves and fishes.

410   HAMILTON, MARIE P. "The Dramatic Suitability of the Man of
       Law's Tale." In Studies in Language and Literature in Honour
       of Maragret Schlauch. Edited by Mieczysław Brahmer, Stanisław
       Helsztyński, and Julain Krzyżanowski. Warsaw: PWN-Polish
       Scientific Publishers, 1966. Reprint. New York: Russell &
       Russell, 1971, pp. 153-63.
           Demonstrates the appropriateness of Chaucer's tale of
       Constance to the Man of Law, citing the elaborate rhetoric of the
       tale and the legally "informed presentation of the trial of
       Constance."

411   JOHNSON, WILLIAM C., Jr. "The Miracles in the Man of Law's
       Tale." Bulletin of the Rocky Mountain Modern Language
       Association 28 (1974):57-65.
           Compares the miracles of Chaucer's Man of Law's Tale with
       those of its source in Nicholas Trivet showing how Chaucer
       emphasizes the human and emotional aspects of the tale and
       deemphasizes the religious. Describes Chaucer's emphasis as
       humanistic.

Canterbury Tales

412   LEWIS, ROBERT ENZER. "Chaucer's Artistic Use of Pope Innocent
       III's De miseria humane conditionis in the Man of Law's
       Prologue and Tale." PMLA 81 (1966):485-92.
          Suggests that Chaucer's uses of materials from Innocent's
       serve several artistic purposes: bridging and unifying the pre-
       existing introductory material and the tale of Constance, high-
       lighting Constance's misfortunes, and underscoring the "serious
       moral tone" of Man of Law's Tale.

413   _____. "Glosses to the Man of Law's Tale from Innocent III's
       De miseria humane conditionis." Studies in Philology 64
       (1967):1-16.
          Compares Chaucer's paraphrases of Innocent III's De miseria
       conditionis humanae (De contemptu mundi)with the Latin manuscript
       glosses that accompany the tale, arguing that the glosses reflect
       Chaucer's own manuscript of De miseria. Either Chaucer or an
       early scribe added the glosses to the tale, using Chaucer's
       original source-text.

414   MILLER, ROBERT P. "Constancy Humanized: Trivet's Constance
       and the Man of Law's Constance." Costerus 3 (1975):49-71.
          Examines Chaucer's modifications in the Man of Law's Pro-
       logue and Tale of Innocent III's De miseria conditionis humanae
       (De contemptu mundi) and Nicholas Trivet's tale of Constance,
       arguing that the changes make the materials appropriate to the
       character of the Man of Law established in General Prologue:
       officious, materialistic, and weak in his understanding of the
       proper relation between law and Providence.

415   PAULL, MICHAEL R. "The Influence of the Saint's Legend Genre
       in the Man of Law's Tale." Chaucer Review 5 (1971):179-94.
          Attributes Chaucer's alterations of Nicholas Trivet's life
       of Constance in Man of Law's Tale to the saint's life genre,
       arguing that his transformation of the dramatic tale into near
       allegory and his enhanced rhetoric are features of hagiography
       from which he developed his own melodramatic form.

416   SCHEPS, WALTER. "Chaucer's Man of Law and the Tale of
       Constance." PMLA 89 (1974):285-95.
          Reads the Man of Law's materials in Canterbury Tales as an
       unfolding characterization of the Man himself that presents him
       as consistently concerned with wealth and rank, expedient in what
       he remembers and how he uses authorities and, above all, tedious
       in his excesses of rhetoric and sentiment.

417   WOOD, CHAUNCEY. "Chaucer's Man of Law as Interpreter."
       Traditio 23 (1967):149-90.
          Assesses Chaucer's tale of Constance as a self-disclosing
       satire of the Man of Law's inability to recognize the hierar-
       chical relation of destiny to Providence. The lawyer is
       motivated by the hope of worldly prosperity; he distorts his

Canterbury Tales

sources; and in his rhetorical commentaries, he consistently
misinterprets the moral implications of his own narrative.

418   WURTELE, DOUGLAS. "'Proprietas' in Chaucer's Man of Law's
       Tale." Neophilologus 60 (1976):577-93.
       Demonstrates that the forensic rhetoric of Man of Law's
Tale follows classical rhetorical exhortations of decorum. Since
such rhetoric was traditionally discouraged in English legal
practice, the Lawyer's use of it either typifies him as a trendy
"newe man" or, as suggested in Man of Law's Prologue, an "amateur
of literature."

       See also entries 88, 127, 190, 216, 222, 224, 257, 285.
For textual issues: 266, 268; sources and analogues: 169, 184,
217, 252; relations to other tales: 549, 563, 566.

THE WIFE OF BATH AND HER TALE

419   ALLEN, JUDSON BOYCE, and GALLACHER, PATRICK. "Alisoun Through
       the Looking Glass; or Every Man His Own Midas." Chaucer
       Review 4 (1970):99-105.
       Explicates the Wife of Bath's Ovidian exemplum of Midas as
an indication of how she misuses authority and a reflection of
her moral weakness. Standard Ovidian commentaries (Giovanni del
Virgilio and Arnulf of Orlean) expose the Wife's distortions of
the exemplary meaning of Midas.

420   AXELROD, STEVEN. "The Wife of Bath and the Clerk." Annuale
       Mediaevale 15 (1974):100-124.
       Questions the traditional assumption of antagonism between
the Wife of Bath and the Clerk, suggesting that the two engage in
"witty banter" rather than "fierce assault." Their "incipient
courtship" is consistent with their portraits, their prologues,
and their tales.

421   BIGGINS, DENNIS. "'O Jankyn, Be Ye There?'" In Chaucer and
       Middle English Studies in Honour of Rossell Hope Robbins.
       Edited by Beryl Rowland. London: George Allen & Unwin, 1974,
       pp. 249-54.
       Collects the suggestions of the Wife of Bath's marital
status from the Canterbury Tales and shows how this evidence
proves her neither wife nor widow at the time of the pilgrimage,
but ambiguously suggests both, enriching her character.

422   BLAKE, N.F. "The Wife of Bath and Her Tale." Leeds Studies
       in English 13 (1982):42-55.
       Reconsiders various critical questions concerning the Wife
of Bath in light of the authority of the Hengwrt manuscript,
denying that the Shipman's Tale was ever intended for the Wife,
challenging the validity of a "Marriage Group," tracing stages of
the Wife's development among the two versions of her tale and the

two of her prologue, and suggesting that her prologue and tale combine with the Friar's and Summoner's tales to form a "cohesive group" concerned with tyranny. Compare East (Entry 429).

423   BURTON, T.L. "The Wife of Bath's Fourth and Fifth Husbands and Her Ideal Sixth: The Growth of a Marital Philosophy." Chaucer Review 13 (1978):34–50.
The Wife of Bath's presentation of her fourth and fifth husbands and the knight in her tale characterize her as a "bossy woman who longs to be mastered in the bedroom" and who "loathes being manacled outside it." She resolves the conflict in fantasy.

424   CAIE, GRAHAM D. "The Significance of the Early Chaucer Manuscript Glosses (with Special Reference to the Wife of Bath's Prologue)." Chaucer Review 10 (1976):350–60.
Examines glosses to the Wife of Bath's Prologue in various manuscripts to show that they are not Chaucerian, but the reactions of contemporary readers. They reveal the readers' reactions as they identify sources of the Wife's material and clarify her misinterpretation and misuse of it.

425   CARRUTHERS, MARY [J]. "The Wife of Bath and the Painting of Lions." PMLA 94 (1979):209–22.
Characterizes the Wife of Bath as an entreprenurial member of the bourgeoisie and discusses the sociopolitical aspects of her parodies of antifeminism and the false gentility of social climbers. In her prologue, she indicates the financial disadvantages of virginity, and her tale inverts the ideals of contemporary deportment books, subverting their illusory gentility.

426   CARY, MEREDITH. "Sovereignty and Old Wife." Papers in Language and Literature 5 (1969):375–88.
Compares Chaucer's Wife of Bath's Tale with its nearly contemporary English analogues and several versions from folklore. Consistent with the female narrator of the tale, all the major roles are female and the expressed values are traditionally associated with women. Transforming a traditionally masculine tale, Chaucer opposes the Wife's "feminine attitude" and "the traditional position of women in his society."

427   COLMER, DOROTHY. "Character and Class in the Wife of Bath's Tale." JEGP: Journal of English and Germanic Philology 72 (1974):329–39.
Argues that the Wife of Bath's fairy romance reflects her sexual obsession and that her discussion of gentilesse extends from her middle-class background. Her rejections of male sexual domination and upper-class moral superiority are consistent with her character.

428   COTTER, JAMES FINN. "The Wife of Bath's Lenten Observance." Papers in Language and Literature 7 (1971):293–97.

The Wife of Bath

Compares the Wife of Bath's lenten practices--extravagant clothing and "dalliance"--and her rhetoric describing them to the Ash Wednesday gospel, clarifying the comedy of her description and the spiritual irony of her actions.

429 EAST, W.G. "By Preeve Which That is Demonstratif." Chaucer Review 12 (1977):78-82.
Argues that the critical attention to the Marriage Argument has obscured the thematic unity of the tales of the Wife of Bath, Friar, and Summoner (Fragment III), all of which address the relative value of authority and experience in Scholastic debate. Compare Blake (entry 422).

430 GILLIAM, D. "'Cast up the Curtyn': A Tentative Exploration into the Meaning of the Wife of Bath's Tale." In Proceedings of the Twelfth Congress of the Australasian Universities Language and Literature Association. Edited by A.P. Treweek. Sydney: Australasian Universities Language and Literature Association, 1970, pp. 435-55.
Reads Wife of Bath's Tale as a double-edged allegory: on one level, the Wife's exhortation to "embrace sexual appetite" since it brings rewards, and on the other, Chaucer's condemnation of sin, signaled by the discussion of gentilesse and echoes of Boethius and Dante.

431 HALLER, ROBERT S. "The Wife of Bath and the Three Estates." Annuale Mediaevale 6 (1965):47-64.
Shows how the concept of the three estates underlies the Wife of Bath's Prologue and Tale: the Wife uses bourgeois statety against her first three husbands, "outclerks" the clerical Jankyn, and through the hag's discussion is more gentle than the knight of her tale. As a cloth merchant, the Wife reflects the social changes of Chaucer's day, prevailing over representatives of traditional social classes.

432 HAMILTON, ALICE. "Helowys and the Burning of Jankyn's Book." Mediaeval Studies 34 (1972):196-207.
Observes similarities in detail and pattern between the book-burning scene of Wife of Bath's Prologue and Peter Abelard's Historia calamitatem, arguing that Abelard's work may have been Chaucer's source, known to him through Jean de Meun and Petrarch.

433 HARWOOD, BRITTON J. "The Wife of Bath and the Dream of Innocence." Modern Language Quarterly 33 (1972):257-73.
Reads the Wife of Bath's Prologue as a complex portrait of the Wife's marital woes and lost innocence which she only partially assuages through the fantasy of her tale. Like the hag of her tale, she knows female desires and the concessions necessary in marriage, but she lacks the hag's power of self-regeneration.

434 HOLLAND, NORMAN N. "Meaning as Transformation: The Wife of Bath's Tale." College English 28 (1967):279-90.

Compares various "modern," "medieval," and "mythic" layers of meaning in Wife of Bath's Tale, privileging a psychoanalytic interpretation that "underlies all others." The meaning of the tale is its process of tranforming the reader's unconscious fantasy into conscious terms: the fantasy is of the phallic aggression of the child who must submit to the mother or hazard castration.

435   KOBAN, CHARLES. "Hearing Chaucer Out: The Art of Persuasion in the Wife of Bath's Tale." Chaucer Review 5 (1971):225-39.
Uses Wife of Bath's Tale to argue that Chaucer's works are best understood orally. Imagining ourselves as listeners to the tale, we can recognize how the exemplary material, the conventions of the plot, and the explicit moralizing on gentility "raise in respective ironic, paradoxical, and hortatory form" the problem of "dignity in fallen human nature."

436   LEVY, BERNARD S. "The Wife of Bath's Queynte Fantasye." Chaucer Review 4 (1970):106-22.
Clarifies the punning references to genitalia in Wife of Bath's Prologue and Tale, arguing that words and phrases like "gentil dedes," "thyng," and "sovereignty" comprise a pattern of bawdy suggestion that characterizes the Wife and the loathly hag as "worldly women." In contrast, the end of the Wife's tale carries covert echoes of baptism.

437   MAGEE, PATRICIA ANNE. "The Wife of Bath and the Problem of Mastery." Massachusetts Studies in English 3 (1971):40-45.
Characterizes the Wife of Bath, not as a radical feminist who wants dominance over males, but as a woman who wants what she can not have and who wants to be dominated. Suggestive parallels between her prologue and tale indicate the difference between what the Wife thinks she wants and "what she 'really' wants."

438   MATTHEWS, WILLIAM. "The Wife of Bath and All Her Sect." Viator 5 (1974):413-43.
Traces the roots of Chaucer's characterization of the Wife of Bath in classical and medieval tradition. In her marital success and her active old age, the Wife differs from the stock character of the old woman found in Ovid's Amores, in Pamphilus, Vetula, Mahieu de Boulogne's Lamentations, Juan Ruiz's El libro de buen amor, and Jean de Meun's Roman de la rose. Chaucer derived her vitality, perhaps, from fabliaux and transformed the stock character.

439   MILLER, ROBERT P. "The Wife of Bath's Tale and Mediaeval Exempla." ELH: A Journal of English Literary History 32 (1965):442-56.
Compares Wife of Bath's Tale to traditional exempla concerned with obedience or fair/foul transformation, identifying the Wife's inversion of traditional interpretations of such exempla, thereby questioning whether or not the knight of the

The Wife of Bath

tale committed "himself utterly to the power of the Fair
Temptress."

440   PATTERSON, LEE. "'For the Wyves Love of Bathe': Feminine
       Rhetoric and Poetic Resolution in the Roman de la Rose and the
       Canterbury Tales." Speculum 58 (1983):656-95.
           Compares the formal and rhetorical aspects of the speeches
       of Jean de Meun's La Vieille and Chaucer's Wife of Bath, arguing
       that the characters reflect the medieval association of poetry
       and sexuality, and that the authors capitalize upon the associa-
       tion to explore and resolve critical literary issues in their
       works. The Wife resolves the conflict between authority, repre-
       sented by the Man of Law, and her own experience, appropriating
       masculine rhetoric for feminine purpose.

441   PRATT, ROBERT A. "Jankyn's Book of Wikked Wyves: Medieval
       Antimatrimonial Propaganda in the Universities." Annuale
       Mediaevale 3 (1962):5-27.
           Authenticates Jankyn's Book of Wicked Wives in Chaucer's
       Wife of Bath's Prologue, describing the history and function of
       such antifeminist collections that combined Theophrastus, Jerome,
       and Walter Map. The popularity of such collections in late-
       medieval universities, especially Oxford, clarifies the character
       of Jankyn.

442   REID, DAVID S. "Crocodilian Humor: A Discussion of Chaucer's
       Wife of Bath." Chaucer Review 4 (1970):73-89.
           Impressionistic reading of the Wife of Bath as caricature,
       her prologue as farce, and her tale as burlesque, resulting from
       the "antic humor" of antifeminism, anticlericism, and class
       antagonism which Chaucer's modifies through his sophisticated
       treatment of popular comedy.

443   ROBERTSON, D.W., Jr. "'And For My Land Hastow Modred Me?':
       Land Tenure, the Cloth Industry, and the Wife of Bath."
       Chaucer Review 14 (1980):403-20.
           Explains and documents the economics of land tenure, the
       cloth industry, and marriage in Chaucer's time, attempting to
       reconstruct the Wife of Bath as Chaucer's audience might have
       seen her. Argues that the Wife embodies the acquisitiveness and
       social disruption associated with the rise of the cloth industry.

444   ROWLAND, BERYL. "On the Timely Death of the Wife of Bath's
       Fourth Husband." Archiv für das Studium der Neueren Sprachen
       und Literaturen 209 (1972):273-82.
           Traces a sub-text of references to death in Wife of Bath's
       Prologue, her false dream, and her fight with Jankyn to suggest
       that the Wife and Jankyn collaborated to murder her fourth hus-
       band. Chaucer leaves the suggestion "tantalizingly ambiguous."

445   _____. "The Wife of Bath's 'Unlawfull Philtrum.'"
       Neophilologus 56 (1972):201-6.

Exemplifies the Wife of Bath's combination of "exegetical and folklore material" by analyzing the traditional association of barley bread with "Priapic loaves" used to excite amorous ardor. The allusion is a subtext to the reference in her Prologue to Christ's multiplication of loaves and fishes.

446   SANDERS, BARRY. "Chaucer's Dependence on Sermon Structure in the Wife of Bath's Prologue and Tale." Studies in Medieval Culture 4 (1974):437-45.
        Identifies manipulation of sermon construction, sermon techniques, and "degenerate pulpit rhetoric" in Wife of Bath's Prologue and Tale, suggesting that such burlesque is part of the Wife's satire of clerical preaching.

447   SCHAUBER, ELLEN, and SPOLSKY, ELLEN. "The Consolation of Alison: The Speech Acts of the Wife of Bath." Centrum 5 (1977):20-34.
        Applies speech-act theory to three Chaucerian female characters, attempting to describe the individualized character of their speech and thereby explain Chaucer's method of characterization. Confrontation, insistence, and confiding syntactically typify the Wife of Bath. The loathly hag of the Wife's tale and Prudence of Tale of Melibee argue more logically and less aggressively than the Wife, and confide not at all.

448   SHAPIRO, GLORIA K. "Dame Alice as Deceptive Narrator." Chaucer Review 6 (1971):130-41.
        Characterizes the Wife of Bath as one whose bravado covers more sentiment and religious conviction than she willingly discloses, identifying tensions between her respect for authority and for experience, her self-deprecation and her assurance, her genuineness and her pretensions, and her suffering and the pain she inflicts upon others.

449   SHUMAKER, WAYNE. "Alisoun in Wonder-Land: A Study in Chaucer's Mind and Literary Method." ELH: A Journal of English Literary History 18 (1951):77-89.
        Assesses the Wife of Bath's portrait and prologue, emphasizing Chaucer's medieval tendency to represent her by generalizations rather than particulars. Even though the Wife is the most realistic of the Canterbury pilgrims, Chaucer characterizes her through her use of authority, not by extrapolating the details of her sketch.

450   SINGER, MARGARET. "The Wife of Bath's Prologue and Tale." In Studies in Chaucer. Edited by G.A. Wilkes and A.P. Reimer. Sydney Studies in English. Sydney: University of Sydney, 1981, pp. 28-37.
        Examines the narrative modes of Wife of Bath's Prologue and Tale, describing the stylistic and rhetorical devices as argument, naturalistic fiction, and romance. The interplay among

The Wife of Bath

these modes reflects the thematic concern with experience and
authority in the prologue and tale..

451   STORM, MELVIN. "Alisoun's Ear." Modern Language Quarterly 42
       (1981):219-26.
           Studies the iconographic significance of the Wife of Bath's
       deafness in one ear, documenting from scriptural and patristic
       sources the suggestion that deafness or hearing with one ear
       signifies abuse of authority and resistence to spiritual truth.

452   THUNDY, ZACHARIAS P. "Matheolus, Chaucer, and the Wife of
       Bath." In Chaucerian Problems and Perspectives: Essays
       Presented to Paul E. Beichner, C.S.C. Edited by Edward Vasta
       and Zacharias P. Thundy. Notre Dame, Ind.: University of
       Notre Dame Press, 1979, pp. 24-58.
           Proposes the thirteenth-century Latin Lamentations of
       Matheolus, translated into French by Jean le Févre, as a source
       of irony in Chaucer's Wife of Bath's Prologue, identifying over
       one hundred verbal parallels between the two and fifteen common
       topics.

453   UTLEY, FRANCIS LEE. "Chaucer's Way with a Proverb: 'Allas!
       Allas! That Evere Love was Synne!'" North Carolina Folklore
       21 (1973):98-104.
           Demonstrates the rich ambiguity of Chaucer's use of
       proverbs by assessing the analogues to a proverb used by the Wife
       of Bath and describing the nuances of her proverbial expression.

454   ZIMBARDO, ROSE A. "Unity and Duality in the Wife of Bath's
       Prologue and Tale." Tennessee Studies in Literature 11
       (1960):11-18.
           Reads Wife of Bath's Prologue as an exploration of the
       tensions between experience and authority, male and female,
       metaphysical and physical. The Wife's "generosity of love"
       enables her to reconcile these opposites within God's order and
       her tale exemplifies this reconciliation through the action and
       advice of the loathly hag.

           See also entries 54, 133, 136, 141, 155, 159, 190, 201,
       229, 241, 257, 260, 272, 322, 766-67. For characterization:
       114, 216, 224, 290, 490; sources and analogues: 169, 176, 178,
       262; relations to other tales: 242, 245, 310, 323-28, 455, 463,
       476-77, 484, 489, 495, 519, 579.

THE FRIAR AND HIS TALE.

455   CARRUTHERS, MARY [J]. "Letter and Gloss in the Friar's and
       Summoner's Tales." Journal of Narrative Technique 2
       (1972):208-14.
           Identifies the thematic importance of "glossing"
       (exegetical interpretation) for a reading of the Friar's and

Summoner's tales as a coherent pair. The overingenious Friar "is revealed" when he ignores literal meanings, while the too-literal Summoner finds no spiritual meaning at all. Their tales extend the concern with glossing begun in the Wife of Bath's Prologue.

456   HAHN, THOMAS, and KAEUPER, RICHARD W. "Text and Context: Chaucer's Friar's Tale." Studies in the Age of Chaucer 5 (1983):67-101.
       Explores the interchange between fiction and history, demonstrating how historical records corroborate Chaucer's depiction of archdeaconate power in Friar's Tale, and how the satire of the tale indicates contemporary attitudes toward this power and its abuse by summoners.

457   HENNEDY, HUGH L. "The Friar's Summoner's Dilemma." Chaucer Review 5 (1971):213-17.
       Clarifies the narrative cleverness of Chaucer's Friar's Tale, evident in the no-escape dilemma of the summoner: by the old woman's curse, he is damned if he fails to repent, and by his own curse and cursed life, he is doomed if he repents and abandons his demonic companion.

458   LENAGHAN, R.T. "The Irony of the Friar's Tale." Chaucer Review 7 (1973):281-94.
       Observes the unusual critical agreement about the double-edged irony of the Friar's Tale in its context. The Friar ridicules the Summoner through the tale, but, ironically, he catches himself "in his own net" when he abuses the intention of his exemplum.

459   MURTAUGH, DANIEL M. "Riming Justice in the Friar's Tale." Neuphilologische Mitteilungen 74 (1973):107-12.
       Traces a pattern of rhyme in Chaucer's Friar's Tale that parallels the tale's theme: "entente" rhymes sequentially with "rente," "hente," and "repente," ironically underscoring the distortion of moral intention and its consequences.

460   NICHOLSON, PETER. "Analogues of Chaucer's Friar's Tale." English Language Notes 17, no. 2 (1979-80):93-98.
       Observes parallels of detail, character, and event among three analogous versions of the same tale: Chaucer's Friar's Tale, an exemplum by Robert Rypen, and one in British Library MS Cotton Cleopatra D.VIII, arguing that the three indicate a specifically English version of the story from which Chaucer derived his version.

461   RICHARDSON, JANETTE. "Friar and Summoner, The Art of Balance." Chaucer Review 9 (1975):227-36.
       Compares the portraits and tales of the Friar and Summoner to demonstrate their superficial contrast and "profound" similarity. Analyzes the structural balance of their tales, and suggests that the characters reflect a sort of psychological

The Friar

projection that depicts the teller's own limitations in his
attempt to satirize the other.

462   STROUD, T.A. "Chaucer's Friar as Narrator." Chaucer Review 8
       (1973):65-69.
            Argues that the deviations of Chaucer's Friar's Tale from
       its analogues characterize the Friar as a pointedly "literal-
       minded narrator."

463   SZITTYA, PENN R. "The Green Yeoman as Loathly Hag: The
       Friar's Parody of the Wife of Bath's Tale." PMLA 90
       (1975):386-94.
            Argues that the three tales of Fragment III of Canterbury
       Tales (Wife of Bath, Friar, Summoner) form a pattern similar to
       that of Fragment I (Knight, Miller, Reeve): an idealized
       narrative is followed by squabbling and parody of the ideal.
       Like the Miller, the Friar parodies the romantic idealism of his
       predecessor's tale while provoking the following teller. The
       parody is evident in verbal echoes, structural parallels, and
       thematic contrasts.

464   WILLIAMS, ARNOLD. "Chaucer and the Friars." Speculum 28
       (1953):499-513. Reprinted in Chaucer Criticism, vol.1, The
       "Canterbury Tales," ed. Richard J. Schoeck and Jerome Taylor
       (Notre Dame, Ind.: University of Notre Dame Press, 1960), pp.
       63-83.
            Describes the history of the mendicant orders and the rise
       of anti-fraternal criticism, demonstrating how Chaucer's Friar-
       pilgrim and the friar of the Summoner's Tale give "artistic form
       to the most important of the charges against the friars"—
       hypocrisy, abuse of confession, secular meddling, etc.

       See also entries 252, 308, 313, 422, 429, 474.

THE SUMMONER AND HIS TALE

465   ADAMS, JOHN F. "The Structure of Irony in the Summoner's
       Tale." Essays in Criticism 12 (1962):126-32.
            Unified theme and structure in the Summoner's Tale indicate
       criticism of fraternal sophistry and hypocritical preaching,
       realized ironically in a punning equation of preaching and
       flatulence and correlation of sophistry and the division of the
       fart.

466   ALFORD, JOHN A. "Scriptural Testament in the Canterbury
       Tales: The Letter Takes Revenge." In Chaucer and Scriptural
       Tradition. Edited by David Lyle Jeffrey. Ottawa: University
       of Ottawa Press, 1984, pp. 197-203.
            Demonstrates how, in Summoner's Tale, bluntly literal
       implications of Biblical texts requite the friar's consistent
       misinterpretation of the spiritual meaning of these texts.

Spiritual and poetic justice combine to repay the friar's "glosyng."

467   CLARK, ROY PETER. "Doubting Thomas in Chaucer's Summoner's
       Tale." Chaucer Review 11 (1976):164-78.
          Identifies a parody of the life of St. Thomas in Chaucer's
       Summoner's Tale, especially the "doubting Thomas" legend.
       Chaucer's frequent use of the name "Thomas," the incredulity of
       the old man, and significant word patterns in the groping scene
       comprise a parodic foil to the action of the tale.

468   FLEMING, JOHN V. "Anticlerical Satire as Theological Essay:
       Chaucer's Summoner's Tale." Thalia 6 (1983):5-22.
          Exposes the topical, antifraternal satire of Summoner's
       Tale, examining its dominant concerns with penance and wrath.
       Throughout the tale, Friar John abuses his fraternal ideals and
       duties, ironically echoing details of contemporary fraternal
       debates. The Summoner's wrath makes him an ironic victim of this
       satire since the proper fraternal ideal of friar's was to save
       the children of wrath through confession, the ideal John
       subverts.

469   HASELMAYER, LOUIS A. "The Apparitor and Chaucer's Summoner."
       Speculum 12 (1937):43-57.
          Documents the criticism of summoners in thirteenth- and
       fourteenth-century historical and episcopal records. Such
       evidence corroborates literary presentations of summoners in
       Chaucer, Langland, and others, showing that "by the end of the
       fourteenth century in England, the apparitors [summoners] had
       become a large and troublesome group of men who took advantage
       . . . of their office to prey upon the people."

470   LANCASHIRE, IAN. "Moses, Elijah and the Back Parts of God:
       Satiric Scatology in Chaucer's Summoner's Tale." Mosaic 14,
       no. 3 (1981):17-30.
          Extends the analyses of Levitan (entry 471) and Szittza
       (entry 473), reading the relationship between Thomas and Friar
       John in Summoner's Tale as a scatological parody of God's rela-
       tions with Moses and Elijah, the purported ancestors of the
       fraternal orders. Thomas's gift to John parodies in complex
       fashion God's favors to the patriarchs.

471   LEVITAN, ALAN. "The Parody of Pentecost in Chaucer's
       Summoner's Tale." University of Toronto Quarterly 40
       (1971):236-46.
          Compares the iconography and exegesis of Pentecost used
       seriously in Dante's Paradiso and parodied in the divided fart at
       the end of Summoner's Tale, showing how Chaucer creates a
       "satiric commentary" on fraternal claims to be imitators of
       Christ's Apostles. Compare Lancashire and Szittya (entries 470
       and 473).

The Summoner

472   PEARCY, ROY J. "Structural Models for the Fabliaux and the
       Summoner's Tale Analogues." Fabula 15 (1974):103-13.
           Analyzes the structure of several fabliaux, demonstrating
       that apparent analogues to the Shipman's Tale depend for their
       humor upon logical disjunctions different from those in Chaucer's
       tale. Superficially, Le Vescie a Prestre and part of the Til
       Eulenspiel account seem analogous to the tale, but the deathbed
       anecdotes of Jean de Meun and another portion of Til Eulenspiel
       better match its deep structure.

473   SZITTYA, PENN R. "The Friar as False Apostle: Antifraternal
       Exegesis and the Summoner's Tale." Studies in Philology 71
       (1974):19-46.
           Explicates the antifraternalism of Summoner's Tale. Its
       pattern of allusion to the Apostles anticipates the wheel scene,
       a parody of Pentecost. Biblical references throughout the tale
       recall the polemical theology used against the friars in
       thirteenth-and fourteenth-century debates. Compare Levitan and
       Lancashire (entries 471 and 470).

474   ZIETLOW, PAUL N. "In Defense of the Summoner." Chaucer Review
       1 (1966):4-19.
           Interprets Summoner's Tale as a successful quitting of the
       Friar and his tale, arguing that the Summoner recognizes the pre-
       tensions of his opponent and assaults them by parodying fraternal
       incoherence and garrulity. Contrasts the personalities and
       styles of the two pilgrims, characterizing the Summoner as openly
       and effectively wicked and the Friar as foolishly vulgar.

           See also entries 169, 178, 252, 308, 313, 422, 429, 455,
       461, 463-64.

THE CLERK AND HIS TALE

475   BREWER, DEREK [S]. "Some Metonymic Relationships in Chaucer's
       Poetry." Poetica (Tokyo) 1 (1974):1-20. Reprinted in
       Chaucer: The Poet as Storyteller (London: Macmillan & Co.,
       1984), pp. 37-53.
           Examines the word "sad" in Chaucer's Clerk's Tale to show
       that meaning in Chaucer's poetry derives, not from extraliterary
       patterns of similarity or metaphor, but from metonymy or contex-
       tual association. As evident in its associations, "sad" means
       "constancy" or "constant in adversity," reflecting Griselda's
       ability to "suppress natural feelings in the name of a higher
       obligation."

476   CARRUTHERS, MARY J. "The Lady, the Swineherd, and Chaucer's
       Clerk." Chaucer Review 17 (1983):221-34.
           The narrative "voice" of the Clerk's Tale emphasizes the
       inhuman cruelty of Walter's treatment of Griselda and the innate
       virtue of her gentilesse, thematically extending the ideals of

truth and integrity articulated in the Wife of Bath's Tale, and
contradicting the stereotype of stern clerkly antifeminism.

477   CHERNISS, MICHAEL D. "The Clerk's Tale and Envoy, the Wife of
      Bath's Purgatory, and the Merchant's Tale." Chaucer Review 6
      (1972):235-54.
            Considers the double irony of the Clerk's Envoy as an index
      to the Merchant's Tale. The envoy ironically offers Griselda as
      a model of wifely conduct, but it also suggests, with double
      irony, that wives can be purgatories on earth for their husbands.
      The theme of marriage as purgatory runs throughout the Merchant's
      Tale, undercutting January's self-delusory notion that it is
      paradise.

478   HAWKINS, HARRIET. "The Victim's Side: Chaucer's Clerk's Tale
      and Webster's Duchess of Malfi." Signs 1 (1975):339-61.
      Reprinted in Poetic Freedom and Poetic Truth: Chaucer,
      Shakespeare, Marlowe, Milton. Oxford: Clarendon Press, 1976,
      pp. 25-54.
            Reads Clerk's Tale as an attack on tyranny, a "horror
      story" that deviates from its sources in order to emphasize the
      cruelty of Walter and the pitiableness of Griselda. Tragic
      fortitude instead of pathos functions in Webster's Duchess of
      Malfi.

479   HENINGER, S.K., Jr. "The Concept of Order in Chaucer's
      Clerk's Tale." JEGP: Journal of English and Germanic
      Philology 56 (1957):382-95.
            Reads Clerk's Tale as an orthodox expression of the
      medieval belief that "divinely ordained order" is mirrored in the
      marital relationship. The tale's overt concern with obedience,
      governance, and degree affirms order and is appropriate to the
      Clerk as a "serious student of medieval philosophy."

480   JOHNSON, LYNN STALEY. "The Prince and His People: A Study of
      the Two Covenants in the Clerk's Tale." Chaucer Review 10
      (1975):17-29.
            Contrasts the obedience of Griselda with the social unrest
      of Walter's people to explore the moral and political theme of
      common profit in Clerk's Tale. Griselda represents the New
      Covenant, and the people the Old, while Walter is the "agent of
      testing." In its emblematic characterization and stark ideology,
      the tale is one of Chaucer's "most artificial."

481   KELLOGG, ALFRED L. "The Evolution of the Clerk's Tale: A
      Study in Connotation." In Chaucer, Langland, Arthur: Essays
      in Middle English Literature, by Alfred L. Kellogg. New
      Brunswick, N.J.: Rutgers University Press, 1972, pp. 276-329.
            Traces the background and development of the tale of
      Griselda in Boccaccio, Petrarch, and Chaucer. Boccaccio's ver-
      sion reflects the "confused state" of the poet's emotions about
      the "double morality" of the tale. Petrarch's Latinizing of

Boccaccio's tale encourages allegorical interpretation through
connotative language and scriptural allusions. Chaucer's version
clarifies and amplifies Petrarch's emphasis, making the tale
dramatically appropriate to the theological Clerk.

482   KRIEGER, ELLIOTT. "Re-Reading Allegory: The Clerk's Tale."
      Paunch 40-41 (1975):116-36.
          Studies Clerk's Tale as a political and moral allegory,
      reading it against Chaucer's "moral balades"--Truth, Lak of
      Stedfastness, and Gentilesse--and arguing that it asserts the
      conservative principle of hierarchy in domestic, political, and
      spiritual relations.

483   LANHAM, RICHARD A. "Chaucer's Clerk's Tale: The Poem not the
      Myth." Literature and Psychology 16 (1966):157-65.
          Questions the validity of psychoanalyzing the characters
      of Clerk's Tale and suggests that as a superb example of clerkly
      rhetorical argument, the tale can better be viewed for its
      psychological effects upon its audience. The tale soothes the
      "irreconcilable" tensions it confronts, allowing each pilgrim
      "good arguments for whatever attitude" he or she has toward the
      tale.

484   LEVY, BERNARD S. "Gentilesse in Chaucer's Clerk's and
      Merchant's Tales." Chaucer Review 11 (1977):306-18.
          Reads the Merchant's presentation of gentilesse as a retort
      to the views of the Wife of Bath and the Clerk. The Wife defines
      gentilesse in terms of "manners, virtue, and sexual indulgence,"
      and the Clerk aligns it with divine grace and noble birth. The
      Merchant's Tale demonstrates that gentilesse cannot be achieved
      through marriage, nor through "inherited" or "natural" virtue.

485   McNAMARA, JOHN. "Chaucer's Use of the Epistle of St. James in
      the Clerk's Tale." Chaucer Review 7 (1973):184-93.
          Pursues the implications of the Clerk's reference to St.
      James at the end of his tale, arguing that St. James's theology
      underlies the plot of the tale, especially Chaucer's version.
      Walter's temptation of Griselda, permitted by God, enables her to
      show her Job-like patience, blending faith and good works as St.
      James advises.

486   MIDDLETON, ANNE. "The Clerk and His Tale: Some Literary
      Contexts." Studies in the Age of Chaucer 2 (1980):121-50.
          Contrasts the context of the Clerk's Tale with other
      medieval versions of the Griselda story to demonstrate how
      Chaucer's frame creates an elaborate, witty bit of literary
      posturing on the part of the Clerk. Through the Clerk's
      "obeisant" response to the Host and the complex irony of his
      envoy, Chaucer creates a Petrarchan man of letters who is aware
      of his audience's lack of sophistication.

487   RAMSEY, ROGER. "Clothing Makes a Queen in the Clerk's Tale."
      Journal of Narrative Technique 7 (1977):104-15.
         Analyzes the clothing imagery of Clerk's Tale and
      associates it with the tale's concern with social degree.

488   REIMAN, DONALD H. "The Real Clerk's Tale: or, Patient
      Griselda Explained." Texas Studies in Literature and Language
      5 (1963):356-73.
         Identifies the theme of Clerk's Tale as the need for a
      transcendent perspective. Griselda does not reflect this
      perspective since she subordinates herself to Walter rather than
      God. The Clerk implies an Aristotelian mean when he details the
      opposed excesses of Walter and Griselda, thus realigning the
      Marriage Group's focus on mastery to the higher concern of the
      sovereignty of God.

489   ROTHMAN, IRVING N. "Humility and Obedience in the Clerk's
      Tale, with the Envoy Considered as an Ironic Affirmation."
      Papers in Language and Literature 9 (1973):115-27.
         Analyzes the Clerk's envoy as an ironic contradiction of
      the virtues of humility and obedience depicted in his tale--by
      implication, a reaffirmation of these virtues aimed at the Wife
      of Bath. In the tale, Chaucer develops these virtues in ways
      that anticipate his envoy.

490   SEVERS, J. BURKE. "Chaucer's Clerks." In Chaucer and Middle
      English Studies in Honour of Rossell Hope Robbins. Edited by
      Beryl Rowland. London: George Allen & Unwin, 1974, pp. 140-
      52.
         Examines Chaucer's fictional clerks in light of contempo-
      rary social history, exploring the poet's realistic use of
      university practice in creating the Clerk-pilgrim, Nicolas and
      Absolon of Miller's Tale, John and Aleyn of Reeve's Tale, the
      astrologer of Franklin's Tale, and the Wife of Bath's fifth
      husband.

491   _____. The Literary Relationships of Chaucer's Clerkes Tale.
      New Haven: Yale University Press; New York: Modern Language
      Association, 1942. Reprint. Hamden, Conn.: Archon Books,
      1972, 380 pp.
         Expands the Clerk's Tale section of Bryan and Dempster
      (entry 252), also by Severs, providing authoritative texts and
      scholarly analysis of the analogues to the tale, and comparing
      the analogues to Clerk's Tale, particularly Petrarch's Latin
      version and its anonymous French translation, Le livre Griseldis.
      Chaucer relied chiefly upon the French text, but close comparison
      reflects the direct influence of Petrarch on Chaucer's habits of
      translation and originality of characterization, narrative tech-
      nique, imagery, and diction. Denies that Chaucer was influenced
      by Boccaccio's version in Decameron.

The Clerk

492   SLEDD, JAMES. "The Clerk's Tale: The Monsters and the
Critics." Modern Philology 51 (1953):73-82. Reprinted in
Chaucer: Modern Essays in Criticism, ed. Edward Wagenknecht
(New York: Oxford University Press, 1959), pp. 226-39;
Chaucer Criticism, Vol. 1, The "Canterbury Tales," ed. Richard
J. Schoeck and Jerome Taylor (Notre Dame, Ind.: University of
Notre Dame Press, 1960), pp. 160-74.

    Assesses Clerk's Tale as a "secular saint's legend," grant-
ing that its action is "frankly marvelous," and exploring its
pathos and sentimentality. Challenges critical attempts to treat
the tale dramatically or to account for its improbability, claim-
ing that such attempts deny the tale the "narrative values"
through which it evokes its "compassionate wonder."

493   STEINMETZ, DAVID C. "Late Medieval Nominalism and the Clerk's
Tale." Chaucer Review 12 (1977):38-54.

    Reads Clerk's Tale as an allegory of the late-medieval
"nominalistic doctrine of justification," accepting Walter as a
flawed reflection of a God, and reading Griselda as one whose
suffering obedience justifies her election. Associates the
Clerk's message with "Occamist principles."

494   STEPSIS, ROBERT. "Potentia Absoluta and the Clerk's Tale."
Chaucer Review 10 (1975):129-46.

    Explains the extreme "willfulness" of Walter in Chaucer's
Clerk's Tale as a reflection of the fourteenth-century idea of
the absolute power of God, an idea important to English thinkers
Thomas Bradwardine and William of Ockham. Describes how the idea
affected the thought of these Oxford philosophers and suggests
that it influences the allegorical tale of Chaucer's Oxford
Clerk.

495   TAYLOR, JEROME. "Frauceys Petrak and the Logyk of Chaucer's
Clerk." In Francis Petrarch, Six Centuries Later: A
Symposium. Edited by Aldo Scaglione. North Carolina Studies
in the Romance Languages and Literatures: Symposia, no. 3.
Chapel Hill: University of North Carolina, 1975, pp. 364-83.

    Identifies the logical basis of Clerk's Tale as a
Petrarchan interpretation of Aristotle—a humanistic application
of logic—and reads the tale as the "substitution of a contrary"
in response to the major premise of Wife of Bath's Tale.

496   USSERY, HULING. "Fourteenth-Century English Logicians:
Possible Models for Chaucer's Clerk." Tennessee Studies in
Literature 18 (1970):1-15.

    Investigates the conditions of the study of logic in
Chaucer's day, assessing his Clerk in light of this information
and suggesting several possible real-life models for the character, notably Ralph Strode.

497   UTLEY, FRANCIS L. "Five Genres in the Clerk's Tale." Chaucer
Review 6 (1972):198-228.

Canterbury Tales

The Merchant

Elaborates the various genres that color Chaucer's Clerk's
Tale, including drama, exemplum, fairy tale, novella, and allegory. Compares the tale to its analogues, and criticizes
attempts to limit it into a single genre, reading it as a fusion
of several genres.

See also entries 141, 154, 159, 208, 260, 319. For
relations to other tales: 292, 324-28, 420, 563, 606.

THE MERCHANT AND HIS TALE

498   BEIDLER, PETER G. "Chaucer's Merchant and the Tale of
       January." Costerus, n.s. 5 (1972):1-25.
       Challenges the traditional critical association of
Chaucer's Merchant and January of the Merchant's tale. Such an
association is based on the invalid a priori assumption that the
Canterbury Tales reflect the biographies of their tellers. The
Merchant is overtly contemptuous of January, while Justinius's
advice correlates with the Merchant's experience. Hence,
Justinus, not January, should be associated with the Merchant.

499   _____. "Chaucer's Merchant's Tale and the Decameron."
       Italica 50 (1973):266-83.
       Notes similarities between Merchant's Tale and two tales of
Boccaccio's Decameron (day 2, tale 10, and day 7, tale 9). Characterizing details, especially of January, reflect Chaucer's
familiarity with Boccaccio's work rather than his use of it as a
direct source.

500   _____. "The Climax in the Merchant's Tale." Chaucer Review 6
       (1971):28-43.
       Challenges Brown's contention (entry 504) that Damian of
Merchant's Tale does not complete the sex act with May, and suggests that Chaucer's adjustment of his sources results in irony.
January is doubly foolish because he witnesses his own cuckolding
and sees only "what he wants to see."

501   BROWN, EMERSON, Jr. "Biblical Women in the Merchant's Tale:
       Feminism, Antifeminism, and Beyond." Viator 5 (1974):387-412.
       Argues that Chaucer does not allow the Merchant's cynical
misogyny to stand unchallenged. The Merchant debases traditon-
ally exemplary women yet his references to them and to the Virgin
remind the audience "of a love greater than anything the Merchant
is capable of comprehending."

502   _____. "Chaucer and a Proper Name: January in the Merchant's
       Tale." Names 31 (1983):79-87.
       Identifies the rich and complex associations of the name
January in Merchant's Tale. Like the Roman god, Janus, January
is associated with keys, vision, and financial success, as well
as with winter and old age.

Canterbury Tales

The Merchant

503   _____. "Chaucer, the Merchant, and Their Tale: Getting
Beyond Old Controversies." Chaucer Review 13 (1978-79):141-
56, 247-62.
Part 1 undercuts critics' observations of inconsistency
between the Merchant's Prologue and Tale by demonstrating the
common attitude toward women, common imagery, and similar, cynical voice of the two. Part 2 hypothesizes whether or not the
Merchant's voice is really Chaucer's own.

504   _____. "Hortus Inconclusus: The Significance of Priapus and
Pyramus and Thisbe in the Merchant's Tale." Chaucer Review 4
(1970):31-40.
Argues that allusions to Priapus and Pyramus and Thisbe at
the end of the Merchant's Tale carry associations evident in traditional commentaries suggesting not only eroticism but ridicule
of sexual frustration, especially Damyan's. Challenged by
Beidler (entry 500).

505   _____. "The Merchant's Tale: Januarie's 'Unlikely Elde.'"
Neuphilologische Mitteilungen 74 (1973):92-106.
Significant details in Chaucer's depiction of January not
only create a sharp word picture but, set against medieval ideas
about old age, also imply "self-deception" and "calculated
futility."

506   BUGGE, JOHN. "Damyan's Wanton Clyket and an Ironic Twiste to
the Merchant's Tale." Annuale Mediaevale 14 (1973):53-62.
Documents the sexual innuendoes of several punning words in
the Merchant's Tale ("clyket," "wyket," and "twiste") and suggests that they emphasize the "phallic motif" of the tale, at
heart a "very elemental sexual joke."

507   BURNLEY, J.D. "The Morality of the Merchant's Tale."
Yearbook of English Studies 6 (1976):16-25.
Covert references and direct allusions to the marriage
liturgy in the Merchant's Tale contrast the tale's dominant
concern with sensual pleasure, thereby establishing an inescap-
able "standard for moral judgement" of the characters and their
actions.

508   CAHN, KENNETH S. "Chaucer's Merchants and the Foreign Exchange: An Introduction to Medieval Finance." Studies in the
Age of Chaucer 2 (1980):81-119.
Details the international monetary practice—banking, exchange, and lending—of fourteenth-century Europe, identifying
types of coins, rates of exchange, and kinds of transactions to
clarify the relative success and honesty of Chaucer's merchants,
especially his Merchant-pilgrim.

509   DALBEY, MARCIA A. "The Devil in the Garden: Pluto and
Proserpine in Chaucer's Merchant's Tale." Neuphilologische
Mitteilungen 75 (1974):408-15.

136

Identifies the allegorical implications of Pluto and Proserpine in the Merchant's Tale: their demonic character derived from Christian tradition, and from *Ovide moralisé*, their embodiment of lust. As such, the gods dictate the actions of the humans in the tale and direct our interpretation.

510 GROVE, ROBIN. "The Merchant's Tale: Seeing, Knowing and Believing." Critical Review 18 (1976):23-38.
Responds sensitively to the rich shifts in tone and attitude in Merchant's Tale, noting how the poetry suggests and counteracts various possible assessments of January, May, and the Merchant, leading to a complex sense of the limits of human perspective and knowledge.

511 HARRINGTON, NORMAN T. "Chaucer's Merchant's Tale: Another Swing of the Pendulum." PMLA 86 (1971):25-31.
Examines the tone and details of Merchant's Tale for the way they characterize the Merchant, reading the tale as a unified, sustained expresson of a derisive voice. The "Juvenalian bitterness" and "pervasive linguistic violence" of the tale align well with its "heightened awareness of sex, particularly in its more ugly, violent, and repellant forms."

512 OTTEN, CHARLOTTE F. "Proserpine: Libratrix suae gentis." Chaucer Review 5 (1971):277-87.
Establishes the typological value of Rebecca, Judith, Abigail, and Esther of Merchant's Tale as "deliverance types," and argues that both Proserpine and May are comic deliverers as well. Finds no bitterness in the tale.

513 PARK, B.A. "The Character of Chaucer's Merchant." English Language Notes 1 (1964):167-75.
Examines the syntax and social backgrounds of Chaucer's portrait of the Merchant to show that, contrary to traditional interpretation, he represents a "typical medieval man of affairs," well to do, and concerned with international finance.

514 PITTOCK, MALCOLM. "The Merchant's Tale." Essays in Criticism 17 (1967):26-40.
Argues that the Merchant misunderstands the implications of his own tale, a narrative about the "nature of, and the relation between different kinds of lechery" which he offers only as a condemnation of marriage. The Merchant's distortions and intrusions reveal Chaucer's dramatic subtlety.

515 ROBERTSON, D.W., Jr. "The Doctrine of Charity in Medieval Literary Gardens." Speculum 26 (1951):24-49.
A seminal article that traces the allegorical value of medieval literary gardens from Beowulf to Chaucer's Merchant's Tale, demonstrating from patristic evidence that such gardens are used "to condemn or satirize cupidity and hold forth Charity as

an ideal." Echoing the Song of Songs, the garden of January
inverts this ideal and reflects the tale's serious morality.

516   ROSENBERG, BRUCE A. "The 'Cherry-Tree Carol' and the
       Merchant's Tale." Chaucer Review 5 (1971):264-76.
       Explores biblical allusions and popular religious motifs in
Merchant's Tale, arguing that the so-called Cherry-Tree Carol of
Mary's pregnancy conflates with allusions to Song of Songs and
other biblical texts to account for May's desire for fruit and
January's blindness at the end of Chaucer's tale.

517   SCHROEDER, MARY C. "Fantasy in the Merchant's Tale."
       Criticism 12 (1970):167-79.
       Interprets January of Merchant's Tale as the Merchant's
"projective self-indulgence," arguing that the Merchant casti-
gates January's "self-delusion" so grotesquely as to suggest his
own lack of balance. January submits to fantasy, but the Merchant fails to see that his overly aggressive realism implies its
own kind of fantasy.

518   SHORES, DAVID L. "The Merchant's Tale: Some Lay Observa-
       tions." Neuphilologische Mitteilungen 71 (1970):119-33.
       Confronts major criticism of Merchant's Tale and argues
that attempts to read it only as a part of the Marriage Group or
as an expression of the Merchant's character deemphasize its
value as a "humorous story about how youth and age do not mix
well in marriage."

519   STEVENS, MARTIN. "'And Venus Laugheth': An Interpretation of
       the Merchant's Tale." Chaucer Review 7 (1972):118-31.
       Challenges the critical view that Merchant's Tale is bitter
and antimatrimonial, reading its Prologue as good-natured ex-
aggeration, and the Tale as a response to the Wife of Bath, not a
commentary on the Merchant's own marriage.

520   TATLOCK, J.S.P. "Chaucer's Merchant's Tale." Modern
       Philology 33 (1935):367-81. Reprinted in Chaucer Criticism,
       vol. 1, The "Canterbury Tales," ed. Richard J. Schoeck and
       Jerome Taylor (Notre Dame, Ind.: University of Notre Dame
       Press, 1960), pp. 175-89; Geoffrey Chaucer: Merchant's Tale,
       ed. Robert J. Blanch, Merrill Literary Casebook Series
       (Columbus, Ohio: Charles E. Merrill Publishing Co., 1970),
       pp. 43-56.
       Explicates the "unrelieved acidity" of the Merchant's Tale,
detailing January's repulsiveness and characterizing May and
Damyan as "paper dolls." The bitterness of the tale is made even
sharper by brilliant style and dramatic and verbal irony.

521   TUCKER, EDWARD F.J. "'Parfite Blisses Two': January's
       Dilemma and the Themes of Temptation and Doublemindedness in
       the Merchant's Tale." American Benedictine Review 33
       (1982):172-81.

Canterbury Tales

Traces the theme of spiritual "doublemindedness" in Merchant's Tale to the epistle of St. James, discusses its development in Bede and its late-medieval popularity. January, onomastically two-faced, properly worries about his spiritual state, but as reflected in the characters of Justinus and Placebo, he is unable to "distinguish between noble and base desire."

522   VON KREISLER, NICHOLAI. "An Aesopic Allusion in the Merchant's Tale." Chaucer Review 6 (1971):30-37.
Explains January's reference to a "panyer ful of herbes" in Merchant's Tale by means of an episode from Life of Aesop, arguing that Chaucer must have known an oral version of Aesop, and showing how the allusion helps characterize January and echoes elsewhere in Merchant's Tale.

523   WENTERSDORF, KARL P. "Theme and Structure in the Merchant's Tale: The Function of the Pluto Episode." PMLA 80 (1965):522-27.
Demonstrates the value and function of the Pluto/Proserpina episode in Merchant's Tale, indicating how it emphasizes the weaknesses of both sexes in marriage, enhances suspense, and combines with other allusions to help unify the tale and imply that the marriage involves elements of rape. The episode underscores January's faults.

See also 141, 159, 240, 260, 322. For sources and analogues: 169, 187, 252, 308-9, 313; relations to other tales: 323-28, 477, 484, 555.

THE SQUIRE AND HIS TALE

524   BRADDY, HALDEEN. "The Genre of Chaucer's Squire's Tale." JEGP: Journal of English and Germanic Philology 41 (1942):279-90. Reprinted in Geoffrey Chaucer: Literary and Historical Studies (Port Washington, N.Y.: Kennikat Press, 1971), pp. 85-95.
Compares the Squire's Tale to several "Oriental analogues" to suggest that the fragmentary tale shows signs of being a framing tale in which the Canacee/falcon plot originally framed three other episodes. The incest motif, familiar in the Oriental frame tales and suggested at the end of Chaucer's fragment, is the probable reason Chaucer did not finish his version.

525   GOODMAN, JENNIFER R. "Chaucer's Squire's Tale and the Rise of Chivalry." Studies in the Age of Chaucer 5 (1983):127-36.
Compares Squire's Tale favorably to other members of its "recognizable genre"--the "composite romances," fashionable in the late fourteenth century and distinctive in their their plot and rhetoric. Similar romances are Generides, Valentine and Orson, Parnatope of Blois, and Huon of Bordeaux.

The Squire

526   HALLER, ROBERT S.   "Chaucer's Squire's Tale and the Uses of
       Rhetoric." Modern Philology 62 (1965):285-95.
           Assesses the rhetorical excesses of Squire's Tale as a
       means to characterize the Squire and to criticize the "pseudo-
       genre" of romance. Dramatically appropriate to a youthful and
       naive love-poet—a fair description of the Squire—the tale
       abuses the rhetorical principles of construction and ornamenta-
       tion, obliquely satirizing romantic sentimentalism.

527   KAHRL, STANLEY J.   "Chaucer's Squire's Tale and the Decline of
       Chivalry." Chaucer Review 7 (1973):194-209.
           Attributes the inept qualities of Chaucer's Squire's Tale
       to the Squire. Especially in contrast to the successful Knight's
       Tale, Squire's Tale reflects the "exoticism and disorder of late-
       medieval court life" in its Eastern setting and rhetorical
       excess.

528   MILLER, ROBERT P.   "Augustinian Wisdom and Eloquence in the F-
       Fragment of Canterbury Tale." Mediaevalia 4 (1978):245-75.
           Examines Squire's Tale and Franklin's Tale in light of
       Augustinian ideals of wisdom wedded to eloquence, reading the
       first tale as a comic portrayal of eloquence without wisdom, and
       the second as a more subtle example of verbal dexterity combined
       with the appurtenances of wisdom, but lacking its substance.
       Franklin's Tale places worldly happiness and worldly words before
       wisdom.

529   NEVILLE, MARIE.   "The Function of the Squire's Tale in the
       Canterbury Scene." JEGP: Journal of English and Germanic
       Philology 50 (1951):167-79.
           Compares Squire's Tale to Knight's Tale to establish sev-
       eral "family traits" of the father-son storytellers. Assesses
       Squire's Tale as part of the Marriage Group, observing how it
       extends the "fairy-tale machinery" of Wife of Bath's and Mer-
       chant's tales, contrasts their approaches to courtesy, and
       prepares for Franklin's Tale.

530   PETERSON, JOYCE E.   "The Finished Fragment: A Reassessment of
       the Squire's Tale." Chaucer Review 5 (1970):62-74.
           Argues that Squire's Tale is complete in the sense that
       enough has been told to characterize the Squire as a snob who is
       without human empathy and whose morality is based on elegance
       rather than charity. The Franklin's interruption of the Squire
       completes Chaucer's purpose of exposing false gentilesse.

531   WOOD, CHAUNCEY.   "The Significance of Jousting and Dancing as
       Attributes of Chaucer's Squire." English Studies 52
       (1971):116-18.
           Suggests that Chaucer's association of dancing and jousting
       in his portrait of the Squire may have been influenced by Henry
       of Lancaster's Le livre se seyntz medicines and may ironically
       contrast the portrait of the Knight.

See also entries 169, 196, 220, 246, 252, 323, 535.

THE FRANKLIN AND HIS TALE

532   BEIDLER, PETER G. "The Pairing of the Franklin's Tale and the
       Physician's Tale." Chaucer Review 3 (1969):275-79.
          Contrasts Dorigen and Virginia to suggest thematic opposi-
       tion between the tales of the Franklin and the Physician and
       Chaucer's intentional pairing of the two.

533   CARRUTHERS, MARY J. "The Gentilesse of Chaucer's Franklin."
       Criticism 23 (1981):283-300.
          Assesses Chaucer's Franklin against a backdrop of
       fourteenth-century social and literary conventions to discover
       that nostalgia is an essential aspect of the character. Senti-
       mental "old-fashionedness" qualifies his moral idealism to
       produce typical Chaucerian ambiguity.

534   DAVID, ALFRED. "Sentimental Comedy in the Franklin's Tale."
       Annuale Mediaevale 6 (1965):19-27.
          Assesses the gentility of the Franklin and his tale, noting
       the bourgeois characteristics of his portrait and contrasting the
       sentimental attitudes of his tale with the courtliness of the
       Knight's. Like his eighteenth-century literary descendants, also
       figures of sentiment, the Franklin is of the middle-class.

535   DUNCAN, CHARLES F., Jr. "'Straw for Youre Gentillesse': The
       Gentle Franklin's Interruption of the Squire." Chaucer Review
       5 (1970):161-64.
          Reads the Franklin's tactful interruption of the Squire and
       the Host's rude rejoinder as dramatic characterizations and evi-
       dence of Chaucer's investigation of complex social relations.

536   FRAZIER, J. TERRY. "The Digression on Marriage in the
       Franklin's Tale." South Atlantic Bulletin 43, no. 1
       (1978):75-85.
          Reads the Franklin's panegyric on marriage as a result of
       his digressive storytelling style, not as an integral part of the
       narrative. The discussion of marriage, Dorigen's complaint, and
       the Franklin's scattered comments on food help characterize him
       as "glib and sprightly and oriented toward the moment."

537   GOLDING, M.R. "The Importance of Keeping 'Trouthe' in The
       Franklin's Tale." Medium Ævum 39 (1970):306-12.
          Describes the opposition and resolution of the dualistic
       notions of 'trouthe' in Franklin's Tale. Conventional courtly
       honor gives way to the more substantial proprieties of real life
       in the "curing" of Aurelius and the maturation of conjugal love
       between Arveragus and Dorigen.

538   HEYDON, PETER N. "Chaucer and the Sir Orfeo Prologue of the
       Auchinleck MS." Papers of the Michigan Academy of Science,

The Franklin

<u>Arts, and Letters</u> 51 (1966):529-45.
Assesses the relations between the opening of Franklin's
Tale and the prologues to two lais of the Auchinleck manuscript,
arguing that redactions of the now-lost prologue to <u>Sir Orfeo</u>
indicate that <u>Orfeo</u> was one of Chaucer's sources, influencing the
character of the Franklin.

539   HUME, KATHRYN.   "The Pagan Setting of the Franklin's Tale and
      the Sources of Dorigen's Cosmology." <u>Studia Neophilologica</u> 44
      (1972):289-94.
      Argues that Dorigen's complaint in Franklin's Tale is more
Boethian than Christian and that the setting of the tale is non-
Christian, indicating that Chaucer focused our attention on
literary, not moral, concerns.

540   _____.   "Why Chaucer Calls the Franklin's Tale a Breton Lai."
      <u>Philological Quarterly</u> 51 (1972):365-79.
      Surveys the characteristic features of the Breton lai,
describing the expectations raised by such a label at the beginning of Franklin's Tale and arguing that Chaucer raised such
expectations to "minimize the religious implications" of magic
and marriage in the tale. Through the label Chaucer sought to
focus attention on <u>gentilesse</u> without confusion from "bourgeois
moral attitudes."

541   KEARNEY, A.M.   "Truth and Illusion in the Franklin's Tale."
      <u>Essays in Criticism</u> 19 (1969):245-53.
      Reads Franklin's Tale as Chaucer's oblique assertion of
male sovereignty as a marital ideal, arguing that the tale
depicts Arveragus as strong in comparsion to Dorigen, and that
its plot challenges the illusory ideal of marital equality. See
Dorothy Colmer's commentary, <u>Essays in Criticism</u> 20 (1970):375-
80, and Kearney's response, <u>Essays in Criticism</u> 21 (1971):109-11.

542   KEE, KENNETH.   "Illusion and Reality in Chaucer's Franklin's
      Tale." <u>English Studies in Canada</u> 1 (1975):1-12.
      Gauges the dramatic effect of the Franklin's interruptions
of his own tale, suggesting that his comments and qualifications,
like his interruption of the Squire, reflect his desire to appear
respectable and orthodox, characterizing him as one who pretends
to chivalric virtues.

543   LANE, ROBERT.   "The Franklin's Tale: Of Marriage and Mean-
      ing." In <u>Portraits of Marriage in Literature</u>. Edited by Anne
      C. Hargrove and Maurine Magliocco. Macomb: Western Illinois
      University, 1984, pp. 107-24.
      Traces a thematic similarity between successful marriage
and effective communication in Franklin's Tale, arguing that both
depend upon shared perspective. Aurelius imposes his subjective
perspective on Dorigen, obscuring meaning and challenging marriage; Arveragus fails to see Dorigen's dilemma from her point of
view.

544 LUENGO, ANTHONY E. "Magic and Illusion in the Franklin's
     Tale." JEGP: Journal of English and Germanic Philology 77
     (1978):1-16.
         Provides historical and literary evidence that Chaucer and
     his audience would have recognized the magician's activities in
     Franklin's Tale as mere "stage magic," arguing therefore that the
     Franklin and the characters in his tale are ironically unable to
     separate appearance and reality.

545 MILLER, ROBERT P. "The Epicurean Homily on Marriage by
     Chaucer's Franklin." Mediaevalia 6 (1980):151-86.
         Compares the Fanklin's "Epicurean" attitude toward marriage
     with its source in the Roman de la rose (Amis's advice on mar-
     riage) to show how Chaucer ironically indicates the weakness of
     the Franklin's position. Traditional assessments of Epicurean
     thought help identify the Franklin's sophistical espousal of "the
     appearance, rather than the essence, of peace and tranquility."

546 MILOSH, JOSEPH. "Chaucer's Too-Well Told Franklin's Tale: A
     Problem of Characterization." Wisconsin Studies in Literature
     5 (1970):1-11.
         Attributes critical dispute over Franklin's Tale to the
     occasional glimpses of rich characterization in the poem,
     glimpses unexpected in the demande d'amour genre that the poem
     exemplifies. Such characterization enriches the essentially
     simple plot.

547 PEARCY, ROY J. "Chaucer's Franklin and the Literary
     Vavasour." Chaucer Review 8 (1973):33-59.
         Assesses Chaucer's Franklin in light of the
     literary/historical tradition of the vavasour, showing how the
     figure from romance informs the Franklin's exchanges with the
     Squire and Host, suggests the genre and theme of Franklin's Tale,
     and enables Chaucer to depict a complex set of contemporary
     social forces.

548 REISNER, THOMAS A., and REISNER, MARY ELLEN. " A British
     Analogue for the Rock-Motif in the Franklin's Tale." Studies
     in Philology 76 (1979):1-12.
         Offers the life of Northumbrian St. Balred as an analogue,
     perhaps a source, for the motif of the removal of the rocks in
     Chaucer's Franklin's Tale. Suggests how Chaucer might have had
     access to the saint's life.

549 ROBERTSON, D.W., Jr. "Chaucer's Franklin and His Tale."
     Costerus, n.s. 1 (1974):1-26. Reprinted in Essays in Medieval
     Culture (Princeton: Princeton University Press, 1980), pp.
     273-90.
         Explains the historical basis for Chaucer's association of
     his Franklin with his Sergeant at Law, exploring the suggestions
     of connivance between them. Assesses the "Epicurean marital
     arrangement" of Franklin's Tale, arguing that in the context of

The Franklin

the hierarchical social relations of the time the tale reflects
illusion, absurdity, and false gentility.

550   SAUL, NIGEL.   "The Social Status of Chaucer's Franklin: A
       Reconsideration." Medium Ævum 52 (1983):10-26.
           Historical assessment of the meaning of "franklin," the
       social function of the class, and the nature of Chaucer's sketch
       of the Franklin demonstrate that Chaucer's portrait and tale re-
       flect many features "uncharacteristic of the class" and thereby
       satirize its social pretensions.

551   SEVERS, J. BURKE.   "Appropriateness of Character to Plot in
       the Franklin's Tale." In Sudies in Language and Literature in
       Honour of Margaret Schlauch. Edited by Mieczysław Brahmer,
       Stanisław Helsztyński, and Julian Krzyżanowski. Warsaw: PWN-
       Polish Scientific Publishers, 1966. Reprint. New York:
       Russell & Russell, 1971, pp. 385-96.
           Argues that Chaucer's characters in Franklin's Tale moti-
       vate plot. Each of the four major characters differs from his or
       her vocational stereotype in precisely the ways that produce the
       happy outcome. The tale is not simply a solution to the Marriage
       Argument, but a well-crafted extension of credible characters.

552   SPECHT, HENRIK. Chaucer's Franklin in the "Canterbury Tales":
       The Social and Literary Background of a Chaucerian Character.
       Publications of the Department of English, University of
       Copenhagen, no. 10. Copenhagen: Akademisk Forlag, 1981, 206
       pp.
           Marshals historical and literary evidence to demonstrate
       the typicality of Chaucer's Franklin and to establish the gen-
       tility of his class. Analyzes the portrait, prologue, and tale
       of the Franklin against information about the legal, manorial,
       and economic conditions of Chaucer's age. Explores the meaning
       of the term "franklin" and demonstrates how the details of
       Chaucer's characterization fit well with the political importance
       and high social standing accorded franklins in his day. Chal-
       lenges critical interpretations of the Franklin as a social
       climber and reads his tale as an expression of genuine gentility.
       Suggests William de Spaygne as a possible real-life model for the
       Franklin.

553   STORM, MELVIN.   "Chaucer's Franklin and Distraint of Knight-
       hood." Chaucer Review 19 (1984):162-68.
           Explicates the reference to twenty pounds in the Franklin's
       address to the Squire at the end of Squire's Tale, explaining how
       that amount, long associated with the enforced knighting of
       landowners (destraint), suggests "social mobility and the in-
       creasingly fiscal nature of social relationships."

554   TRAVERSI, DEREK. "The Franklin's Tale." In The Literary
       Imagination: Studies in Dante, Chaucer, and Shakespeare.
       Newark: University of Delaware Press, 1982, pp. 87-119.

Reads Franklin's Tale as an ambiguous extension of the
Marriage Argument wherein romantic setting and sensibility
qualify the tale's presentation of marriage, reminding us that
the ideals of gentility and generosity, however admirable and
desirable, solve human problems no more surely than do
"realistic" solutions such as the Wife of Bath's.

555   WHITE, GERTRUDE M. "The Franklin's Tale: Chaucer or the
        Critics." PMLA 89 (1974):454-62.
             Reads Franklin's Tale as thematically opposite to
        Merchant's Tale. Contrasts between the tales clarify the
        Franklin's celebration of the power of truth, corroborated in
        Chaucer's lyrics, Truth, Gentilesse, and Lak of Stedfastnesse.

             See also entries 79, 133, 137, 208, 217, 224, 244, 322,
        490. For sources and analogues: 169, 252; relations to other
        tales: 323-28, 528-30, 558.

THE PHYSICIAN AND HIS TALE

556   AMOILS, E.R. "Fruitfulness and Sterility in the Physician's
        and Pardoner's Tales." English Studies in Africa 17
        (1974):17-37.
             Argues that "the theme of spiritual fertility and the re-
        lated concept of the defeat of death" thematically weld the tales
        of the Physician and Pardoner. Parson's Tale and Roman de la
        rose--an important source for the two linked tales--are indexes
        to these themes.

557   BENSON, C. DAVID. "The Astrological Medicine of Chaucer's
        Physician and Nicholas of Lynn's Kalendarium." American Notes
        and Queries 22 (1984):62-66.
             Demonstrates the acceptance of astrological medicine in
        Nicholas of Lynn's Kalendarium and suggests, therefore, that
        Chaucer's Physician follows "educated medical opinion of his day"
        when he consults the stars.

558   BROWN, EMERSON. "What is Chaucer Doing with the Physician and
        His Tale?" Philological Quarterly 60 (1981):129-49.
             Confronts three aspects of Chaucer's Physician's Tale: its
        narrative "flaws" when compared to its analogues, its tale/teller
        relationship, and its place in the Canterbury sequence. At-
        tributes the uncertain morality of the tale to the character of
        the Physician, a healer who has significant difficulty in identi-
        fying causes, linking the tale to those of the Franklin and
        Pardoner as the center of a sequential triad concerned with the
        causes of evil in the world.

559   FICHTE, JOERG O. "Incident--History--Exemplum--Novelle: The
        Transformation of History in Chaucer's Physician's Tale."
        Florilegium 3 (1983):1-7.

Canterbury Tales

The Physician

Analyzes the dominant narrative features of Physician's
Tale and its earlier analogues to argue that, within Canterbury
Tales, the story is neither historical nor exemplary. Rather,
its context, method, intention, and reception define it as a
novella, Chaucer's own discovery of the literary genre usually
associated with Boccaccio.

560   HAINES, R. MICHAEL. "Fortune, Nature, and Grace in Fragment
        C." Chaucer Review 10 (1976):220-35.
            Identifies the thematic focus on the fortune-nature-grace
        topos in the Physician's and Pardoner's tales, suggesting that
        the focus was a conscious attempt by Chaucer to link the tales
        and align them with a similar concern in a section of Parson's
        Tale, unifying the Canterbury Tales.

561   LONGSWORTH, ROBERT. "The Doctor's Dilemma: A Comic View of
        the Physician's Tale." Criticism 13 (1971):223-33.
            Reads Physician's Tale as a comic reflection of the
        Doctor's limited moral outlook. He attempts to lend moral
        credibility to his tale, but fails through disorganization,
        misinterpretation of the exemplum of Jephthah's daughter, and
        clumsy moralizing.

562   MANDEL, JEROME H. "Governance in the Physician's Tale."
        Chaucer Review 10 (1976):316-25.
            Examines the "governor-governed relationship" in Physi-
        cian's Tale, contrasting Apius, Virginius, and God in their
        respective roles as governors of the state, the family, and the
        cosmos. Ironically, Apius and Virginius err as governors, giving
        Virginia opportunity to submit to God.

563   MIDDLETON, ANNE. "The Physician's Tale and Love's Martyrs:
        'Ensamples Mo Than Ten' as a Method in the Canterbury Tales."
        Chaucer Review 8 (1973):9-32.
            Presents Physician's Tale in light of Chaucer's use of
        exemplary material, comparing the tale thematically to its
        sources and generically to Legend of Good Women, Clerk's Tale,
        and Man of Law's Tale. In Physician's Tale, Chaucer undercuts
        facile exemplary conclusions to engage us in "the process of
        determining" the purpose of telling tales. Such engagement is
        the crowning achievement of Canterbury Tales.

564   RAMSEY, LEE C. "'The Sentence of It Sooth Is': Chaucer's
        Physician's Tale." Chaucer Review 6 (1972):185-97.
            Approaches Physician's Tale as a piece of misapplied moral-
        izing. As in other Chaucerian narratives, the implications of
        the tale escape its narrator, in this case ironically high-
        lighting the theme of the impossibility of maintaining virtue in
        a world where the only defense against sin is knowledge.

565   ROBBINS, ROSSELL HOPE. "The Physician's Authorities." In
        Studies in Language and Literature in Honour of Margaret

<u>Schlauch</u>. Edited by Mieczysław Brahmer, Stanisław
Helsztyński, and Julian Krzyżanowski. Warsaw: PWN-Polish
Scientific Publishers, 1966. Reprint. New York: Russell &
Russell, 1971, pp. 335-41.
    Indicates the accuracy of Chaucer's list of medical author-
ities in his portrait of the Physician. Chaucer's catalog
matches contemporary medical sources better than most
commonplace lists.

566   ROWLAND, BERYL. "The Physician's 'Historial Thyng Notable'
       and the Man of Law." <u>ELH: A Journal of English Literary
       History</u> 40 (1973):165-78.
       Provides background to Chaucer's Man of Law, his Physician,
and the tradition of animosity between their professions, demonstrating the appropriateness of Physician's Tale to its teller by
identifying its antilegal bias.

567   TROWER, KATHERINE B. "Spiritual Sickness in the Physician's
       and Pardoner's Tales: Thematic Unity in Fragment VI of the
       <u>Canterbury Tales</u>." <u>American Benedictine Review</u> 29 (1978):67-
       86.
       Argues for a "symbolic" connection between the Physician
and the Pardoner. Both are "potential healers"; both seek wealth
"by capitalizing on human sickness"; and both tales "focus on the
process of dying as a terminal rather than a transcendental
event." Physician's Tale is a "prelude to the Pardoner's entire
performance."

568   USSERY, HULING. <u>Chaucer's Physician: Medicine and Literature
       in Fourteenth-Century England</u>. Tulane Studies in English, no.
       19. New Orleans: Tulane University, 1971, 158 pp.
       Surveys historical records to explain the various branches
of medical practice in Chaucer's age and to identify physicians
contemporary with him. Describes Chaucer's Doctor of Physic as a
"secular cleric," and suggests several possible real-life models.
Argues that the Physician's character is more realistic and less
ironic than often assumed, challenging interpretive criticism
with social history. Reads Physician's Tale as a straightforward
narrative, appropriate to its teller, especially in its morality
and erudition.

569   WALLER, MARTHA S. "The Physician's Tale: Geoffrey Chaucer
       and Fray Juan Garcia de Castrojeriz." <u>Speculum</u> 51 (1976):292-
       306.
       Suggests that Chaucer's Physician's Tale was influenced by
Juan Garcia de Castrojeriz's <u>Regimiento de Principis</u>, a heavily
glossed adaptation of Aegidius Romanus's <u>De regime principium</u>.
Cites various parallels in concept and wording between the
Spanish text and Chaucer's additions to Jean de Meun's tale of
Virginia.

       See also entries 169, 252, 319, 532.

THE PARDONER AND HIS TALE

570   BISHOP, IAN. "The Narrative Art of the Pardoner's Tale."
       Medium Ævum 36 (1967):15-24. Reprinted in Chaucer--The
       "Canterbury Tales": A Casebook, ed. J.J. Anderson (London:
       Macmillan & Co., 1974), pp. 209-221.
            Attributes the success of Chaucer's tale of the three
       rioters to its economy of characterization and description, and
       its "double perspective" of naturalism and near allegory. Sparse
       naturalistic details intertwine ironically with allegorical sug-
       gestions in the plot, especially in the characterizatuion of the
       Old Man.

571   CONDREN, EDWARD I. "The Pardoner's Bid for Existence."
       Viator 4 (1973):177-205.
            Combines the critical tendencies to view the Pardoner
       either psychologically or exegetically, arguing that the figural
       implications of his tale reflect his complex personality. His
       prologue reveals his attempt to rely on his "technical virtuosity
       as a performer," but in the figures of the Old Man and the riot-
       ers his tale reflects his fears and his failure.

572   CURRIE, FELICITY. "Chaucer's Pardoner Again." Leeds Studies
       in English 4 (1971):11-22.
            Argues that the Pardoner intends to sting the consciences
       of the Canterbury pilgrims to his own advantage with his tale of
       death. The Host's virulent response and the laughter of the
       other pilgrims indicate that he effectively aims his tale at the
       "lewed peple" and "gentils" alike.

573   DELASANTA, RODNEY. "Sacrament and Sacrifice in the Pardoner's
       Tale." Annuale Mediaevale 14 (1973):43-52.
            Summarizes earlier study of Eucharistic parody in the Par-
       doner's Prologue and Tale, and develops this theme by documenting
       the orthodox sacrificial understanding of the sacrament and
       demonstrating the ironic importance of sacrifice in the tale.

574   DeNEEF, A. LEIGH. "Chaucer's Pardoner's Tale and the Irony of
       Misrepresentation." Journal of Narrative Technique 3
       (1974):85-96.
            Studies the literal and metaphoric levels of the Pardoner's
       Prologue and Tale, arguing that the Host's rejection of the
       teller represents the failure of any of the pilgrims to derive
       proper spiritual benefit from the Pardoner's exemplum--their
       failure to separate properly the wheat and chaff of his
       performance.

575   GLASSER, MARC. "The Pardoner and the Host: Chaucer's
       Analysis of the Canterbury Game." CEA Critic 46, nos. 1-2
       (1983-84):37-45.

Reads Pardoner's Prologue and Tale as a pointed assault on the Host, helping to justify the Host's vitriolic rebuke of the Pardoner. The Pardoner's self-description parodies the Host's treatment of the pilgrims, and his assault on the "tavern vices" criticizes the Host's profession. The Pardoner's tale mocks the Host's conception and plan for the Canterbury pilgrimage.

576 HALVERSON, JOHN. "Chaucer's Pardoner and the Progress of Criticism." Chaucer Review 4 (1970):184-202.
Surveys recent criticism of the Pardoner and his tale, noting how critical trends respond to historical ones and assessing the Pardoner's persona as a modern "put-on," a game-player who hazards deception and "occasional extravagances" in contests of wit and verbal dexterity. The Pardoner's uncanny presentation of death is more important than his sexual secret or the theological undertones of his tale. Continues Sedgewick (entry 589).

577 JUNGMAN, ROBERT E. "The Pardoner's Quarrel with the Host." Philological Quarterly 55 (1976):279-81.
The Pardoner/Host quarrel at the end of Pardoner's Tale grows out of the same Pauline text (1 Timothy 6) as the Pardoner's duplicitous homiletic theme and illustrates how false teaching leads to quarreling.

578 KELLOGG, ALFRED L., and HASELMAYER, LOUIS A. "Chaucer's Satire of the Pardoner." PMLA 66 (1951):251-77. Reprinted in Chaucer, Langland, Arthur: Essays in Middle English Literature, by Alfred L. Kellogg. New Brunswick, N.J.: Rutgers University Press, 1972, pp. 212-44.
Documents the history of the office of pardoner in the Middle Ages, emphasizing attempts to restrict its abuse, and exemplifying the criticism of pardoners from fourteenth-century records. Chaucer's presentation of the Pardoner satirizes not an individual but the conditions that made abuse possible.

579 KERNAN, ANNE. "The Archwife and the Eunuch." ELH: A Journal of English Literary History 41 (1974):1-25.
The Pardoner's interruption of the Wife of Bath reveals rich parallels between their characters and their tales. In addition to "casual parallels," there are substantial associations: both reflect cupidity and sterility; their prologues are autobiographical; and their tales include evocative projections of the tellers, hers of the Hag and his of the Old Man.

580 KHINOY, STEPHAN A. "Inside Chaucer's Pardoner?" Chaucer Review 6 (1972):255-67.
Assesses the Pardoner's performance as a puzzle that obscures the proper relation between word and meaning posing a dilemma for pilgrims and readers alike. If we accept his rhetoric and his relics as valid, we become his dupes; if we reject them, we become as cynical as he is. The Host's rebuttal—an echo of Reason's discussion of meaning in Jean de Meun's Roman

The Pardoner
   de la rose--rejects both the relics and the Pardoner's meaning,
avoiding the dilemma.

581   KNIGHT, STEPHEN. "Chaucer's Pardoner in Performance." Sydney
      Studies in English 9 (1983):21-37.
         Exemplifies the dramatic benefits of oral, public per-
      formance of Pardoner's Prologue and Tale, reading them as
      "monologue theatre." Argues that an ideological conflict between
      public and private values underlies the power and thematic impact
      of the Pardoner's performance.

582   LAWTON, DAVID. "The Pardoner's Tale: Morality and Context."
      In Studies in Chaucer. Edited by G.A. Wilkes and A.P. Reimer.
      Sydney Studies in English. Sydney: University of Sydney,
      1981, pp. 38-63.
         Discusses the interplay between frame and tale in the
      Pardoner's performance, assessing its penitential message and its
      encouragement that humanity reject this message. The Pardoner is
      a type of preacher who profers potent penitential material under
      the guise of falseness; the Host typifies those who reject repen-
      tence along with falseness in the manner described by False
      Seeming in Roman de la rose.

583   MANNING, STEPHEN. "Chaucer's Pardoner: Sex and Non-Sex."
      South Atlantic Bulletin 39 (1974):17-26.
         Investigates the oral imagery of Pardoner's Prologue Tale
      and portrait, observing psychoanalytic and semiotic patterns of
      aggression, false signs, phallicism, and castration, concluding
      that the Pardoner is caught in the "vicious circle of his own
      sinfulness" and is "unconsciously in search of pardon."

584   MERRIX, ROBERT P. "Sermon Structure in the Pardoner's Tale."
      Chaucer Review 17 (1983):235-49.
         Surveys the structural development of sermons in the Middle
      Ages and compares Chaucer's Pardoner's Tale to the university
      sermon of the late-medieval period, arguing that the tale dupli-
      cates the structure of such sermons and their relationship
      between theme and form.

585   MILLER, CLARENCE H., and BOSSE, ROBERTA B. "Chaucer's
      Pardoner and the Mass." Chaucer Review 6 (1972):171-84.
         Addresses Pardoner's Prologue and Tale as a "distorted
      reflection" of the liturgy and meaning of the mass, arguing that
      various structural parallels and specific details and references
      to the mass constitute the "inner consistency" of the Pardoner's
      materials.

586   PETERSON, JOYCE E. "With Feigned Flattery: The Pardoner as
      Vice." Chaucer Review 10 (1976):326-36.
         Places the Pardoner in the tradition of the Vice figure of
      morality plays and interprets in this light the pilgrims' re-
      sponses to the Pardoner, particularly the Host's.

Canterbury Tales

587 PITTOCK, MALCOLM. "The Pardoner's Tale and the Quest of
Death." Essays in Criticism 24 (1974):107-23.
     Explores the contrast between "notional awareness" and
"substantial knowledge" in Pardoner's Prologue and Tale, reading
the rioters' quest as an increasingly symbolic objective correla-
tive for their spiritual death, and the Old Man as an indicator
of their limited perspective and a symbol of Providence. The
Pardoner's performance is self-delusory: he thinks his tale is
about avarice when it is about sin and death.

588 ROWLAND, BERYL. "Chaucer's Idea of the Pardoner." Chaucer
Review 14 (1979):140-54.
     Studies the Pardoner as a "testicular pseudohermaphrodite
of the feminine type," documenting traditional notions of
hermaphroditism, positive and negative, and showing how the
significant dualism in Chaucer's presentation of the character
capitalizes upon such notions.

589 SEDGEWICK, G.G. "The Progress of Chaucer's Pardoner, 1880-
1940." Modern Language Quarterly 1 (1940):431-58. Reprinted
in Chaucer: Modern Essays in Criticism, ed. Edward
Wagenknecht (New York: Oxford University Press, 1959), pp.
126-58; edited slightly in Chaucer Criticism, Vol. 1, "The
Canterbury Tales," ed. Richard J. Schoeck and Jerome Taylor
(Notre Dame, Ind.: University of Notre Dame Press, 1960), pp.
190-220.
     Surveys criticism of the Pardoner, denying several
"heresies" of interpretation and demonstrating that the
Pardoner's materials present a "powerfully consistent work of
art." Through the sketch of the Pardoner in General Prologue,
his interruption of the Wife of Bath, his headlink, prologue,
tale, and exchange with the Host, Chaucer "extorts"
interpretation from us, evoking a "fully-rounded" charlatan--
impudent, effective, and contradictory. Criticial survey updated
in Halverson (entry 576).

590 STORM, MELVIN. "The Pardoner's Invitation: Quaestor's Bag or
Becket's Shrine?" PMLA 97 (1982):810-18.
     Reads the Pardoner's performance as a threat to the
spiritual success of the Canterbury pilgrimage, noting parallels
between the rioters' fatal tree and the Pardoner's "alestake,"
and arguing that the Host's rejection of the Pardoner's relics—
offered as an alternative to Becket's shrine--is a "turning
point" toward Canterbury as the heavenly Jerusalem.

591 TRISTAM, PHILIPPA. "'Olde stories longe tyme agoon': Death
and the Audience of Chaucer's Pardoner." In Death in the
Middle Ages. Edited by Herman Braet and Werner Verbeke.
Mediaevalia Lovaniensa, 1st ser., studia 9. Louvan: Louvan
University Press, 1983, pp. 179-90.
     Contrasts the conception of death in Chaucer's Pardoner's
Tale with that of contemporary English depictions, arguing that

Canterbury Tales

The Pardoner

Chaucer offers a "deliberate challenge to the charnel imagination" of his time. In refusing to personify death and in presenting his Old Man as spiritually and physically prepared for death, Chaucer counteracts contemporary trends.

See also entries 54, 135, 253, 260, 272, 304. For style and rhetoric: 253, 260, 272, 304; sources and analogues: 178, 252; relations to other tales: 556, 558, 560, 567.

THE SHIPMAN AND HIS TALE

592   ABRAHAM, DAVID H. "Cosyn and Cosynage: Pun and Structure in the Shipman's Tale." Chaucer Review 11 (1977):319-27.
Identifies cosen/cosenyge puns in Shipman's Tale and argues that they structure the tale. Midway through the tale, and midway through the sixteen occurrences of the word in the tale, the word shifts its relational meaning (cousin) to meaning "deception" (cozen), paralleling the deceptive manipulation of relations in the plot.

593   FRIES, MAUREEN. "An Historical Analogue to the Shipman's Tale?" Comitatus 3 (1972):19-32.
Demonstrates the "numerous details of language and plot" in the Shipman's Tale that recall Edward III's naval victory over Spain and the subsequent marriage of Pedro the Cruel to Blanche of Bourbon. Through the tale, Chaucer makes ironic comedy of these historical events well-known to his original audience.

594   GIBSON, GAIL McMURRAY. "Resurrection as Dramatic Icon in the Shipman's Tale." In Signs and Symbols in Chaucer's Poetry. Edited by John P. Hermann and John J. Burke, Jr. University: University of Alabama Press, 1981, pp. 102-12.
Identifies echoes of a "comic Resurrection drama" in the Shipman's Tale. Signaled by verbal images of new clothing and significant repetition of "arisings" on the third day, the tale ironically recalls the Resurrection play of the cycle dramas in which Magdelen (wife) meets Christ (monk) in a garden and informs his disciples, particularly Peter (merchant).

595   GUERIN, RICHARD. "The Shipman's Tale: The Italian Analogues." English Studies 52 (1971):412-19.
Reassesses and synthesizes critical opinion and textual evidence pertaining to the Italian analogues of Chaucer's Shipman's Tale, concluding that "it seems not unreasonable" that Chaucer's version was influnced by his reading of Sercambi's Novelle, no. 31, and tales 8.1 and 8.2 of Boccaccio's Decameron.

596   McCLINTOCK, MICHAEL W. "Games and Players of Games: Old French Fabliaux and the Shipman's Tale." Chaucer Review 5 (1970):112-36.
Contrasts Shipman's Tale with several analogues and as-

sesses the relations among the tale's characters, arguing that
Chaucer complicates the simple fabliau by focusing on the
"gamesmanship" of the three characters, producing not simple
laughter but moral reaction to manipulation and maneuvering.

597   MILLICHAP, JOSEPH R. "Source and Theme in the Shipman's
       Tale." University of Dayton Review 10, no. 3 (1974):3-6.
       Compares Chaucer's Shipman's Tale to its analogues to
suggest that Chaucer's produced the tale's "ironic treatment of
morality." Chaucer uses a monk rather than a soldier, emphasizes
the theme of abused friendship, underscores the husband's futile
awareness of his cuckolding, and contrasts bawdry with innocence.

598   NICHOLSON, PETER. "The Shipman's Tale and the Fabliaux."
       ELH: A Journal of English Literary History 45 (1978):583-96.
       Reads Shipman's Tale as something of an anti-fabliau in
which "mercantile thinking," characterization, and the surprizing
harmony of the ending reflect a bourgeois sensibility that
counteracts the slapstick and vulgarity expected in a fabliau.

599   SCATTERGOOD, V.J. "The Originality of the Shipman's Tale."
       Chaucer Review 11 (1977):210-31.
       Reads Shipman's Tale as a critique of the limitations of
the bourgeois sensibility of the merchant in the tale, his
literal-mindedness, and his single-minded pursuit of his financial goals. The merchant is cuckolded because he accepts his
wife and the monk at face value and goes about his business with
little imagination or inquisitiveness.

600   SILVERMAN, ALBERT H. "Sex and Money in Chaucer Shipman's
       Tale." Philological Quarterly 32 (1953):329-36.
       Identifies the sex/money puns of Shipman's Tale to show
that the "chief ironic point" of the tale is the
"commercialization of marriage," and suggests possible dramatic
tensions between the Shipman and Merchant.

       See also entries 272, 422. For sources and analogues:
252, 308-9, 313, 323, 388.

THE PRIORESS AND HER TALE

601   BRENNAN, JOHN P. "Reflections on a Gloss to the Prioress's
       Tale from Jerome's Adversus Jovinianum." Studies in Philology
       70 (1974):243-51.
       Surveys the scholarship on glosses to Chaucer manuscripts
and discusses a gloss to the Prioress's Tale to argue that
Chaucer is "responsible for most of the substantive glosses" to
manuscripts of the Canterbury Tales. The gloss from Jerome's
Adversus Jovinianum suggests a two-stage composition process for
the Prioress's Tale and a sense of ironic characterization likely
to be Chaucer's rather than a scribe's.

Canterbury Tales

The Prioress

602   COLLETTE, CAROLYN P. "Sense and Sensibility in the Prioress's Tale." _Chaucer Review_ 15 (1981):138-50.
       Assesses the sentiment of the Prioress's Tale in light of the fourteenth-century "fashion in religious taste" and shows how the Prioress's "myopic" emphasis on "love, emotion, and pity" is consonant with the fashionable concern for "deep emotional response."

603   FRANK, HARDY LONG. "Chaucer's Prioress and the Blessed Virgin." _Chaucer Review_ 13 (1979):346-62.
       Demonstrates the influence of the late-medieval Cult of the Virgin on the portrait and tale of Chaucer's Prioress, citing parallels between contemporary Marian epitomes and Madame Eglantine, especially her name and oaths, the courtliness of her sketch, and the anti-Semitism of her tale.

604   FRANK, ROBERT WORTH, Jr. "Miracles of the Virgin, Medieval Anti-Semitism, and the Prioress's Tale." In _The Wisdom of Poetry: Essays in Early English Literature in Honor of Morton W. Bloomfield._ Edited by Larry D. Benson and Siegfried Wenzel. Kalamzoo, Mich.: Medieval Institute Publications, 1982, pp. 177-88.
       Documents the conventionality of anti-Semitism in medieval tales of the Virgin, tracing the roots of the convention in social, doctrinal, and literary history, and arguing that Chaucer selected his Prioress's Tale for its intensity of pathos, not to condemn its teller for anti-Semitism.

605   FRIEDMAN, ALBERT B. "The Prioress's Tale and Chaucer's Anti-Semitism." _Chaucer Review_ 9 (1974):118-29.
       Challenges the critical attempts to absolve Chaucer of anti-Semitism, since they lead to misunderstandings of the Prioress. Anti-Semitism, an historical fact, is "incidental" to this tale, which illustrates the Prioress's apt reverence for Mary and her "indulgence in pathos and sentimentality."

606   HOY, MICHAEL. "The Tales of the Prioress and the Clerk." In _Chaucer's Major Tales._ Edited by Michael Hoy and Michael Stevens. London: Norton Bailey, 1969, pp. 41-59.
       Contrasts the relative success of the Prioress's and Clerk's tales, arguing that the pattern of alternating realism and idealism in Prioress's Tale evokes pathos in the modern reader, while the flat style and emblematic characters of Clerk's Tale produces only melodrama.

607   KNOEPFLMACHER, U.C. "Irony Through Scriptural Allusion: A Note on Chaucer's Prioress." _Chaucer Review_ 4 (1970):180-83.
       Identifies two echoes of Matthew's gospel in Chaucer's sketch of the Prioress—a detail of her table manners and her feeding of her dogs—and argues that the details are richly ambivalent rather than satiric.

608   MADELEVA, Sister M. "Chaucer's Nuns." In Chaucer's Nuns and
       Other Essays. New York: D. Appleton & Co., 1925, pp. 3-42.
       Reprinted in A Lost Language and Other Essays (New York:
       Sheed & Ward, 1951), pp. 31-60.
            Documents Chaucer's familiarity with the life of nuns by
       assessing the portraits, prologues, and tales of the Prioress and
       Second Nun in light of the liturgy and practice of convent life,
       noting parallels between the Rule of St. Benedict and the nuns'
       behavior, and identifying details that derive from their daily
       cycle of prayer.

609   POWER, EILEEN. "Madam Eglentyne: Chaucer's Prioress in Real
       Life." In Medieval People. [10th ed.] London: Methuen; New
       York: Barnes & Noble, 1963, pp. 73-95.
            Reconstructs the life of a medieval nun, conflating
       Chaucer's portrait of the Prioress in General Prologue and the
       historical records of episcopal visits to convents.

610   RIDLEY, FLORENCE. The Prioress and the Critics. University
       of California English Studies, no. 30. Berkeley: University
       of California Press, 1965, 51 pp.
            Summarizes the critical assessments of Chaucer's Prioress.
       Examines contemporary attitudes toward Jews and compares
       Prioress's Tale to its analogues to deny that Chaucer satirizes
       anti-Semitism. The portrait, the tale, and the opinions of the
       Host and the Nun's Priest show mild satire of "a kind-hearted,
       silly, somewhat misdirected woman" who is unaware of her own
       worldliness.

611   WOOD, CHAUNCEY. "Chaucer's Use of Signs in His Portrait of
       the Prioress." In Signs and Symbols in Chaucer's Poetry.
       Edited by John P. Hermann and John J. Burke, Jr.. University:
       University of Alabama Press, 1981, pp. 81-101.
            Examines the details of the Prioress's portrait to demon-
       strate Chaucer's unsympathetic depiction of a "nun who is not a
       nun." The details are either "calculatedly equivocal" or
       indications of the ambivalence of the Prioress's morality.
       Surveys previous criticism.

            See also entries 94, 136, 154, 208, 241, 247, 252, 637,
       905.

THE TALE OF SIR THOPAS

612   BURROW, J.A. "Chaucer's Sir Thopas and La Prise de Nuevile."
       Yearbook of English Studies 14 (1984):44-55. Reprinted in
       English Satire and the Satiric Tradition, ed. Claude Rawson
       (Oxford: Basil Blackwell, 1984), pp. 44-55.
            Compares Chaucer's Sir Thopas to the thirteenth-century La
       Prise de Nuevile, a satire of Flemish weavers that burlesques the
       chanson de geste. The similarities of technique and detail

Sir Thopas

between the two suggest that even if Chaucer did not know the
Prise, he was aware of the parodic tradition of the poem.

613   . "Sir Thopas: An Agony in Three Fits." Review of
English Studies, n.s. 22 (1971):54–58.
    Three manuscript divisions of Sir Thopas (not indicated in
modern editions) mark a "principle of progressive diminution."
The number of stanzas in each fit (18, 9, 4 1/2) and the narrative materials in these fits contract proportionately "towards
nothingness," suggesting a numerological joke evident to sophisticated members of Chaucer's audience.

614   . "Sir Thopas in the Sixteenth Century." In Middle
English Studies: Presented to Norman Davis in Honour of his
Seventieth Birthday. Edited by Douglas Gray and E.G. Stanley.
Oxford: Clarendon Press, 1983, pp. 69–91.
    Surveys the literary allusions to Sir Thopas in the six-
teenth century, noting its consistent associatiion with balladry
and rusticity, and gauging degrees of sensitivity to its humor.
Considers references by Dunbar, Skelton, Wyatt, Puttenham,
Warton, Drayton, Spenser, Lyly, and Shakespeare.

615 CONLEY, JOHN. "The Peculiar Name 'Thopas.'" Studies in
Philology 73 (1976):42–61.
    Explores the possible medieval associations of the name
"Thopas" by investigating lapidaries, biblical commentaries, and
heraldic sources. Denies editorial association of the name with
chastity and suggests instead a generalized, ironic meaning of
excellence.

616 GAYLORD, ALAN T. "Chaucer's Dainty 'Dogerel': The 'Elvyssh'
Prosody of Sir Thopas." Studies in the Age of Chaucer 1
(1979):83–104.
    Surveys the prosodic delights of Sir Thopas and argues
that, far from being a piece of weak verse as the Host suggests,
or mere parody, it is a work of substantial virtuosity that
exposes "romance pretensions" and underscores the artistry of
Chaucer's more typical verse.

617 WOOD, CHAUNCEY. "Chaucer and Sir Thopas: Irony and
Concupiscence." Texas Studies in Literature and Language 14
(1972):389–403.
    Identifies the sexual undertones of Tale of Sir Thopas and
argues that the portrait of Chaucer in the Thopas prologue depicts a concupiscent man, citing parallels to Dante's Commedia
and imagery of hares and elves. The Host interrupts Chaucer's
tale because the tale does not manifest the sexuality the Host
expects from the teller.

See also entries 126, 136, 243, 252, 272, 343, 379.

THE TALE OF MELIBEE

618   BORNSTEIN, DIANE. "Chaucer's Tale of Melibee as an Example of the Style clergial." Chaucer Review 12 (1978):236-54.
        Compares the prose style of Chaucer's Tale of Melibee to that of its French source, showing how Chaucer cultivated the style clergial (chancellory style) of the original, especially in his use of "introductory phrases, doublets, subordinate clauses, and trailing sentence structures."

619   BRINTON, LAUREL J. "Chaucer's Tale of Melibee: A Reassessment." English Studies in Canada 10 (1984):251-64.
        Surveys criticism of Chaucer's Tale of Melibee and isolates three major concerns of the tale as it relates to its context. The tale clarifies the importance of reasonableness in worldly affairs, it reflects the themes of sovereignty and proper counsel found elsewhere in Canterbury Tales, and it "participates" in the interaction between "sentence" and "solaas" in the tales.

620   HOFFMAN, RICHARD L. "Chaucer's Melibee and Tales of Sondry Folk." Classica et Medievalia 30 (1969):552-77.
        Surveys critical reaction to Tale of Melibee and extends Strohm's reading of the tale as a religious allegory (entry 624) and a key to the rest of Canterbury Tales. The name "Sophia" and Sophia's wounds recall Christ and the Crucifixion, while "Melibee" signifies all who drink too deeply of the honey of worldly pleasure. The many sententiae of the tale particularize the message of the Crucifixion and link it allusively to the rest of the pilgrims. Includes a list of correspondences between Melibee and the other tales.

621   OWEN, CHARLES A., Jr. "The Tale of Melibee." Chaucer Review 7 (1973):267-80.
        Explores how the Tale of Melibee sustains the thematic concern for good women found elsewhere in Chaucer's works and parallels the Parson's concern for forgiveness. The allegory of the tale never overwhelms its literal level even though its drama interacts with political, moral, and spiritual allegory.

622   PALOMO, DOLORES. "What Chaucer Really Did to Le Livre de Mellibee." Philological Quarterly 53 (1974):304-20.
        Compares Tale of Melibee stylistically to its source, Renaud's Le livre de Mellibee, arguing for the ironic and dramatic value of Chaucer's version. By heightening the style of the piece beyond decorous limits, Chaucer effects a "very subtle stylistic parody" that helps to characterize its teller, contribute to the Marriage Argument, and give the Host "his comeuppance."

623   STILLWELL, GARDINER. "The Political Meaning of Chaucer's Tale of Melibee." Speculum 19 (1944):433-44.

Melibee

     Notes various parallels between Chaucer's Tale of Melibee and contemporary political events, associating Prudence with Philippa, Joan, and Anne; Melibee with Richard; and the pacifist message of the poem with the problem of the French wars.

624   STROHM, PAUL. "The Allegory of the Tale of Melibee." _Chaucer Review_ 2 (1967):32-42.
     Reads Tale of Melibee as an allegorical exhortation to spiritual passivity and submission to God, documenting the theological notion that self-defense against sin is spiritual vanity. Chaucer's sensitivity to this significance, which was available in his sources, is evident in his creation of the name "Sophia," meaning wisdom, for Melibee's daughter.

     See also entries 163-64, 243, 252, 272, 328, 343, 447.

THE MONK AND HIS TALE

625   BEICHNER, PAUL E. "Daun Piers, Monk and Business Admistrator." _Speculum_ 34 (1959):611-19. Reprinted in _Chaucer Criticism_, Vol 1, "The Canterbury Tales," ed. Richard J. Schoeck and Jerome Taylor (Notre Dame, Ind.: University of Notre Dame Press, 1969), pp. 52-62.
     Assesses Chaucer's portrait of the Monk as a depiction of a "monastic official not a cloisterer on a holiday." The portrait better represents human nature than satire, since the Monk's high office and his social responsibilities account for his apparent deviations from monastic ideals.

626   BERNDT, DAVID E. "Monastic _Acedia_ and Chaucer's Characterization of Daun Piers." _Studies in Philology_ 68 (1971):435-50.
     Reconciles the apparent conflict between the Monk's worldly sketch in General Prologue with his ascetic tale by reading them both as manifestations of an acedious personality. Details of the Monk's actions and physiognomy match discussions of _acedia_ in Cassian, Gregory, and Pernaldus, suggesting that Chaucer consciously represented "this complex psychological phenomenon."

627   DELASANTA, RODNEY K. "'Namoore of this': Chaucer's Priest and Monk." _Tennessee Studies in Literature_ 13 (1968):117-32.
     Contrasts Chaucer's Monk and Nun's Priest, demonstrating how their tales are theologically opposed. The Monk's dreary view of fortune is undercut by the Nun's Priest's orthodox and lively assertion of Providence, making of the Monk a "theological lummox."

628   FRY, DONALD K. "The Ending of the Monk's Tale. _JEGP: Journal of English and Germanic Philology_ 71 (1972): 355-68.
     Through manuscript discussion and demonstration of dramatic propriety, substantiates the Ellesmere arrangement of the Monk's

tragedies where the contemporary accounts, or so-called "modern instances," are at the end. The Knight interrupts the Monk for philosophical reasons and because Pedro of Cyprus, one of the Monk's subjects, was his former commander.

629   LOCK, F.P. "Chaucer's Monk's Use of Lucan, Suetonius, and 'Valerie.'" English Language Notes 12 (1975):251-55.
         Shows how the Monk's interpretations of his exemplary tragedies characterize him as intellectually weak. He blames fortune for the falls in his narratives, but the sources he cites offer more cogent reasons in several notable cases: Adam, Ugolino, and Julius Caesar.

630   OLSSON, KURT. "Grammar, Manhood, and Tears: The Curiosity of Chaucer's Monk." Modern Philology 76 (1978):1-17.
         Analyzes the various aspects of the character of Chaucer's Monk to show how the element of "idle curiosity" appears in his portrait, prologue, and tale. Patristic authority explains how curiosity dominates his roles as grammarian, tragedian, hunter, and "outridere."

631   WHITE, ROBERT B., Jr. "Chaucer's Daun Piers and the Rule of St. Benedict: The Failure of An Ideal." JEGP: Journal of English and Germanic Philology 70 (1971):13-30.
         Summarizes the monastic Rule of St. Benedict and demonstrates that, directly or by inference, all of the monastic vows are compromisd in Chaucer's portrait of the Monk, presenting the character as a "satiric consummation of all possible monastic faults."

         See also entries 212, 360, 638. For genre: 212, 727, 736; sources and analogues: 169, 185, 252.

THE NUN'S PRIEST AND HIS TALE

632   ALLEN, JUDSON BOYCE. "The Ironic Fruyt: Chauntecleer as Figura." Studies in Philology 66 (1969):25-35.
         Compares the description of Chauntecleer to exegetical commentaries and shows that "allegorical clues" in Nun's Priest's Tale "force themselves upon us." Yet, the relation between the efficio and the cock-as-preacher tradition is ironic: "mock epic, mock sermon, and mock allegory" comprise a gentle criticism of "taking exegetical method too seriously."

633   BESSERMAN, LAWRENCE L. "Chaucerian Wordplay: The Nun's Priest and his Womman Divyne." Chaucer Review 12 (1977):68-73.
         Reveals the multiple meanings of the Nun's Priest's assertion that he "kan noon harm of womman divyne," exemplifying how Chaucer's rich semantic ambiguity functions.

634   BLAKE, N.F. "Reynard the Fox in England." In Aspects of the
       Medieval Animal Epic. Edited by E. Rombauts and A.
       Welkenhuysen. Mediaevalia Lovaniensia, 1st ser., studia 3.
       Louvain: Louvain University Press; The Hague: Nijhoff, 1975,
       pp. 53-65.
           Places Nun's Priest's Tale in the context of four other
       Middle English tales of the fox and argues that, like the others,
       its source was not a version of the French Roman de Renart, but
       rather a moral fable of the preaching tradition.

635   BLOOMFIELD, MORTON W. "The Wisdom of the Nun's Priest's
       Tale." In Chaucerian Problems and Perspectives: Essays
       Presented to Paul E. Beichner, C.S.C. Edited by Edward Vasta
       and Zacharias P. Thundy. Notre Dame, Ind.: University of
       Notre Dame Press, 1979, pp. 70-82.
           Formally a beast-epic of the wisdom literature tradition,
       the Nun's Priest's Tale mocks its epic conventions--dreams,
       pursuit, rhetoric, and language. Yet this mockery of the too
       serious ironically affirms the wisdom of proper perspective.
       Compares Chaucer's tale to Robert Henryson's Taill of Schir
       Chantecleir and the Foxe.

636   BOULGER, JAMES D. "Chaucer's Nun's Priest's Tale." In
       Literary Studies in Memory of Francis A. Drumm. Edited by
       John H. Dorenkamp. Worcester, Mass.: College of the Holy
       Cross; Wetteren, Belgium: Cultura Press, 1974, pp. 13-32.
           Assesses the humor in Nun's Priest's Tale, describing how
       it modifies both morality and skepticism, and characterizing the
       Priest as a gaudium spiritus who mediates between the Parson's
       morality and the Host's mirth. The tale encourages the faithful
       acceptence of a providential world, "with all the moral folly,
       intellectual pretension, and human fallibility in it."

637   BROES, ARTHUR T. "Chaucer's Disgruntled Cleric: The Nun's
       Priest's Tale." PMLA 78 (1963):156-62.
           Affirms the dramatic appropriateness of Nun's Priest's Tale
       to its teller by detailing how and where the tale "twits" the
       Prioress's fastidiousness, her domination of the Priest, and the
       mawkishness and grotesquery of her tale.

638   DEAN, NANCY. "Chaucerian Attitudes towards Joy with Particu-
       lar Consideration of the Nun's Priest's Tale." Medium Ævum
       44 (1975):1-13.
           Examines the range of heavenly and earthly joys depicted in
       Canterbury Tales and evaluates their moral validity in Boethian
       terms and in terms of contemporary values. Suggests that Chaucer
       prefers the "serene intellectual joy" of the Nun's Priest to the
       Knight's and Monk's "strenuous view of living."

639   FRIEDMAN, JOHN BLOCK. "The Nun's Priest's Tale: The Preacher
       and the Mermaid's Song." Chaucer Review 7 (1973):250-66.

Examines the appropriateness of the Nun's Priest's Tale to
its teller, assessing its similarities to exemplary sermons and
arguing that the Priest's theme is antifeminist. Form and theme
are consistent with the Priest's occupation.

640   HOY, MICHAEL. "The Nun's Priest's Tale." In Chaucer's Major
       Tales. Edited by Michael Hoy and Michael Stevens. London:
       Norton Bailey, 1969, pp. 135-62.
       Explores Chaucer's manipulation of oppositions and changing
perspective that produce irony and constructive satire in Nun's
Priest's Tale. The masterful shifts of style and rhetoric in the
tale deftly contrast the rustic and the courtly, the learned and
the lewd, the human and the animal, holding them in dynamic tension that requires interpretive participation from the audience.

641   KAUFFMAN, CORRINE E. "Dame Pertelote's Parlous Parle."
       Chaucer Review 4 (1970):41-48.
       Uses medieval herbals to demonstrate that Pertolote's
laxatives in Nun's Priest's Tale, supposed cures for
Chauntecleer, would have been extremely dangerous, possibly
fatal. Pertelote's misinformation perhaps extends Chaucer's
satire of women in the tale.

642   LUMIANSKY, R.M. "The Nun's Priest in the Canterbury Tales."
       PMLA 68 (1953):896-903.
       Characterizes the Nun's Priest as an intellectual but timid
man by assessing the dramatic interplay of the pilgrims. The
Host's complaint about his wife and his altercation with the Monk
provoke the Priest's antifeminist comments and his rebuttal of
the Monk's Tale. The Host returns the favor by praising the
Priest in language he earlier applied to the virile Monk.

643   MANN, JILL. "The Speculum Stultorum and the Nun's Priest's
       Tale." Chaucer Review 9 (1975):262-82.
       Suggests that Nigel of Longchamps's Speculum stultorum
inspired Chaucer's ironic use of beast fable in Nun's Priest's
Tale since both emphasize the disjuncture between animal and
human nature and the difficulty of "applying moral analysis to
animals." Chaucer's reference to the Speculum in his tale and
the similarity of the two suggest that Chaucer was lampooning the
moralizing of comic fables.

644   MANNING, STEPHEN. "The Nun's Priest's Morality and the
       Medieval Attitude Towards Fables." JEGP: Journal of English
       and Germanic Philology 59 (1960):403-16.
       Exemplifies a range of medieval attitudes toward fables and
their moral value, suggesting that the Nun's Priest's exhortation
to find a moral in his tale is ironic commentary on those who
felt that a poem "had to have some moral in order to justify its
existence."

645 MYERS, D.E. "Focus and 'Moralite' in the Nun's Priest's Tale." Chaucer Review 7 (1973):210-20.
Assesses Nun's Priest's Tale from three widening perspectives: as a simple fable, the tale moralizes against flattery; as a rhetorical address to a court audience, it advises rulers; in the dramatic context of Canterbury Tales, it reflects back on the Priest who advises the Knight and the Monk but fails to see the tale's reflexive allegory about a "preacher-prelate"—himself.

646 PRATT, ROBERT A. "Some Latin Sources of the Nonnes Preest on Dreams." Speculum 52 (1977):538-70.
Investigates Chaucer's debt to Robert Holcot's commentary on the Book of Wisdom for the dream materials of Nun's Priest's Tale. Influenced by exemplary tales from Cicero, Albertus Magnus, and Valerius Maximus, Chaucer transformed Holcot's commentary in the debate on dreams between Pertelote and Chauntecleer.

647 ____. "Three Old French Sources of Nonnes Preestes Tale." Speculum 47 (1972):422-44, 646-68.
Explores the relations among Nun's Priest's Tale and its analogues, demonstrating that Chaucer's tale was based upon Marie de France's Del cok e del gupil, enriched by Pierre de St. Cloud's Roman de Renart and the anonymous Renart le contrefait. Chaucer's tale parallels each analogue in ways significant enough for all of them to be considered sources.

648 SCHEPS, WALTER. "Chaucer's Anti-Fable: Reductio ad Absurdum in the Nun's Priest's Tale." Leeds Studies in English 4 (1971):1-10.
Examines Chaucer's manipulation of the generic features of Nun's Priest's Tale as a beast fable and argues that the multiple moralizations of the tale, its sharp differentiation of human and bestial, and its illustrious depiction of Chauntecleer all parody the genre. The tale is an "anti-fable."

649 SCHRADER, RICHARD J. "Chauntecleer, the Mermaid and Daun Burnel." Chaucer Review 4 (1970):284-90.
Argues that the references to the mermaid and to Burnel the ass in Nun's Priest's Tale indicate Chauntecleer's culpability in his encounters with the fox. The allusions suggest that his pride and his improper relations with Pertelote endanger him morally as well as physically.

650 SHALLERS, A. PAUL. "The Nun's Priest's Tale: An Ironic Exemplum." ELH: A Journal of English Literary History 42 (1975):319-37.
Accounts for the rich ambiguity of Nun's Priest's Tale by tracing the influence upon it of both the idealistic tradition of cock-and-fox homiletic exempla and the naturalistic tradition of Roman de Renart. Chaucer balances the two, producing a "shifting

focus" and simultaneously exploring humility and challenging our ability to practice the virtue successfully.

651   YATES, DONALD N. "Chauntecleer's Latin Ancestors." Chaucer Review 18 (1983):116-26.
      Analyzes similarities of detail and style between Nun's Priest's Tale and Alcuin's De gallo, Ademar's fable Gallus et vulpes, and especially Isengrimus to show how elements of these "prototypes" recur in Chaucer's tale even though his immediate sources may lack them.

      See also entries 22, 201, 215-16, 218, 249, 260, 272, 347. For style and rhetoric: 135, 137, 141, 152, 172, 226; sources and analogues: 252; relations to other tales: 282, 610, 617.

THE SECOND NUN AND HER TALE

652   BEICHNER, PAUL E. "Confrontation, Contempt of Court, and Chaucer's Cecilia." Chaucer Review 8 (1974):198-204.
      Shows how Chaucer intensifies the trial scene of Second Nun's Tale, eliminating the repetition of his Latin source (the Mobritian analogue) and increasing Cecilia's contentiousness and Almachius's stupidity. The changes emphasize the trial rather than Cecilia's martyrdom.

653   CLOGAN, PAUL M. "The Figural Style and Meaning of the Second Nun's Prologue and Tale." Medievalia et Humanistica, n.s. 3 (1972):213-40.
      Argues that the "chief function" of the Prologue to the Second Nun's Tale is to isolate the "figural meaning" of the legend of St. Cecilia. The idleness stanzas establish an eschatological paradox between action and passion, the invocation to Mary explores the mystery of virginity and fruitfulness, and the name-etymologies signal the major figural images of the tale, especially marriage and light.

654   EGGEBROTEN, ANNE. "Laughter in the Second Nun's Tale: A Redefinition of the Genre." Chaucer Review 18 (1984):55-61.
      Identifies the generic humor of Second Nun's Tale in its presentation of faithlessness. The tale encourages laughter at Valerian's shocked confrontation with Cecilia's virginity and Tiburce's stunned recognition of truth; it encourages ridicule of Almachius's stupidity. These responses depend upon the confidence of medieval faith, reflected elsewhere in the saint's life genre.

655   GRENNEN, JOSEPH E. "Saint Cecilia's 'Chemical Wedding': The Unity of Canterbury Tales, Fragment VIII." JEGP: Journal of English Germanic Philology 65 (1966):466-81.
      Demonstrates how the Second Nun's life of St. Cecilia anticipates the Canon's Yeoman's "wholesale condemnation of

The Second Nun

alchemy." The themes of busyness, good works, and wisdom appear
in both tales, and a pattern of covert alchemical details in the
Nun's tale precedes the Yeoman's overt concern.

656   LUECKE, JANEMARIE. "Three Faces of Cecilia: Chaucer's Second
       Nun's Tale." American Benedictine Review 33 (1982):335-48.
            Proposes a connection between virginity and busyness in
       Second Nun's Tale, tracing the correlation to early Christian
       ideals of female sexual freedom, and arguing that in Chaucer's
       late-medieval context the story reflects the Nun's aggressive
       sense of her spiritual role and vocation.

657   PECK, RUSSELL A. "The Ideas of 'Entente' and Translation in
       Chaucer's Second Nun's Tale." Annuale Mediaevale 8 (1967):17-
       37.
            Examines a thematic relation between poetic and spiritual
       translation in Second Nun's Prologue and Tale, arguing that this
       theme unifies them and is reflected in Canon's Yeoman's and
       Parson's tales. Also identifies in the Nun's Prologue and Book
       of the Duchess a common concern with poetry as a cure for the
       malaise of their narrators.

658   REAMES, SHERRY L. "The Cecilia Legend as Chaucer Inherited It
       and Retold It: The Disappearance of an Augustinian Ideal."
       Speculum 55 (1980):38-57.
            Compares Chaucer's Second Nun's Tale to the thirteenth-
       century story of Cecilia in Jacob of Voragine's Legenda Aurea and
       the sixth-century passio of the saint to show how the two later
       versions reflect "theological pessimism." Chaucer's version
       emphasizes divine power and reduces the efficacy of human choice
       and understanding in the operation of grace.

659   _____. "The Sources of Chaucer's Second Nun's Tale."
       Modern Philology 76 (1978):111-35.
            Assesses the complex relations among Chaucer's Second Nun's
       Tale and its analogues, arguing that Chaucer followed Jacob of
       Voragine's Legenda Aurea for the first half of his tale, estab-
       lishing that Chaucer's second half is closer to the version by
       Antonio Bosio (ca. 1600) than to other Latin or Middle English
       versions, and demonstrating that this second half is a freer
       translation by Chaucer than is normally assumed.

            See also entries 88, 167, 252, 608, 665.

THE CANON'S YEOMAN AND HIS TALE

660   CAMPBELL, JACKSON J. "The Canon's Yeoman as Imperfect
       Paradigm." Chaucer Review 17 (1982):171-81.
            Describes the Canon's Yeoman's Prologue and Tale as confes-
       sional, reflections of the Yeoman's partial conversion. While he
       does not completely reject alchemy, his disassociation from it is

Canterbury Tales

a reform that anticipates—is an "imperfect paradigm" of—the
penitential process "that the Parson is soon to make explicit."

661 DUNCAN, EDGAR H. "The Literature of Alchemy and Chaucer's
     Canon's Yeoman's Tale: Framework, Theme and Characters."
     Speculum 43 (1968):633-56.
        Documents Chaucer's borrowing from alchemical literature,
     and shows how he attacked the pretensions and deceptions of
     alchemy though the Yeoman. Since Chaucer was so well educated in
     the literature, we cannot be certain whether or not the Yeoman's
     opinion is his.

662 GARDNER, JOHN [CHAMPLIN]. "The Canon's Yeoman's Prologue and
     Tale: An Interpretation." Philological Quarterly 46
     (1967):1-17.
        Characterizes the Canon's Yeoman as a comic figure, corre-
     lates the Yeoman's Canon with the priest of part 2 of the tale,
     and reads the Yeoman's pursuit and rejection of alchemy as an
     allegory of false religion that shields a more subtle allegory of
     Christian truth.

663 HARRINGTON, DAVID V. "Dramatic Irony in the Canon's Yeoman's
     Tale." Neuphilologische Mitteilungen 66 (1965):160-66.
        Characterizes the priest of Canon's Yeoman's Tale as
     covetous and gullible, an abuser of his vocation whose personal-
     ity encourages the reader to blame the alchemical deception of
     the tale as much on him as on the canon.

664 McCRACKEN, SAMUEL. "Confessional Prologue and the Topography
     of the Canon's Yeoman." Modern Philology 68 (1971):289-91.
        Finds a tripartite structure of introduction, confession,
     and tale in several of the Canterbury tales and argues that the
     Canon Yeoman's performance matches this paradigm even though the
     manuscript rubrics of Pars prima and Pars secunda obscure the
     parallels.

665 ROSENBERG, BRUCE A. "The Contrary Tales of the Second Nun and
     the Canon's Yeoman." Chaucer Review 2 (1968):278-91.
        Establishes the cohesion of Fragment VIII of Canterbury
     Tales (Second Nun's Tale and Canon's Yeoman's Tale) by comparing
     the oppositions between their images of alchemy, color, and
     vision with the thematic oppositions between charity and revela-
     tion in the Nun's Tale and cupidity and natural science in the
     Yeoman's.

        See also entries 219-20, 223, 252, 257, 260, 655, 657, 666.

THE MANCIPLE AND HIS TALE

666 BRODIE, ALEXANDER H. "Hodge of Ware and Geber's Cook:
     Wordplay in the Manciple's Prologue." Neuphilologische

165

Canterbury Tales

The Manciple

Mitteilungen 72 (1971):62-68.
Reads the Manciple's Prologue as a complex set of inter-
linked puns that grow out of the Canon's Yeoman's Tale of alchemy
and parody the Cook as a mortally drunk, mock-knight.

667 CAMPBELL, JACKSON J. "Polonius among the Pilgrims." Chaucer
Review 7 (1972):140-46.
Characterizes the teller of the Manciple's Tale as a
"folksy babbler," full of sententiousness and misplaced moralism.
Suggests that the characterizations of the Manciple in General
Prologue and Manciple's Prologue only hint at the personality
that dominates the tale.

668 DAVIDSON, ARNOLD B. "The Logic of Confusion in the Manciple's
Tale." Annuale Mediaevale 19 (1979):5-13.
Reads the apparent inconsistencies of the Manciple's Tale
as intentional attempts by the Manciple to manipulate his
audience as he manipulates the Cook in his Prologue and his
employers in the General Prologue. Through the Manciple's
dishonesty, Chaucer asserts Christian truth ironically.

669 FULK, R.D. "Reinterpreting the Manciple's Tale." JEGP:
Journal of English and Germanic Philology 78 (1979):485-93.
Explicates Manciple's Tale as a cogent warning from the
Manciple to the Cook. After asserting the insignificance of
social rank and the inherent danger of anger, the Manciple warns
the Cook, his social equal, to restrain his tongue or beware the
consequences.

670 HARWOOD, BRITTON J. "Language and the Real: Chaucer's
Manciple." Chaucer Review 6 (1972):268-79.
Contrasts Manciple's Tale and its analogues to show that
the subject of the tale is language that the Manciple uses to
"sneer at those who can be distracted from empirical reality by
language." The tale ironically anticipates the Parson's proper
use of language.

671 SCATTERGOOD, V.J. "The Manciple's Manner of Speaking."
Essays in Criticism 24 (1974):124-46.
Demonstrates the close integration of the Manciple's
Prologue and Tale via their central concern with self-control in
speech. The Manciple's verbal dexterity results from his cynical
sense of expediency, yet he does not disguise completely his
moral weaknesses.

672 SEVERS, J. BURKE. "Is the Manciple's Tale a Success?" JEGP:
Journal of English and Germanic Philology 51 (1952):1-16.
Compares Manciple's Tale to its analogues, demonstrating
how Chaucer adjusts it to suit the worldly Manciple and the prologue to his tale. Stark characterization and elaborate rhetoric
in the tale suggest that the Manciple presents an exemplum of
expediency.

166

673   WOOD, CHAUNCEY. "Speech, the Principle of Contraries, and
       Chaucer's Tales of the Manciple and the Parson." Mediaevalia
       6 (1980):209-29.
           Identifies the "principle of contraries" in medieval
       aesthetics and the understanding of speech in medieval thought,
       demonstrating how the theme of speech unites the Manciple's and
       Parson's prologues and tales. The Manciple is a "paradigm of the
       improper use of speech," and the Parson uses speech only for
       doctrine.

       See also entries 22, 135, 137, 167, 169, 252, 308.

THE PARSON AND HIS TALE

674   ALLEN, JUDSON BOYCE. "The Old Way and the Parson's Way: An
       Ironic Reading of the Parson's Tale." Journal of Medieval and
       Renaissance Studies 3 (1973):255-71.
           Marshals exegetical evidence for reading Chaucer's tone as
       consistently ironic and documents the suggestion that the end of
       a literary piece has no special weight in medieval aesthetics,
       arguing that Parson's Tale ironically offers love rather than
       penance as the true way to God. Challenged by Wenzel (entry
       681).

675   BROWN, EMERSON, Jr. "The Poet's Last Words: Text and Meaning
       at the End of the Parson's Prologue." Chaucer Review 10
       (1976):236-42.
           Questions Manly's emendation (entry 31) of the last lines
       of the Parson's Prologue, followed in modern editions, and demon-
       strates the authenticity of the original on the grounds of
       manuscript evidence, syntactic precedent in the Canterbury Tales,
       and literary quality.

676   DELASANTA, RODNEY. "Penance and Poetry in the Canterbury
       Tales." PMLA 93 (1978):240-47.
           Asserts Chaucer's earnest intent in the Parson's peni-
       tential treatise by examining the symbolic and dramatic stategies
       of the Parson's Prologue. As the Pilgrims ride into sight of
       Canterbury, Chaucer introduces a number of eschatological images
       that suggest the neccesity of penance to salvation.

677   _____. "The Theme of Justice in the Canterbury Tales."
       Modern Language Quarterly 31 (1970):298-307.
           Explicates the images and symbols of judgment and closure
       in the Parson's Prologue, assessing scriptural, astrological, and
       numerological signals that the pilgrims are at the penultimate
       stage of a spiritual journey as well as a physical one.

678   FINLAYSON, JOHN. "The Satiric Mode and the Parson's Tale."
       Chaucer Review 6 (1971):94-116.

The Parson

Compares Canterbury Tale to other satires to define the
"flexible satiric mode" of the work, dependent upon shifting
narrative perspective especially in General Prologue. In this
light, Parson's Tale is not an index to the whole work, but one
among many perspectives that "qualify and modify each other and
provide a comprehensive complex which, in its wholeness, may be a
sort of truth." Characterizes the Parson as pedantic and somewhat dour. Challenged by Wenzel (entry 681).

679   PATTERSON, LEE W. "The Parson's Tale and the Quitting of the
       Canterbury Tales." Traditio 34 (1978):331-80.
           Locates Parson's Tale in the genre of the "penitential
       manual," attributes its organization to Chaucer rather than his
       sources, and discusses its possible date of composition and
       thematic relevance to the other Canterbury tales. Following
       "lines of influence" from the other tales, Parson's Tale must
       have been written late; it "dismisses" earlier tales by
       redefining the act of speaking as penitential rather than
       expressive.

680   PFANDER, H.G. "Some Medieval Manuals of Religious Instruction
       in England and Observations on Chaucer's Parson's Tale."
       JEGP: Journal of English and Germanic Philology 35
       (1936):243-58.
           Surveys medieval religious manuals available in England in
       Chaucer's day and describes Parson's Tale as a manual of the
       "confessional type." Notes parallels between this tale and other
       manuals, especially the fragmentary MS Lambeth 182, and suggests
       that the tale is a translation of a Latin original also trans-
       lated in Lambeth 182.

681   WENZEL, SIEGFRIED. "Chaucer's Parson's Tale: 'Every Tales
       Strengthe.'" In Europäische Lehrdictung: Festschrift für
       Walter Naumann zum 70. Geburstag. Edited by Hans Gerd Rötzer
       and Herbert Walz. Darmstadt: Wissenschaftliche
       Buchgesellschaft, 1981, pp. 86-98.
           Surveys critical interpretation of Parson's Tale.
       Describes the "rhetorical weighting" of its prologue, arguing
       that the Parson's replacement of the Host as guide follows the
       models of Alain de Lille and Dante. The tale has more authority
       in the collection than the tales that precede it. Challenges
       Allen (entry 674) and Finlayson (entry 678).

682   _____. "The Source of Chaucer's Seven Deadly Sins." Traditio
       30 (1974):351-78.
           Tentatively suggests a new "source" for the Deadly Sins
       section of Chaucer's Parson's Tale: several unpublished
       manuscripts (grouped here by their first words, Quoniam and
       Primo) that reflect more significant parallels to the Parson's
       discussion than have been previously discovered.

683   ____. "The Source of the 'Remedia' of the Parson's Tale."
         Traditio 27 (1971):433-54.
         Demonstrates significant parallels between the "Remedia"
sections of Chaucer's Parson's Tale and several unpublished
manuscripts, here designated Postquam. The tradition of the
Parson's treatise is complex, but the Postquam group of
manuscripts appears to be the source of the "Remedia" sections.

         See also entries 159, 163-64, 224, 252, 278. For relations
to other tales: 145, 251, 253, 300, 556, 560, 621, 657, 670,
673, 688.

THE RETRACTION

684   CAMPBELL, A.P. "Chaucer's Retraction: Who Retracted What?"
         Revue de l'Université d'Ottawa 35 (1965):35-53; Humanities
         Association Bulletin 16, no. 1 (1965):75-97.
         Surveys and rejects much of the criticism of Chaucer's
Retraction, arguing for a reading based on Chaucer's frequent use
of ironic reversal and on the characters of the Parson and the
narrator. The narrator follows tradition by closing with a
prayer and overturns the Parson's staid rejection of fables.

685   GORDON, JAMES D. "Chaucer's Retraction: A Review of
         Opinion." In Studies in Medieval Literature in Honor of
         Professor Albert Croll Baugh. Edited by MacEdward Leach.
         Philadelphia: University of Pennsylvania Press, 1961, pp. 81-
         96.
         Traces the history of interpretation of Chaucer's Retrac-
tion from the early rejection of it as inauthentic, hypotheti-
cally the result of Chaucer's late-life senility or monkish
addition, to more recent acceptance and attempts to reconcile its
tone with the rest of Chaucer's corpus.

686   KNAPP, ROBERT S. "Penance, Irony, and Chaucer's Retraction."
         Assays: Critical Approaches to Medieval and Renaissance Texts
         2 (1983):45-67.
         Explores the semiotic affinity among retraction, irony, and
penance, reading Chaucer's Retraction as an extension of the
sustained irony of Canterbury Tales and as a penitential, self-
canceling sign that points to the similarity and vast disparity
between, on the one hand, speech acts or tales among men, and, on
the other, the Word that mediates between God and man.

687   SAYCE, OLIVE. "Chaucer's Retractions: The Conclusion of the
         Canterbury Tales and Its Place in Literary Tradition." Medium
         Ævum 40 (1971):230-48.
         Documents the conventional nature of Chaucer's Retraction
by exploring the rhetorical commonplaces of medieval prologues
and conclusions, and by identifying analogous epilogues in
French, Latin, and German. Chaucer uses commonplace language and

The Retraction

conventional form. but he includes several signals of his "ironic and humorous detachment" from his literary confession.

688   WURTELE, DOUGLAS. "The Penitence of Geoffrey Chaucer."
       Viator 11 (1980):335-61.
       Surveys criticism of Chaucer's Retraction and divides the piece into two portions: the Parson's concluding address and an "interpolated middle" that lists Chaucer's literary "sins." In light of the penitential theory of Parson's Tale, modified from Pennafort's Summa casuum de poenitentia, the Retraction suggests Chaucer's hope for his spiritual future.

       See also entries 160, 208, 745.

Troilus and Criseyde

CRITICAL TRADITION

689   KAMINSKY, ALICE R. Chaucer's "Troilus and Criseyde" and the
       Critics. Athens: Ohio University Press, 1980, 259 pp.
           Surveys and compares critical approaches to Chaucer's
       Troilus and Criseyde in a discursive manner, classifying the ap-
       proaches under broad categories and identifying their strengths
       and weaknesses. Boccaccio's and Chaucer's biographies are major
       touchstones for the historical school; Boethian thought for the
       philosophical; genre and structure for the formalists; courtly
       love and character for the psychologists.

690   SHEPHERD, G.T. "Troilus and Criseyde." In Chaucer and
       Chaucerians: Critical Studies in Middle English Literature.
       Edited by D.S. Brewer. London: Thomas Nelson & Sons;
       University: University of Alabama Press, 1966. Reprint.
       Nelson's University Paperbacks, 1970, pp. 65-87. Reprinted in
       Chaucer and His Contemporaries: Essays on Medieval Literature
       and Thought, ed. Helaine Newstead (Greenwich, Conn.: Fawcett
       Publications, 1968), pp. 143-63
           Indicates how modern assumptions have produced inadequate
       interpretations of Troilus and Criseyde. Fourteenth-century
       notions of war and sex, nonnovelistic narration, separation of
       narration and argument, and subordination of character to action
       make it a distinctly medieval tragic romance. Its illumination
       of an "other order" is more important than the tragic action
       itself.

       See also entries 47, 711, 715.

TEXTUAL ISSUES

691   ROOT, ROBERT K. The Textual Tradition of Chaucer's Troilus.
       Chaucer Society Publications, 1st ser., no. 99. London: K.
       Paul, Trench, Trübner, & Co.; Oxford University Press, 1916.
       Reprint. New York: Johnson Reprint, 1967, 296 pp.

Troilus and Criseyde

Textual Issues

Textual analysis of the sixteen manuscripts and two early printed editions of Chaucer's Troilus and Criseyde that describes the texts and analyzes their variants line by line. Accounts for the complex relations among the texts by theorizing that Chaucer revised his poem. Designates the first unrevised version alpha, the revision from which most later texts derive, beta. A third version, gamma, refers to a group of corrupt manuscripts that derive from a common unreliable exemplar. Windeatt (entries 24 and 693) and Hanna (in entry 21) challenge this analysis, arguing that the variations are all scribal.

692   WINDEATT, BARRY A. "The Scribes as Chaucer's Early Critics." Studies in the Age of Chaucer 1 (1979):119-42.
      Analyzes scribal variations and glosses in the manuscripts of Troilus and Criseyde to display the "earliest line-by-line literary criticism of Chaucer's poetry." Distinctively Chaucerian diction and syntax are evident where scribes adjust or explain Chaucer's original language, most often his concise expressions and compressed images. Revised as "The Scribal Medium," in Windeatt's edition of Troilus (entry 24).

693   ____. "The Text of Troilus." In Essays on "Troilus and Criseyde." Edited by Mary Salu. Chaucer Studies, no. 3. Cambridge: D.S. Brewer; Totowa, N.J.: Rowman & Littlefield, 1979, pp. 1-22.
      Examines the manuscript variants of Troilus and Criseyde and directly challenges Root's theory (entry 691) of multiple versions of the poem. The major discrepancies between the alpha and beta families of manuscripts reflect Chaucer's habits of translation rather than a change in his design for the poem. Discrepancies among all three groups of manuscripts suggest minor adjustments by the author or, more likely, scribal alteration. Revised as "The Text of the Troilus," in Windeatt's edition of Troilus (entry 24).

      See also entries 20, 24, 729.

SOURCES AND LITERARY RELATIONS

694   ANDERSON, DAVID. "Theban History in Chaucer's Troilus." Studies in the Age of Chaucer 4 (1982):109-33.
      Documents medieval understanding that the Trojan War followed soon after the Theban War, and argues that Chaucer's references to Thebes in Troilus and Criseyde constitute a "satirical counterpoint" to Troilus's and Pandarus's attention to "courtly business" rather than the "momentous events" of the war.

695   BENSON, C. DAVID. The History of Troy in Middle English Literature: Guido delle Colonne's "Historia destructionis Troiae" in Medieval England. Cambridge: D.S. Brewer; Totowa, N.J.: Rowman & Littlefield, 1980, 174 pp.

Appraises Guido delle Colonne's impact on Middle English poetry and serves the double function for Chaucerians of identifying Guido's influence on Chaucer's Troilus and Criseyde, and Chaucer's influence on Lydgate's Troy Book and Henryson's Testament of Cresseid. Chaucer borrowed his historian/narrator from Guido as well as his manipulation of proverbs and his concern with fortune. In turn, Lydgate's view of history is due to his emulation of Chaucer. Henryson's poem reflects the same withdrawal from history into fiction as does Chaucer's.

696   EBEL, JULIA. "Troilus and Oedipus: The Genealogy of an Image." English Studies 55 (1974):15-21.
Describes the direct influence of Statius's Thebaid on Troilus and Criseyde, separating this influence from that of other medieval tales of Thebes, including Boccaccio's Filostrato. Chaucer makes direct use of the "pivotal role" of Oedipus in Statius, equating Troilus to Oedipus through verbal echo and images of blindness.

697   FRANK, ROBERT WORTH, Jr. "Troilus and Criseyde: The Art of Amplification." In Medieval Literature and Folklore Studies: Essays in Honor of Francis Lee Utley. Edited by Jerome Mandel and Bruce A. Rosenberg. New Brunswick, N.J.: Rutgers University Press, 1970, pp. 155-71.
Analyzes Chaucer's expansions of Boccaccio's Filostrato in Troilus and Criseyde to show how he complicated the view of love. Such additions as sententiae, increased social context, complexities of character, and Troilus's long speeches enable Chaucer to examine love from many perspectives.

698   GARBÁTY, THOMAS [J]. "The Pamphilus Tradition in Ruiz and Chaucer." Philological Quarterly 46 (1967):457-70.
Identifies the parallels in plot and detail among the Latin Pamphilus de amore, the Roman de la rose, Juan Ruiz's Libro de buen amor, and Chaucer's Troilus and Criseyde, arguing that the deviations of Troilus from its acknowledged source--Boccaccio's Filostrato--should be attributed to Chaucer's familiarity with these other works rather than Boccaccio's Filocolo. The Pamphilus tradition influenced Chaucer's characterization.

699   KNAPP, PEGGY ANN. "Boccaccio and Chaucer on Cassandra." Philological Quarterly 56 (1977):413-17.
Contrasts the Cassandras in Chaucer's Troilus and Criseyde and Boccaccio's Filostrato to show how Chaucer changed the character, sharpening its focus upon the ravages of fortune.

700   LEWIS, C.S. "What Chaucer Really Did to Il Filostrato." Essays and Studies 17 (1932):56-75. Reprinted in Chaucer Criticism, vol.2, "Troilus and Criseyde" & the Minor Poems, ed. Richard J. Schoeck and Jerome Taylor (Notre Dame, Ind.: University of Notre Dame Press, 1961), pp. 16-33; Chaucer's

Troilus and Criseyde

Sources

"Troilus": Essays in Criticism, ed. Stephen A. Barney
(Hamden, Conn.: Archon Books, 1980), pp. 37-54.
     Compares Troilus and Criseyde to its immediate source,
Boccaccio's Filostrato, describing the changes Chaucer made in
"medievalizing" the story. The poem's historical pose, its
rhetorical amplification, its consistent sententiousness, and
especially its representation of the conventions of courtly love
place it in the tradition of medieval romance and distinguish it
from Boccaccio and rising Italian humanism. See Young (entry
740).

701   PRATT, ROBERT A. "Chaucer and Le Roman de Troyle et de
       Criseida." Studies in Philology 53 (1956):509-39.
           Parallels passages from Boccaccio's Filostrato, Beauvau's
       Le roman de Troyle et de Criseida, and Chaucer Troilus and
       Criseyde to show that Chaucer used the French translation of
       Boccaccio as well as the original. Suggests that the French
       version was his primary source and a means to sophisticate his
       knowledge of the Italian language.

702   WETHERBEE, WINTHROP. Chaucer and the Poets: A Essay on
       "Troilus and Criseyde." Ithaca: Cornell University Press,
       1984, 249 pp.
           Addresses Troilus and Criseyde as a poem about Chaucer's
       confrontation with previous poetry, especially classical poetry
       as he observed its treatment in Dante's Commedia. Through
       Troilus, the narrator of Chaucer's poem explores and rejects the
       medieval courtly love found in Roman de la rose. Significant al-
       lusions to Vergil, Ovid, Statius, and Dante define the roles of
       Troilus and Criseyde as epic actors rather than as courtly
       lovers, directing attention to the narrator's difficulty in ac-
       cepting his characters and their actions. The narrator confronts
       the opposition between Christian and pagan poetry, acknowledging
       the power and the limits of ancient verse, and, in his Epilogue,
       accepting the Dantean role of Christian poet. A contrast between
       mere making and true poetry underlies this acceptance, particu-
       larly as Dante adumbrated it in his fictional account of
       Statius's "conversion" to Christianity through poetry.

703   WIMSATT, JAMES I. "Guillaume de Machaut and Chaucer's Troilus
       and Criseyde." Medium Ævum 45 (1976):277-93.
           Demonstrates the influence of various poems by Guillaume de
       Machaut on Chaucer's Troilus and Criseyde, especially Jugement
       dou roy de Navarre and Remede de Fortune on Troilus's psychology
       and Pandarus's advice, and Paradis d'Amour and Mireoir amorereux
       on Antigone's song.

704   WINDEATT, BARRY. "Chaucer and the Filostrato." In Chaucer
       and the Italian Trecento. Edited by Piero Boitani.
       Cambridge: Cambridge University Press, 1983, pp. 163-83.
           Explains the cumulative effect of Chaucer's "in-etched"
       alterations of Boccaccio's Filostrato in his Troilus and

<u>Criseyde</u>. Chaucer expands the conceptual breadth of the story by emphasizing the characters's reflectiveness about love and increasing references to death, time, fortune, and God. Compare to "The <u>Troilus</u> as Translation" in Windeatt's edition of <u>Troilus</u> (entry 24).

705   YOUNG, KARL. <u>The Origin and Development of the Story of Troilus and Criseyde</u>. Chaucer Society Publications, 2d ser., no. 41. London: K. Paul, Trench, Trübner & Co., 1908. Reprint. New York: Gordian Press, 1968, 195 pp.
       Traces the development of the story of Troilus and Criseyde from its earliest roots in Dares and Dictys's chronicles to Chaucer's poem, acknowledging the importance of Boccaccio's <u>Filostrato</u> as Chaucer's source, but arguing also for the direct influence upon Chaucer of Boccaccio's sources, Benoît de Sainte-Maure's <u>Roman de Troie</u> and Guido delle Colonne's <u>Historia Troiana</u>, (Historia destructionis Troiae) Also argues for the influence of Boccaccio's <u>Teseida</u> and <u>Filocolo</u> on Chaucer's <u>Troilus</u>. Examines Chaucer's debt to each of these sources by identifying common motifs, patterns, and passages. Theorizes about Chaucer's references to Lollius.

       See also, for relations to works by Boccaccio, entries 6, 10, 24, 180, 185, 708, 718, 721, 733-34, 740-41, 743, 748, 758-60, 780, 791-92, 799, 801, 803; for relations to other works: 722, 731, 743-44, 746, 757, 759, 761, 768, 791, 794, 803.

STYLE AND IMAGERY

706   BREWER, DEREK S. "The Ages of Troilus, Criseyde and Pandarus." <u>Studies in English Literature</u> (Tokyo), English number (1972):3-15. Reprinted in <u>Tradition and Innovation in Chaucer</u> (London: Macmillan & Co., 1982), pp. 80-88.
       Examines the references to youth and aging in <u>Troilus and Crisyde</u> to determine the ages of the main characters, even though "novelistic" accuracy is impossible. Troilus may be about nineteen, Criseyde a few years older, and Pandarus a "middle-aged trendy."

707   BURJOREE, D.M. "The Pilgrimage of Troilus's Sailing Heart in Chaucer's <u>Troilus and Criseyde</u>." <u>Annuale Mediaevale</u> 13 (1972):14-31.
       Explores Chaucer's nautical metaphors in <u>Troilus and Criseyde</u>, especially the "sailing heart" of Troilus. Establishes the commonplace nature of nautical imagery in classical, patristic, and medieval tradition, and documents Chaucer's extension of the tradition to include the "spiritual pilgrimage" of Troilus's love. See Stevens (entry 717).

708   CORSA, HELEN STORM. "Dreams in <u>Troilus and Criseyde</u>." <u>American Imago</u> 27 (1970):52-65.

Studies the psychoanalytic implications of the three dreams in Troilus and Criseyde, arguing that the "Oedipal fantasy" at the "very core" of Boccaccio's Filostrato is emphasized in Chaucer's version.

709   COTTEN, MICHAEL E.   "The Artistic Integrity of Chaucer's Troilus and Criseyde." Chaucer Review 7 (1972):37-43.
Observes two image patterns in books 4 and 5 of Troilus and Criseyde that fuse characterization and allegory. Criseyde's association with the moon (and Troilus's with the sun) suggests both her inconstancy and the theme of Boethian fortune. Infernal imagery communicates the pain of lost love and the eschatology of worldly pleasure. Compare to Stokes (entry 774).

710   CRAMPTON, GEORGIA RONAN.   "Action and Passion in Chaucer's Troilus." Medium Ævum 43 (1974):22-36.
The medieval "do and suffer" topos of rhetoric, philosophy, and literature informs the main characters of Troilus and Criseyde. With fair consistency, Pandarus acts, Troilus suffers, and Criseyde vacillates between action and passion.

711   DONALDSON, E. TALBOT.   "Chaucer in the Twentieth Century." Studies in the Age of Chaucer 2 (1980):7-13.
Suggests that the twentieth century is the first in which Chaucer has been "fully appreciated and understood," and examines several passages of Troilus and Criseyde that describe Criseyde to show how Chaucer provokes us to create characters through rich ambiguity and such "devious devices" as uncertain syntax, subjunctive mood, overstatement, understatement, and "just plain lies."

712   GORDON, IDA L.   "The Narrative Function of Irony in Chaucer's Troilus and Criseyde." In Medieval Miscellany Presented to Eugene Vinaver by Pupils, Colleagues, and Friends. Edited by F. Whitehead, A.H. Diverres, and F.E. Sutcliffe. Manchester: Manchester University Press; New York: Barnes & Noble, 1965, pp. 146-56.
Exemplifies various kinds of irony in Troilus and Criseyde, demonstrating how the narrator's tentative comments ironically communicate Criseyde's accession to her love tryst with Troilus, and how her accession comments obliquely on both the frailty and value of courtly love.

713   KORETSKY, ALLEN C.   "Chaucer's Use of the Apostrophe in Troilus and Criseyde." Chaucer Review 4 (1970):242-66.
Examines Chaucer's use of exclamatio—rhetorical apostrophe—in the design of Troilus and Criseyde and the characterization of the narrator and major actors. Following medieval rhetorical theory, Chaucer uses the device to "dilate and amplify" his material and to represent "deeply felt emotion."

Troilus and Criseyde

714   LANHAM, RICHARD A. "Opaque Style and Its Use in Troilus and
       Criseyde." Studies in Medieval Culture 3 (1970):169-76.
          Examines the uniformity of Pandarus's and Troilus's
       rhetoric in Troilus and Criseyde, reading the poem as a comedy of
       self-victimization. Troilus is a prisoner, trapping himself in
       courtly conventions; Pandarus devotes himself to "folk wisdom
       rather than principle." In contrast, Criseyde is a victim of her
       adaptation to the conventions of her changing environment.

715   LAWTON, DAVID. "Irony and Sympathy in Troilus and Criseyde:
       A Reconsideration." Leeds Studies in English 14 (1983):94-
       115.
          Argues that "sympathetic" and "ironic" readings of Troilus
       and Criseyde are compatible once we accept that the "stable"
       irony of the poem results from our "foreknowledge of the oucome
       of the events." The poem corroborates this irony while exploring
       both spiritual and "ludic" ideas of love; it limits our sympathy
       for the characters when we witness their passions "overborne by
       circumstance."

716   SHARROCK, ROGER. "Second Thoughts: C.S. Lewis on Chaucer's
       Troilus." Essays in Criticism 8 (1958):123-37. Reprinted as
       "Troilus and Criseyde: Poem of Contingency," in Chaucer's
       Mind and Art, ed. A.C. Cawley, Essays Old and New, no. 3
       (London: Oliver & Boyd, 1969), pp. 140-54.
          Responds to C.S. Lewis's discussion (entry 236) of courtly
       love in Troilus and Criseyde, identifying the features of Troilus
       that emphasize human limitation: colloquialisms, proximity of
       the ludicrous and the sublime, the human vulnerability of the
       lovers, and the "contingent, fortuitous character of ordinary
       life." Reads the final stanzas as a spiritual counterpoint to
       the poem's theme of the contingency of material life.

717   STEVENS, MARTIN. "The Winds of Fortune in the Troilus."
       Chaucer Review 13 (1979):285-307.
          Identifies the recurrent nautical winds-of-fortune metaphor
       in Troilus and Criseyde, showing how it reflects the poem's
       dominant concern with "destinal forces" and how the characters
       adapt the metaphor to fit their own outlooks. Only the narrator
       properly views destiny as Providence. See Burjoree (entry 707).

718   TAYLOR, DAVIS. "The Terms of Love: A Study of Troilus's
       Style." Speculum 51 (1976):76-90. Revised in Chaucer's
       "Troilus": Essays in Criticism, ed. Stephen A. Barney
       (Hamden, Conn.: Archon Books, 1980), pp. 231-56.
          Examines the style of Troilus's speeches in comparision
       with those of Boccaccio's Troilo and against a background of
       three "recurrent conventions that distinguish medieval love
       poetry": superlatives; quantitative terms (e.g., "ful," "al,"
       "hele"); and balanced, repetitive internal monologues. Troilus's
       style is more conventional than Troilo's, but it suggests a
       strong sense of individuality and energetic, internal struggle.

719   VAN, THOMAS A. "Imprisoning and Ensnarement in Troilus and
       the Knight's Tale." Papers in Language and Literature 7
       (1971):3-12.
           Identifies images of imprisonment and ensnarement in
       Troilus and Criseyde and in Knight's Tale as reflections of the
       characters' attempts to control others, "shadowed over" by the
       cosmic patterns that thwart human desire. The ending of each
       poem reminds us of the importance of human choice in spiritual
       affairs.

720   WIMSATT, JAMES I. "Medieval and Modern in Chaucer's Troilus
       and Criseyde." PMLA 92 (1977):203-16.
           Investigates the interaction in Troilus and Criseyde of
       modern realism and emphasis on epic, romance, and philosophy. In
       the poem, fortune reflects all of the "medieval" elements, ironi-
       cally undercutting the freedom of the lovers. Yet the realistic
       treatment of "genre scenes" of everyday activity makes their love
       vital and attractive.

721   _____. "Realism in Troilus and Criseyde and the Roman de la
       Rose." In Essays on "Troilus and Criseyde." Edited by Mary
       Salu. Chaucer Studies, no. 3. Cambridge: D.S. Brewer;
       Totowa, N.J.: Rowman & Littlefield, 1979, pp. 43-56.
           Argues that Troilus and Criseyde and Roman de la rose
       reflect, in different ways, the realism of two traditions:
       cosmic allegories and the arts of love. The allegories operate
       in a "sphere of realism" by focusing on love as typical of human
       life; the arts of love produce a more immediate "circumstantial
       realism."

722   WINDEATT, BARRY. "'Love that Oughte Ben Secree' in Chaucer's
       Troilus." Chaucer Review 14 (1979):116-31.
           Contrasts the different representations of social privacy
       in Chaucer's Troilus and Criseyde and Boccaccio's Filostrato to
       show how Chaucer increased his lovers's concern with secrecy. In
       his poem, social conditions and courtly demands require such
       secrecy, reflecting the poet's larger concern with the difficul-
       ties of contrasting idealized literary standards of behavior with
       actual social conditions.

           See also entries 125, 137, 141, 154, 221-22, 740, 746, 751,
       778, 784.

STRUCTURE AND GENRE

723   ADAMSON, JANE. "The Unity of Troilus and Criseyde." Critical
       Review 14 (1971):17-37.
           Reads Troilus and Criseyde as a sensitive representation of
       the contradictions of human life. Criseyde manifests an intense
       but inactive self-consciousness and Troilus tries to conceptual-
       ize his vital feelings. Through them, Chaucer represents

humanity's impossible desire to experience and understand simultaneously.

724   BESSENT, BENJAMIN R.   "The Puzzling Chronology of Chaucer's
       Troilus."   Studia Neophilologica 41 (1969):99–111.
            Clarifies the precise chronology of Troilus and Criseyde
       evident through temporal and astrological references in the poem,
       and suggests that Chaucer used chronology primarily to present
       Criseyde favorably.

725   BRENNER, GERRY.   "Narrative Structure in Chaucer's Troilus and
       Criseyde."   Annuale Mediaevale 6 (1965):5–18.   Revised
       slightly in Chaucer's "Troilus": Essays in Criticism, ed.
       Stephen A. Barney (Hamden, Conn.:   Archon Books, 1980), pp.
       131–44.
            Surveys discussions of the structure of Troilus and
       Criseyde and argues that Chaucer yokes a symmetrical structure, a
       "metaphor of harmony and order," to an ironic structure of dis-
       ordering inversions, wrenched foreshadowings, and multiple points
       of view.   The combination parallels the other "unresolvable
       antinomies" of the poem, for example, fate and free will,
       Christian and pagan, tragic and comic, poetic convention and
       human reality, etc.

726   CLOUGH, ANDREA.   "Medieval Tragedy and the Genre of Troilus
       and Criseyde."   Medievalia et Humanistica, n.s. 11 (1982):211–
       27.
            As a "romance tragedy," Troilus and Crisyde marks an impor-
       tant stage in the development between medieval de casibus tragedy
       and Elizabethan tragedy.   Emotional, philosophical, and psycho-
       logical, Chaucer's poem combines romance and tragedy in a new
       form that anticipates the likes of Marlowe's Hero and Leander and
       Shakespeare's Romeo and Juliet.

727   FARNHAM, WILLARD.   "Fall of Princes: Chaucer and Lydgate."
       In The Medieval Heritage of Elizabethan Tragedy.   Berkeley:
       University of California Press, 1936.   Reprint.   Oxford:
       Basil Blackwell, 1970, pp. 129–60.
            Places Chaucer's Monk's Tale and Troilus and Criseyde in
       the medieval, Boccaccian tradition of de casibus tragedy.   Reads
       Monk's Tale as a "sterile confinement of Chaucer's spirit," yet
       appropriate to its fictional teller.   Assesses Troilus as an
       "inspired glorification of Boccaccio's conception of tragedy"
       that benefits from its focus on a single tragic protagonist and
       its careful exploration of the theme of contemptus mundi in the
       work.

728   HART, THOMAS ELWOOD.   "Medieval Structuralism: 'Dulcarnoun'
       and the Five-Book Design of Chaucer's Troilus."   Chaucer
       Review 16 (1981):129–70.
            Explores the elaborate geometrical and numerical relations
       that underlie the structure of Troilus and Criseyde, citing tra-

ditional sources, graphing the results, and arguing that Chaucer
followed Geoffrey of Vinsauf's advice to compose poetry on architectural principles. Demonstrates how the number of lines in
each book derive from a Pythagorean theorem cited by Criseyde and
how the pentagon and circle can be used to generate several
patterns of diction and image.

729   HUSSEY, S.S. "The Difficult Fifth Book of Troilus and
       Criseyde." Modern Language Review 67 (1972):721-29.
         Attributes several "oddities" of book 5 of Troilus and
Criseyde to the possibility that Chaucer did not revise and
integrate this book as he did the others. The book lacks a
proem, contains much rhetorical "padding," and jumbles its
sources. Manuscript evidence supports the argument.

730   McALPINE, MONICA E. The Genre of "Troilus and Criseyde."
       Ithaca: Cornell University Press, 1978, 252 pp.
         Argues that de casibus tragedy serves as a foil to the
Boethian complexity of Chaucer's Troilus and Criseyde, contrasting the single omniscient point of view of the genre with the
poem's multiple perspectives. The conclusion of Troilus encom-
passes the comedy of Troilus's achievement of pagan wisdom and
the tragedy of Criseyde's infidelity, modified by the audience's
recollection of the integrity of their love and the narrator's
efforts to "conclude his own performance." Such self-conscious
contrasts and closures effectively communicate the Boethian truth
of the limitations of all human effort and interpretation.

731   McCALL, JOHN P. "The Five-Book Structure of Chaucer's
       Troilus." Modern Language Quarterly 23 (1962):297-308.
         Parallels the theme and structure of the five books of
Troilus and Criseyde with those of Boethius's Consolation of
Philosophy, arguing that Chaucer imitated the structure of the
Consolation, inverted its "dramatic movement," and thereby made
his tragedy a "companion piece" to Boethius's comedy.

732   MACEY, SAMUEL L. "Dramatic Elements in Chaucer's Troilus."
       Texas Studies in Literature and Language 12 (1970):301-23.
         Discusses Troilus and Criseyde in light of Aristotelian
dramatic theory, assessing its five-act structure, scene
divisions, rising and falling action, structural balance, and observance of the unities. The poem employs the major techniques
of classical drama, but its Christian ethos and its epilogue make
interpretation as an Aristotelian tragedy impossible.

733   MEECH, STANFORD B. Design in Chaucer's Troilus. Syracuse,
       N.Y.: Syracuse University Press, 1959. Reprint. New York:
       Greenwood Press, 1969, 541 pp.
         Close comparative reading of Chaucer's Troilus and Criseyde
and Boccaccio's Filostrato, assessing Chaucer's achievement by
observing his appropriations from Boccaccio's work and deviations
from it. Chaucer's expands the poem's chronology and spatiality,

Troilus and Criseyde

its astrological machinery, and its atmosphere of inevitability,
universalizing Boccaccio's message about love: in all earthly
matters, expectations clash with actualities. Chaucer intensifies the courtly atmosphere of the poem and increases its irony
both by sharpening the imagery and by juxtaposing conflicting
scenes and songs. He defines his characters more sharply and
presents their virtues and limitations with broader understanding
and greater compassion. Yet his sense of determinism is strong.

734   MORGAN, GERALD. "The Significance of the Aubades in Troilus
       and Criseyde." Yearbook of English Studies 9 (1979):221-35.
          Analyzes the Proem and aubades (dawn songs) of Troilus and
       Criseyde, book 3, to clarify the poem's comparison between human
       and divine love. Chaucer's alterations of Boccaccio's Filostrato
       in these passages emphasize the insufficiency of earthly love and
       the "essential goodness of love itself."

735   PECK, RUSSELL A. "Numerology and Chaucer's Troilus and
       Criseyde." Mosaic 4, no. 4 (1972):1-29.
          Surveys the nature, function, and background of numerology
       in medieval poetry and argues for its significance in Troilus and
       Criseyde. Numerology underscores the contrast between the poem's
       five-part structure and its emphatically worldly setting.
       "Numerical metaphors" help define the characters.

736   ROBERTSON, D.W., Jr. "Chaucerian Tragedy." ELH: A Journal
       of English Literary History 19 (1951):1-37. Reprinted in
       Chaucerian Criticism, vol.2, "Troilus and Criseyde" & the
       Minor Poems, ed. Richard J. Schoeck and Jerome Taylor (Notre
       Dame, Ind.: University of Notre Dame Press, 1961), pp. 86-
       121.
          Defines Chaucerian tragedy in Boethian and Christian terms,
       explaining the importance of fortune, reason, and duty to under-
       standing the pattern of tragedy in Monk's Tale and Troilus and
       Criseyde. Troilus, like all Chaucer's tragic protagonists,
       echoes Adam's fall by abandoning human reason and likeness to God
       and subjecting himself to fortune. His is the tropological
       pattern of "every mortal sinner."

737   SALTER, ELIZABETH. "Troilus and Criseyde: A Reconsidera-
       tion." In Patterns of Love and Courtesy: Essays in Memory of
       C.S. Lewis. Edited by John Lawlor. London: Edward Arnold;
       Evanston, Ill.: Northwestern University Press, 1966, pp. 86-
       106.
          Reads Troilus and Criseyde as a reflection of Chaucer "at
       work," observing his "gradually changing purposes" and his
       various modifications of tone and atmosphere. By virtue of its
       magnitude and "imaginative strength," the poem varies and
       fluctuates; its unity is coordinate rather than subordinate,
       communicating through significant breaks and pauses. Its
       greatness lies more in the questions about humanity it raises
       than in the answers it provides.

Structure and Genre

738   UTLEY, FRANCIS L. "Scene-Division in Chaucer's Troilus and
       Criseyde." In Studies in Medieval Literature in Honor of
       Professor Albert Croll Baugh. Edited by MacEdward Leach.
       Philadelphia: University of Pennsylvania Press, 1961, pp.
       109-38.
            Analyzes Troilus and Criseyde as a series of eighty-three
       identifiable "scenes," demonstrating the skillful use of dialogue
       in the poem, its manipulation of visual image, its contrasts, and
       its deft shifts of tempo. Includes an "Analysis of Scenes" in
       schematic outline, indicated by line number.

739   VAN DYKE, CAROLYN. "The Errors of Good Men: Hamartia in Two
       Middle English Poems." In Hamartia: The Concept of Error in
       the Western Tradition: Essays in Honor of John M. Crossett.
       Edited by Donald V. Stump et al. Texts and Studies in
       Religion, no. 16. New York: Edwin Mellen Press, 1983, pp.
       171-91.
            Assesses Sir Gawain and the Green Knight and Troilus and
       Criseyde in light of Aristotle's tragic theory, arguing that the
       poems and the theory reflect a similar paradox. The theory as-
       sumes and the poems generate double responses from the audience:
       the hero's error is innocent in that it is ignorant or limited,
       but he is nevertheless culpable before universal law. In the
       poems, ignorance and culpability parallel the Christian
       universals of mercy and justice.

740   YOUNG, KARL. "Chaucer's Troilus and Criseyde as Romance."
       PMLA 53 (1938):38-63.
            Extends and details Lewis's discussion (entry 700) of
       Chaucer's "medievalization" of Boccaccio's Filostrato, arguing
       that the romantic features of Troilus and Criseyde enhance its
       "glamor and strangeness." More than Filostrato, the poem dis-
       tances us through setting and action, heightens the courtly
       atmosphere of the plot, and introduces romantic scenes. The
       "psychology" of the characters is not inimical to the poem's
       romance genre.

            See also entries 689-90. For structure: 3, 159, 751-52,
       769, 781; for genre: 1, 6, 9, 90, 152, 177, 212, 216, 700, 721.

PHILOSOPHY AND MORAL VISION

741   apRoberts, Robert P. "The Boethian God and the Audience of
       the Troilus." JEGP: Journal of English and Germanic
       Philology 69 (1970):425-36.
            Compares the departures from Troy of Chaucer's and
       Boccaccio's Criseydes to demonstrate how fate operates in Troilus
       and Criseyde. The operation of fate and the poem's omniscient
       point of view allow the reader to witness a Boethian interaction
       of destiny and free will in which foreknowledge is not causal.

Troilus and Criseyde

Philosophy and Moral Vision

742   BLOOMFIELD, MORTON W. "Distance and Predestination in Troilus
       and Criseyde." PMLA 72 (1957):14-26. Reprinted in Chaucer
       Criticism, vol. 2, "Troilus and Criseyde" & the Minor Poems,
       ed. by Richard J. Schoeck and Jerome Taylor (Notre Dame, Ind.:
       University of Notre Dame Press, 1961), pp. 196-210; Chaucer's
       "Troilus": Essays in Criticism, ed. Stephen A. Barney
       (Hamden, Conn.: Archon Books, 1980), pp. 75-90.
           Describes the unique narrator of Troilus and Criseyde: an
       observor of an action he has no power over. This vantage is the
       "artistic correlative to the concept of predestination" insofar
       as it compels the reader to regard the story from the distance of
       foreknowledge. Troilus's apotheosis brings him close to this
       superior vantage, but the narrator and the reader leap to the
       even higher vantage of Christian consolation.

743   DiPASQUALE, PASQUALE, Jr. "'Sikernesse' and Fortune in
       Troilus and Criseyde." Philological Quarterly 49 (1970):152-
       63.
           Chaucer combines the twin Boethian themes of security and
       fortune in Troilus and Criseyde and resolves them theologically
       in the manner stated in Boccaccio's Genealogy of the Gods.
       Criseyde desires secure protection and Troilus pursues fleshly
       delights; both submit to fortune.

744   FREIWALD, LEAH RIEBER. "Swich Love of Frendes: Pandaras and
       Troilus." Chaucer Review 6 (1971):120-29.
           Characterizes the relationship between Troilus and Pandarus
       as Aristotelian "imperfect" friendship, correlative to Jean de
       Meun's "contrarie" friendship. Because imperfect, the friendship
       wanes as it becomes mutually useless, reflecting another aspect
       of Chaucer's "theme of the frailty and vanity of earth-bound
       affection. Compare to Cook (entry 786).

745   GALLAGHER, JOSEPH E. "Theology and Intention in Chaucer's
       Troilus." Chaucer Review 7 (1972):44-66.
           Argues that the retraction of Troilus and Criseyde as
       "worldly vanitee" reflects Chaucer's recognition that his poem is
       not moral. In Troilus, Chaucer represents the insubstantiality
       of the world, but does not willfully reject it, even in his
       epilogue. Hence, his Retraction is necessary in Canterbury
       Tales.

746   GORDON, IDA L. The Double Sorrow Of Troilus: A Study of
       Ambiguities in "Troilus and Criseyde." Oxford: Clarendon
       Press, 1970, 162 pp.
           Investigates the techniques for creating ambiguity in
       Troilus and Criseyde, exploring their relations to allegory and
       irony, and assessing the function of ambiguity in the poem. The
       polysemy of the word "love"--caritas and cupiditas--carries
       ambiguity at every point, often ironically. Similarly, Chaucer's
       appropriation of his sources, especially Boethius, evokes irony
       and verges on allegory when the original contexts clash with

Troilus and Criseyde

Chaucer's use of them. The interventions of the narrator and the
dualistic presentation of the major characters encourage readers
to view love as both a heavenly ideal and an earthly reality,
clarifying their ambiguous tension and challenging us to resolve
this double allegory of love.

747   HOWARD, DONALD R. "The Philosophies of Chaucer's Troilus."
       In The Wisdom of Poetry: Essays in Early English Literature
       in Honor of Morton W. Bloomfield. Edited by Larry D. Benson
       and Siegfried Wenzel. Kalamazoo, Mich.: Medieval Institute
       Publications, 1983, pp. 151-75.
            Surveys the major criticism of philosophical themes in
       Troilus and Criseyde and reconciles the apparent disjunction
       between pagan and Christian philosophies in the poem. Pandarus
       embodies the poet's view of pagan thought, humanistically combin-
       ing "Heraclitean flux, skepticism, hedonism, Horatian carpe diem,
       [and] stoic resignation." The epilogue reflects his awareness
       that all we know is human vanity and mutability.

748   HUBER, JOHN. "Troilus's Predestination Soliloquy: Chaucer's
       Changes from Boethius." Neuphilologische Mitteilungen 66
       (1965):120-25.
            Compares Troilus's predestination soliloquy (Troilus and
       Criseyde, 4:958-1073) with its source in Boethius's Consolation
       of Philosophy to show how Chaucer emphasizes Troilus's desire to
       abdicate personal responsibility by denying human freedom.

749   LOCKHART, ADRIENNE R. "Semantic, Moral, and Aesthetic
       Degeneration in Troilus and Criseyde." Chaucer Review 8
       (1973):100-118.
            Argues that the debasement of certain ideal concepts in
       Troilus and Criseyde is a structural metaphor for its moral and
       artistic concerns. "Honour," "worthiness," "gentilesse,"
       "manhod," and "trouthe" degenerate semantically through the poem,
       and Pandarus distorts these virtues, reflecting Chaucer's recog-
       nition that such ideals cannot be sustained in either life or
       poetry.

750   MOORMAN, CHARLES. "'Once More unto the Breach': The Meaning
       of Troilus and Criseyde." Studies in the Literary Imagination
       4, no. 2 (1971):61-71.
            Defines and assesses various kinds of determinism in
       Troilus and Criseyde--fortune, courtly love, and individual
       personality--and suggests that Chaucer conflates them in order to
       represent the "confusion and ambiguity" of "earthly motives and
       events."

751   ROWE, DONALD W. O Love O Charite! Contraries Harmonized in
       Chaucer's "Troilus." Carbondale: Southern Illinois
       University Press, 1976; London: Feffer & Simmons, 1976, 210
       pp.

Reads Troilus and Criseyde as a "sacramental revelation of God," tracing its spiritual resolution of opposites to the Chartrian Neoplatonic tradition of concordia discors. Identifies the contrasting styles of books 1 and 2 and their respective emphases on spiritual and social worlds, arguing that book 3 combines both styles and "forms of behavior." The individual psychologies of the characters blend with their representative values, combining realism and allegory. Structure, imagery, and diction pose thematic and generic paradoxes that reflect the narrator's lack of control over his material and leads the reader through the "rational motion" of discovering the Creator in the created, spiritual love in its earthly reflection.

752   STRAUSS, JENNIFER. "Teaching Troilus and Criseyde." Southern Review (Adelaide) 5 (1972):13-20.
        Identifies the incongruity of three focal scenes in Troilus and Criseyde (the consummation, Troilus's ascent, and the narrator's epilogue), arguing that their incongruity reveals the poem's exploratory nature. It examines love from various perspectives, and in leaving them unresolved, portrays the insufficiency of any single human perspective.

753   WENZEL, SIEGFRIED. "Chaucer's Troilus of Book IV." PMLA 79 (1964):542-47.
        Shows how Troilus's noble adherence to reason in book 4 of Troilus and Criseyde participates in a epistemological pattern in which reason is higher than passion but lower than the "intelligence" that comes from a divine perspective. Troilus's ascent is a "reward" for his adherence to his human, limited ideal.

        See also entries 2-3, 6-8, 154-55, 244, 689, 702, 732, 734, 739, 755-56, 758, 802-03. For fortune and determinism: 170-71, 209-10, 216, 218, 317, 736, 791, 801.

LOVE, SEX, AND MARRIAGE

754   BRADDY, HALDEEN. "Chaucer's Playful Pandarus." Southern Folklore Quarterly 34 (1970):71-81.
        Argues that Pandarus and Criseyde share incest in Troilus and Criseyde. A pun on the meaning of "deth" as coition, first found here in English, and several suggestive passages imply the relationship. See apRoberts (entry 763) and Rudat (entry 789).

755   DENOMY, ALEXANDER J. "The Two Moralities of Chaucer's Troilus and Criseyde." Transactions of the Royal Society of Canada, 3d ser., 44, no. 2 (1950):35-46. Reprinted in Chaucer Criticism, vol. 2, "Troilus and Criseyde" & the Minor Poems, ed. Richard J. Schoeck and Jerome Taylor (Notre Dame Ind.: University of Notre Dame Press, 1961), pp. 147-59.

Troilus and Criseyde

Love, Sex, and Marriage

Contrasts Chaucer's Troilus and Criseyde and Andreas Capellanus's De amore, defining irresistability and unique ennobling power as the essential characteristics of courtly love. Chaucer repudiates such love in Troilus by emphasizing its incompatibility with Christianity.

756　HEIDTMANN, PETER. "Sex and Salvation in Troilus and Criseyde." Chaucer Review 2 (1968):246-53.
　　　Questions the traditional polarization of caritas and cupiditas by arguing that Troilus's ascent at the end of Troilus and Criseyde shows that earthly love has ennobled the lover and made him worthy of the heavens.

757　HELTERMAN, JEFFREY. "Masks of Love in Troilus and Criseyde." Comparative Literature 26 (1974):14-31.
　　　Explores the influence of Italian literary presentations of love on Troilus and Criseyde by paralleling Troilus's love with Dante's in Vita nuova and detailing the influence of Petrach's sonnets to Laura on Chaucer's language and imagery.

758　HOWARD, DONALD R. "Courtly Love and the Lust of the Flesh: Troilus and Criseyde." In The Three Temptations: Medieval Man in Search of the World. Princeton: Princeton University Press, 1966, pp. 76-160.
　　　Interprets Troilus and Criseyde as a supreme expression of the courtly love tradition that presents Christian ideals in an earthly context. Through the pre-Christian setting of the poem, Chaucer represents love as a moral act that evokes Christian awareness without being an allegory of sin. Explicitly exploring the tension between fortune and love, the poem implicitly contrasts pagan and Christian love. In this way, Troilus develops an historically important "double truth" in the expression of courtly love and intensifies both the moral and the romantic elements beyond its immediate source, Boccaccio's Filostrato.

759　KIRBY, THOMAS. Chaucer's "Troilus": A Study in Courtly Love. Louisiana State University Studies, no. 39. University: Louisiana State University Press, 1940. Reprint. Gloucester, Mass.: Peter Smith, 1959, 346 pp.
　　　Examines the nature and function of courtly love in Troilus and Criseyde, surveying the backgrounds of the courtly love tradition, comparing Troilus to Boccaccio's Filostrato, and contrasting the characterizations of the major actors in the two poems. Traces the roots of courtly love to Ovid and explores the tradition of love in troubadour lyrics, Chrétien de Troyes, Andreas Capellanus, and Italian dolce stil nuovo. Describes Filostrato as a "typical courtly love document" and assesses Chaucer's intensification of the story, particularly by increasing the importance of Pandarus, the complexity of Criseyde, and the aggressiveness of Diomede in contrast to the passive fatalism of Troilus. In comparison with Filostrato, Troilus emphasizes the ennobling, transcendant effects of love.

760   MAGUIRE, JOHN B. "The Clandestine Marriage of Troilus and
       Criseyde." Chaucer Review 8 (1974):262-78.
            Describes the nature of medieval "clandestine" marriage,
       valid and fairly common in Chaucer's day, although not performed
       in church, arguing that the relationship between Troilus and
       Criseyde is such a marriage. The suggestions of clandestine mar-
       riage in Troilus and Criseyde include Chaucer's focus on marital
       "trouthe," the attitude and words of Pandarus, and several of the
       poet's modifications of Boccaccio's Filostrato. Compare Kelly
       (entry 235).

761   WOOD, CHAUNCEY. The Elements of Chaucer's "Troilus." Durham:
       Duke University Press, 1984, 216 pp.
            Focuses upon the aspects of Troilus and Criseyde which
       criticize erotic love, tracing the poem's transformations of
       Boccaccio's Filostrato and assessing external and internal
       evidence of attitudes toward love and sexuality. Contemporary
       negative treatments of sexual love, especially those of John
       Gower to whom Troilus is dedicated, clarify the proper subordina-
       tion of sex to will and the significance of Troilus's debasement.
       Venus's domination of the action--more evident than in
       Filostrato--indicates the sexual nature of the lovers' attrac-
       tion, while recurrent images associated with the three major
       characters underscore the immorality of their love.

            See also entries 159, 229, 232, 235, 238, 697, 716, 746,
       758, 763, 785. For courtly love and its tradition: 233-34, 236-
       37, 689, 700, 750, 778; for spiritual love: 751, 762, 779-80.

CRISEYDE

762   apROBERTS, ROBERT P. "The Central Episode of Chaucer's
       Troilus." PMLA 77 (1962):373-85.
            Examines Criseyde's motives in surrendering to Troilus to
       demonstrate how these motives lend the character the "very feel
       of life." Chaucer's lack of emphasis on sexual desire is
       consistent with his goal of presenting "perfect human love."

763   _____. "The Growth of Criseyde's Love." In Medieval Studies
       Conference, Aachen, 1983: Language and Literature. Edited by
       Wolf-Dietrich Bald and Horst Weinstock. Bamberger Beiträge
       zur Englischen Sprachwissenschaft, no. 15. Frankfurt: Peter
       Lang, 1984, pp. 131-41.
            Criticizes "sexpot" readings of Troilus and Criseyde and
       traces the gradual development of Criseyde's attraction to
       Troilus from her first sight of him to the consummation scene
       where her resistence to love fails and she accepts her emotions.
       Her resistence reveals the value she places on love and her
       reluctance to jeopardize her honor.

Troilus and Criseyde

764   BECHTEL, ROBERT B. "The Problem of Criseyde's Character."
       Susquehanna University Studies 7, no. 2 (1963):109-18.
            Surveys early critical assessments of Criseyde--as
       betrayer, as instrument of fate, as fearful--and concludes that
       the character is a vehicle through whom Chaucer expresses the
       ecstasy of human love and its transitoriness.

765   BURNLEY, J.D. "Criseyde's Heart and Weakness of Women: An
       Essay in Lexical Interpretation." Studia Neophilologica 54
       (1982):25-38.
            Chaucer's description of Criseyde includes traditional,
       Scholastic connotations of feminine mutability in the phrases
       "slydyng of corage" and "tendre herte"; the physiognomic detail
       of straight eyebrows indicates the same.

766   CORRIGAN, MATTHEW. "Chaucer's Failure With Women: The
       Inadequacy of Criseyde." Western Humanities Review 23
       (1969):107-20.
            Criticizes Chaucer's depictions of Alison of Bath and, es-
       pecially, Criseyde as reflections of the prejudices of his age.
       The narrator of Troilus and Criseyde obscures our direct appre-
       hension of Criseyde as essentially "a magnificent exemplum of
       medieval woman."

767   DAVID, ALFRED. "Chaucerian Comedy and Criseyde." In Essays
       on "Troilus and Criseyde." Edited by Mary Salu. Chaucer
       Studies, no. 3. Cambridge: D.S. Brewer; Totowa, N.J.:
       Rowman & Littlefield, 1979, pp. 90-104.
            Sets Criseyde's comic pattern of cyclical change against
       Troilus's single, tragic ride on Fortune's wheel, demonstrating
       how she is "constant in her mutability" and how, through her,
       Chaucer affirms the important but limited validity of worldly
       survival, anticipating the Wife of Bath.

768   DONALDSON, E. TALBOT. "Briseis, Briseida, Criseyde, Cresseid,
       Cressid: Progress of a Heroine." In Chaucerian Problems and
       Perspectives: Essays Presented to Paul E. Beichner, C.S.C.
       Edited by Edward Vasta and Zacharias P. Thundy. Notre Dame,
       Ind.: University of Notre Dame Press, 1979, pp. 3-12.
            Demonstrates that other attributes besides infidelity com-
       plicate the Criseyde character developed from Homer to
       Shakespeare. Chaucer's figure combines deep passion with the
       attractiveness of Dares's Briseis and the insecurity of Benoît's
       Briseida. Although passion is also evident in Henryson's and
       Shakespeare's characters, only Shakespeare reflects Chaucer's
       feminist awareness.

769   GROSS, LAILA. "The Two Wooings of Criseyde."
       Neuphilologische Mitteilungen 74 (1973):113-25.
            Demonstrates the similarity of Pandarus's wooing of
       Criseyde for Troilus and Diomedes wooing of her for himself, and
       the consistency of Criseyde's reaction to the wooings.

770   HOWARD, DONALD R. "Experience, Language, and Consciousness:
       Troilus and Crisyede, II, 596-931." In Medieval Literature
       and Folklore Studies: Essays in Honor of Francis Lee Utley.
       Edited by Jerome Mandel and Bruce A. Rosenberg. New
       Brunswick, N.J.: Rutgers University Press, 1970, pp. 173-92.
       Revised slightly in Chaucer's "Troilus": Essays in Criticism,
       ed. Stephen A. Barney (Hamden, Conn.: Archon Books, 1980),
       pp. 159-80.
          Examines the process of Criseyde's falling in love with
       Troilus as a poetic tour de force of the representation of con-
       sciousness. Chaucer enables his audience to share Criseyde's
       abstract thoughts and to participate with her visually (observing
       Troilus), auricularly (Antigone's song), and subconsciously (her
       dream), thereby creating a full experience of consciousness
       through language.

771   MIESZKOWSKI, GRETCHEN. "The Reputation of Criseyde: 1155-
       1500." Transactions of the Connecticut Academy of Arts and
       Sciences 43 (1971):71-153. Reprinted separately (Hamden,
       Conn.: Archon, 1971).
          Documents the early, negative understanding of Criseyde as
       a fickle women, even a seductress, and assesses the effect of
       this reputation upon the meaning of Troilus and Criseyde. Benoît
       de Sainte-Maure's Roman de Troie, Guido delle Colonne's Historia
       destructionis Troiae, and Boccaccio's Filostrato define
       Criseyde's negative reputation, one reflected in other versions
       of the tale and in allusions to Criseyde by other poets, such as
       John Gower. Chaucer manipulates this reputation from the start
       of his poem, creating a tension between the audience's negative
       attitude toward the character and the narrator's positive
       opinion, effectively detaching readers from the narrator even
       while engaging them in the love story. Fifteenth-century
       depictions of Criseyde attest the contemporary sensitivity to
       Chaucer's sophisticated narrative techniques.

772   ROWLAND, BERYL. "Chaucer's Speaking Voice and Its Effects on
       His Listeners' Perception of Criseyde." English Studies in
       Canada 7 (1981):129-40.
          Evokes a sense of Chaucer's performance of his poetry by
       citing classical and medieval oratorical and rhetorical
       treatises, and suggests that the narrator's positive opinion of
       Criseyde would have been emphatic and persuasive in performance.

773   SCHIBANOFF, SUSAN. "Criseyde's 'Impossible' Aubes." JEGP:
       Journal of English and Germanic Philology 76 (1977):326-33.
          Observes the presence of adynata, or listed impossibili-
       ties, in Criseyde's ironic dawn-songs, suggesting that they
       derived from antifeminist songs of female deception and therefore
       foreshadow Criseyde's infidelity to Troilus.

774   STOKES, M. "The Moon in Leo in Book V of Troilus and
       Criseyde." Chaucer Review 17 (1982):116-29.

Criseyde

Explains the astrological significance of Criseyde's
promise to return to Troilus before the moon leaves Leo,
associating Criseyde with the changeable moon and Trolius with
the royal lion. Identifies several techniques that distance the
audience from book 5 of Troilus and Criseyde and compares its
astral allegory with that of Complaint of Mars. Compare to
Cotten (entry 709).

775   TAYLOR, WILLENE P. "Supposed Antifeminism in Chaucer's
       Troilus and Criseyde." Xavier University Studies 9, no. 2
       (1970):1-18.
            Reads Legend of Good Women as mock penance for Troilus and
       Criseyde. Troilus is not antifeminist, even though the nar-
       rator's changing view of Criseyde raises the possibility. The
       apparent apology to the God of Love in the Legend is a "mock
       palinode" to Troilus, an example of Chaucer's humane, non-
       judgmental comedy.

            See also entries 54, 79, 136, 171, 706, 709-12, 714, 723-
       24, 793, 796, 909.

TROILUS

776   BARNEY, STEPHEN A. "Troilus Bound." Speculum 47 (1972):
       445-58.
            Studies Chaucer's theme of bondage in association with
       fortune, love, and sin as it characterizes Troilus. The theme
       recurs in Troilus's speeches, reflecting that he is bound by love
       to truth and therefore a "model of heroic steadfastness and
       tragic incapacity." Surveys Chaucer's use of the theme in works
       before Troilus.

777   BARON, F. XAVIER. "Chaucer's Troilus and Self-Renunciation in
       Love." Papers in Language and Literature 10 (1974):5-14.
            Attributes Troilus's hesitancy to act to his "self-
       renunciation in love" as well as his vanity and fatalism. At the
       end of Troilus and Criseyde, self-renunciation looms as an
       essential aspect of Troilus's idealized "nobility and
       magnificence."

778   GREEN, RICHARD F. "Troilus and the Game of Love." Chaucer
       Review 13 (1979):201-20.
            Contrasts Troilus's "comic ineptitude as a love-talker"
       with the sociable love-talk of Pandarus and Criseyde and the
       expedient palaver of Diomedes. Troilus lacks verbal dexterity,
       but he makes it up in sincerity and "trouthe," reflecting the
       ambivalent status of courtly love in literature and society.

779   HASKELL, ANN S. "The Doppelgängers in Chaucer's Troilus."
       Neuphilologische Mitteilungen 72 (1971):723-34.

Explores the significant "twoness" in Troilus and Criseyde
by observing Troilus's three doubling relationships: with Hector
as a public double, with Pandarus as a "fractional" double without whom Troilus is incapable of sustaining the love affair, and
with Diomedes as his "unrestrained opposite" who heralds
Troilus's death.

780   HATCHER, ELIZABETH R. "Chaucer and the Psychology of Fear:
       Troilus in Book V." ELH: A Journal of English Literary
       History 40 (1973):307-24.
            Contrasts Troilus with Boccaccio's Filostrato to clarify
       the psychological subtleties in Troilus's responses to Criseyde's
       departure. His initial refusal to doubt her, his dream of the
       boar, and his consultation of Cassandra all reflect his growing
       fear of the truth and, ironically, make Criseyde appear worse to
       him than she really is--the bitterest irony of Troilus's tragedy.

781   MANN, JILL. "Troilus' Swoon." Chaucer Review 14 (1980):319-
       45.
            Argues that Troilus's swoon in Troilus and Criseyde is a
       stage in the ongoing growth of the relation between the lovers, a
       development that levels the social and emotional discrepancies
       between them and thereby provides a sound basis for the consum-
       mation scene that follows.

782   MARTIN, JUNE HALL. "Troilus." In Love's Fools: Aucassin,
       Troilus, Calisto and the Parody of the Courtly Lover.
       Coleccion Tamesis, ser. A, no. 21. London: Támesis Books,
       1972, pp. 37-70.
            Characterizes Troilus as a comic parody of the typical
       courtly lover, contrasting him with courtly heroes like Tristan
       and Chrétien's Lancelot. Analyzes Chaucer's satire of conven-
       tional details and attitudes: the hero's prowess and willingness
       to act, the lovers' need for secrecy, the pains of love, and the
       religion of love.

783   MASI, MICHAEL. "Troilus: A Medieval Psychoanalysis."
       Annuale Mediaevale 11 (1970):81-88.
            Psychoanalyzes Troilus in medieval fashion, assessing the
       effects of his first sight of Criseyde, his exercise of imagina-
       tion to fix her image mentally, and his melancholic dream of the
       boar. The stages of fascination and the nature of the dream are
       familiar from Aristotle and Galen.

784   WHITMAN, FRANK H. "Troilus and Criseyde and Chaucer's
       Dedication to Gower." Tennessee Studies in Literature 18
       (1973):1-11.
            Contrasts the presentations of a "knight in love" in
       Chaucer's Troilus and Criseyde and John Gower's Vox Clamantis,
       reading Chaucer's Troilus as a depiction of the debilitating
       effects of improper love, and assessing the narrator's sympathy
       for Troilus as comic irony. Cites examples of juxtaposition,

Troilus

bathos, and unreasonable behavior as indications that the poem ridicules Troilus's sentiments.

See also entries 696, 706-7, 709-10, 714, 723, 744, 748, 753, 774.

PANDARUS

785   CARTON, EVAN. "Complicity and Responsibility in Pandarus' Bed and Chaucer's Art." PMLA 94 (1979):47-61.
        Argues that the involvement of Pandarus, the narrator, and the reader determines the plot of Troilus and Criseyde. Pandarus is a paradigm of involvement in his overt manipulation of the lovers. The narrator's intrusions engage the reader in imagining implied actions. Pandarus's sexual encounter with Criseyde (3:1555-82) brings together these levels of "complicity."

786   COOK, RICHARD G. "Chaucer's Pandarus and the Medieval Ideal of Friendship." JEGP: Journal of English and Germanic Philology 69 (1970):407-24.
        Assesses Pandarus's actions in Troilus and Criseyde in light of medieval ideals of friendship and Boccaccio's Pandaro. Pandarus's protestations of friendship for Troilus conflict with his devious actions to represent both the "world's notion of what a friend is" and the "moralist's notion" of what he is not—an example of Chaucer's double vision. Compare to Freiwald (entry 744).

787   ROBBIE, MAY G. "Three-Faced Pandarus." California English Journal 3, no. 1 (1967):47-54.
        Praises Pandarus as a courtly intermediary, friend to Troilus, and kinsman to Criseyde, arguing that he fulfills traditional expectations in each role and acts with good intent.

788   ROWLAND, BERYL. "Pandarus and the Fate of Tantalus." Orbis Litterarum 24 (1969):3-15.
        Psychoanalyzes Pandarus as a hermaphrodite who derives double, vicarious sexual satisfaction from contributing to the relationship between Troilus and Criseyde.

789   RUDAT, WOLFGANG. "Chaucer's Troilus and Criseyde: The Narrator-Reader's Complicity." American Imago 40 (1983):103-13.
        Psychoanalyzes Pandarus's motives in aiding Troilus to gain Criseyde's love, arguing that the affair serves Pandarus as "vicarious sexual indulgence." Traces suggestions of incest and references to Oedipus, and dicusses images of sexual "death" in Pandarus's teasing of Criseyde. Compare Braddy (entry 754).

790   RUTHERFORD, CHARLES S. "Pandarus as Lover: 'A Joly Wo' or 'Loves Shotes Keene'?" Annuale Mediaevale 13 (1972):5-13.

Characterizes Pandarus as a role-player whose one unmasked moment in Troilus and Criseyde—his love lament early in book 2—preserves Troilus from appearing absurd. Pandarus's private moment clarifies the power of love and helps us to accept Troilus's debilitation without ridicule.

See also entries, 131, 133, 706, 710, 714, 744, 747, 779.

MINOR CHARACTERS

791   GREENFIELD, STANLEY B. "The Role of Calkas in Troilus and Criseyde." Medium AEvum 36 (1967):141-51.
       Contrasts Chaucer's Calkas in Troilus and Criseyde with analogous characters in Benoît and Boccaccio, showing how Chaucer ridicules astrological prophecy and offers instead a Boethian sense of destiny.

792   KIERNAN, K[EVIN] S. "Hector the Second: The Lost Face of Troilustratus." Annuale Mediaevale 16 (1975):52-62.
       Compares Hector in Chaucer's Troilus and Boccaccio's Filostrato, showing how Chaucer enlarged Hector's role as a foil to Troilus's questionable heroism and lack of response to apparent destiny. Through Hector, Chaucer emphasizes Troilus's abrogation of responsibility.

793   SCHIBANOFF, SUSAN. "Argus and Argyve: Etymology and Characterization in Chaucer's Troilus." Speculum 51 (1976):647-58.
       Traces the traditional etymologizing of "Argyve," the name of Criseyde's mother, arguing that the name characterizes the woman, ironically contrasts Criseyde with her mother, and reflects Chaucer's awareness of contemporary conflicts between naturalistic and conventional theories of naming.

794   SUNDWALL, McKAY. "Deiphobus and Helen: A Tantalizing Hint." Modern Philology 73 (1975):151-56.
       Suggests that Chaucer knew Vergil's account of the eventual marriage of Deiphobus and Helen, and that amorousnes was implicit in their relationship in Troilus and Criseyde. When Pandarus maneuvers the tryst between the titular lovers, Deiphobus and Helen's relationship helps to cement the bond and provides ironic overtones.

See also entries 171, 240, 699, 779.

THE NARRATOR

795   HUPPÉ, BERNARD F. "The Unlikely Narrator: The Narrative Stategy of the Troilus. In Signs and Symbols in Chaucer's Poetry. Edited by John P. Hermann and John J. Burke, Jr. University: University of Alabama Press, 1981, pp. 174-91.

Examines the conflict between comedy and tragedy in the proems of Troilus and Crisyde. The narrator's misplaced sense of tragedy and his loss of control of his material in the proem to book 4 foreshadow the "shock of recognition" we feel at the genuine tragedy in Troilus's apotheosis. Chaucer uses the narrator and the "allurement of love" to produce this shock.

796 SALTER, ELIZABETH. "Troilus and Criseyde: Poet and Narrator." In Acts of Interpretation: The Text in Its Context, 700-1600: Essays on Medieval and Renaissance Literature in Honor of E. Talbot Donaldson. Edited by Mary J. Carruthers and Elizabeth D. Kirk. Norman, Okla.: Pilgrim Books, 1982, pp. 281-91.

Challenges the critical separation of poet and narrator in Troilus and Criseyde, arguing that the evidence of tension between the plot and the narrator's opinions--especially the ambiguous characterization of Criseyde--reflects the poet's emotional struggle with his material rather than that of a "sentimental narrator."

797 WASWO, RICHARD. "The Narrator of Troilus and Criseyde." ELH: A Journal of English Literary History 50 (1983):1-25.

Explores the conflicting views of the narrator of Troilus and Criseyde, attributing such conflict not to differences of method but to contradictions within the poem that result from Chaucer's social status and the upheavals of his day. Because Chaucer addressed a socially superior audience, his poem reflects "irony of dislocation," not "irony of complicity."

See also entries 81, 85-86, 162, 167, 171, 702, 717, 742, 766, 775, 785, 798, 802.

THE ENDING

798 DONALDSON, E. TALBOT. "The Ending of Chaucer's Troilus." In Early English and Norse Studies Presented to Hugh Smith. Edited by Arthur Brown and Peter Foote. London: Methuen, 1963, pp. 26-45. Revised slightly in Speaking of Chaucer (New York: W.W. Norton & Co., 1970), pp. 84-101; Chaucer's "Troilus": Essays in Criticism, ed. Stephen A. Barney (Hamden, Conn.: Archon Books, 1980), pp. 115-30.

Observes that Chaucer's narrators assure us, "by a modesty prologue or by . . . notable simplicity," that they report only naked fact. Tension between these ruses and "a complex of implications" create the "ultimate significance" of his poetry, especially at the end of Troilus and Criseyde where the narrator's "simple view of reality" paradoxically suggests a complex contemptus mundi.

799 DRONKE, PETER. "The Conclusion of Troilus and Criseyde." Medium Ævum 33 (1964):47-52.

Compares the epilogue of Troilus and Crisyde to its sources in Boccaccio's Filostrato and Teseida, reading Chaucer's ending as an affirmation of love. Troilus's ascent to the fixed stars and the narrator's celebration of Troilus's "beatitude" indicate the positive tone of the ending.

800   FARNHAM, ANTHONY E. "Chaucerian Irony and the Ending of the Troilus." Chaucer Review 1 (1967):207-16.
       Explores the quality and breadth of Chaucer's irony by examining the "feyned love" of Troilus and Criseyde. At the end of the poem, Chaucer advises spiritual love--in this context an ironic acknowledgment that all human love, spiritual or physical, falls "far short of perfection and truth."

801   KEAN, P.M. "Chaucer's Dealings with a Stanza of Il Filostrato and the Epilogue of Troilus and Criseyde." Medium Ævum 33 (1964):36-46.
       Examines a pattern of word and image Chaucer used in his Troilus and Criseyde, not found in Boccaccio's Filostrato. Following Boethius, Chaucer associates blindness with both love and destiny, and he represents the struggle of human will against these forces, welding the opening of his poem to its epilogue.

802   REISS, EDMUND. "Troilus and the Failure of Understanding." Modern Language Quarterly 29 (1968):131-44.
       Argues that Troilus's apotheosis at the end of Troilus and Criseyde and the dream of Scipio in Parliament of Fowls, do not imply contemptus mundi. The dreamer of Parliament goes beyond contempt to explore love, and the narrator of Troilus surpasses Troilus's failure to understand his view of the cosmos by affirming Christian love.

803   STEADMAN, JOHN M. Disembodied Laughter: "Troilus" and the Apotheosis Tradition: A Reexamination of Narrative and Thematic Concerns. Berkeley: University of California Press, 1972, 190 pp.
       Examines the philosophical traditions behind the closing stanzas of Troilus and Criseyde. Like ascents in Cicero's Somnium Scipionis, Lucan's Pharsalia, Dante's Paradiso, and Boccaccio's Teseida, Troilus's ascent preserves the "pagan decorum" of the poem while satisfying Christian eschatological doctrine. Chaucer's ending fuses the pagan apotheosis of the hero with the Boethian commonplaces interspersed throughout the poem, bringing into sharp focus the epistemological crux of the work: the contrast between human ignorance and divine knowledge, itself a Boethian topos. Troilus's laughing rejection of false felicity and the narrator's advice to embrace divine love epitomize the ironic tension evident throughout the work, tension between heroic tragedy and Troilus's comic ignorance of philosophical and moral truth.

The Ending

804   UTLEY, FRANCIS LEE. "Stylistic Ambivalence in Chaucer, Yeats,
       and Lucretius--The Cresting Wave and the Undertow."
       University Review (Kansas City) 37 (1971):174-98.
           Includes a close reading of the epilogue to Chaucer's
       Troilus and Criseyde, emphasizing its ambivalence and its rapid
       changes of direction that underscore the poem's paradoxical
       rejection of the lovers and empathy with them.

805   YEAGER, R.F. "'O Moral Gower': Chaucer's Dedication of
       Troilus and Criseyde." Chaucer Review 19 (1984):87-99.
           Explains Chaucer's dedication of Troilus and Criseyde to
       John Gower as a clarification of the poem's earnest meaning.
       Chaucer's reference capitalizes upon Gower's reputation as a
       reformer, a classicist, and a moral advocate. The reference
       associates the addresses to the young people who might mis-
       construe the poem with the Trinity who perceives truth unclouded,
       suggesting that Gower (and Ralph Strode) are ideal human
       interpreters.

           See also entries 85, 147, 190, 224, 702, 716, 742, 747,
       753, 756, 795.

Dream Poems

806   CLEMEN, WOLFGANG. Chaucer's Early Poetry. Translated by
C.A.M. Sym. London: Methuen & Co., 1963, 224 pp.
    A cogent introduction to Chaucer's apprenticeship to
poetry, analyzing his development through the early poems and the
emergence of his individual voice. Genuine feeling modifies the
elaborate conventions of Book of the Duchess, offering a means to
control grief. In House of Fame, association of dissimilar
models and styles produces wry, ironic poetry intended for an
audience of initiates. Parliament of Fowls welds satire and
allegory. Imitation of French poetry and resistence to it are
evident in An A.B.C., Complaint unto Pity, Complaint to his Lady,
Complaint of Mars, and Anelida and Arcite.

807   HIEATT, CONSTANCE B. The Realism of Dream Vision: The Poetic
Exploration of the Dream-Experience in Chaucer and His Contemporaries. De Proprietatibus Litterarum, Series Practica, no.
2. The Hague: Mouton, 1967, 117 pp.
    Explores the psychological validity of Middle English dream
poetry, comparing it to actual dreams, tracing its literary and
philosophical roots, and examining its form and allegory. In
Chaucer's dream poems, the dream is "primarily a structural
framework," even though he self-consciously exploits philosophy
and psychology. The verisimilar dream frame of Book of the
Duchess, in contrast to Pearl, expresses human sympathy rather
than transcendant theology. House of Fame refuses to be "pinned
down," its dream "largely an excuse for fantastic situations."
Parliament of Fowls uses the fantasy of dreams to rich thematic
effect, and the Prologue to the Legend of Good Women explores the
conventions of courtly poetry. Also examines the dreams of Piers
Plowman, Parliament of the Three Ages, and Winner and Waster.

808   HUPPÉ, BERNARD F., and ROBERTSON, D.W., Jr. Fruyt and Chaf:
Studies in Chaucer's Allegories. Princeton: Princeton
University Press, 1963, 165 pp.
    Interprets Book of the Duchess and Parliament of Fowls
allegorically, reading them against a "set of symbolic referents"
derived from the tradition of biblical exegesis and patristic

interpretation common to such authors as Augustine, Hugh of St. Victor, Alain de Lille, Petrarch, and Boccaccio. As well as an elegy for Blanche, Book of the Duchess is a Christian consolation, as is evident in the correspondence between the narrator's and Alcyone's grief, and in such significant allegorical commonplaces as the narrator's eight-year sickness, Christ as Physician and Hunter, and the complex interrelations of the poem's time, the ecclesiastical year, and the liturgical day. Parliament of Fowls explores the "vanity of the world" and those who love it, allegorically exalting philosophical detachment over earthly passion. The juxtaposition of the dream of Scipio, the allegorical garden, and the image of Nature as God's vice-regent signal the poem's thematic focus on a Christian alternative to eroticism.

809   LAWLOR, JOHN. "The Earlier Poems." In Chaucer and Chaucerians: Critical Studies in Medieval Literature. Edited by D.S. Brewer. London: Thomas Nelson & Sons; University: University of Alabama Press, 1966. Reprint: Norwich: Nelson's University Paperbacks, 1970, pp. 39-64.
       Reads Book of the Duchess, House of Fame, Parliament of Fowls, Anelida and Arcite, and Complaint of Mars as similar in the way they keep their audiences distant and in their "unerring eye for pretence." Similar stylistic devices such as dream frames, narrative naiveté, and dramatic dialogue enable Chaucer to address an audience of social superiors with freedom.

810   WHITMAN, F[RANK] H. "Exegesis and Chaucer's Dream Visions." Chaucer Review 3 (1969):229-38.
       Argues that Chaucer's dream visions are "essentially moral," combining the suggestiveness of Macrobian dreams with exegetical responses to classical literature and reflecting the technique of moving from experience to written authority as a form of contemplation.

811   WINDEATT, BARRY, ed. and tr. Chaucer's Dream Poetry: Sources and Analogues. Chaucer Studies, no. 7. Cambridge: D.S. Brewer; Totowa, N.J.: Rowman & Littlefield, 1982, 186 pp.
       Translates into modern prose various sources and analogues of Chaucer's Book of the Duchess, Parliament of Fowls, House of Fame, and Prologue to the Legend of Good Women. Includes anonymous visions and love-question poems as well as complete poems or selections by Guillaume de Machaut, Jean Froissart, Eustache Deschamps, Oton de Granson, Jean de Condé, Nicole de Margival, Boccaccio, Alain de Lille, and Cicero. A short introduction describes Chaucer's techniques for "coordinating" his sources to create new poetry.

812   WINNY, JAMES. Chaucer's Dream-Poems. London: Chatto & Windus; New York: Barnes & Noble, 1973, 158 pp.
       Introduces the literary tradition of dream visions and Macrobius's categories of dreams. Studies Book of the Duchess, House of Fame, and Parliament of Fowls, concentrating upon the

reciprocal relations between the dream and frame and their combination of courtly sentiment with comic colloquialism. <u>Book of the Duchess</u> embodies "implicit criticism" of courtly love, contrasting "romantic ideals" with the "demands of everyday life" as expressed by the narrator. <u>House of Fame</u> attempts to represent the "nature and behaviour of the creative consciousness." <u>Parliament of Fowls</u> links the concerns and techniques of the earlier poems with the later sophistication of <u>Canterbury Tales</u>, exploring the courtly and colloquial aspects of love and art.

See also entries 1-3, 6, 10, 17, 57, 72, 78, 82, 131, 152, 211, 216, 249, 827, 850, 861, 890, 902.

Book of the Duchess

813   BLAKE, N.F. "The Textual Tradition of the Book of the
        Duchess." English Studies 62 (1981):237-48.
            Describes the textual history of Book of the Duchess and
        discusses significant variants among its three manuscripts and
        Thynne's edition, challenging the authenticity of lines 31-96,
        288, and 886 derived from Thynne and accepted by modern editors.

814   BOARDMAN, PHILLIP C. "Courtly Language and the Strategy of
        Consolation in the Book of the Duchess." ELH: A Journal of
        English Literary History 44 (1977):567-79.
            Explains the narrator's inability to understand the Black
        Knight's laments of Book of the Duchess as an undercutting of
        facile poetic consolation. Chaucer commemorates the lady while
        exposing the inability of courtly language to console through
        blunt recognition of death and confrontation with the transitori-
        ness of human life.

815   BRONSON, BERTRAND H. "The Book of the Duchess Re-opened."
        PMLA 67 (1952):863-81. Reprinted in Chaucer: Modern Essays
        in Criticism, ed. Edward Wagenknecht (New York: Oxford
        University Press, 1959), pp. 271-94.
            Initiates the modern recognition of Book of the Duchess as
        psychological consolation, examining the role of the narrator in
        the poem and arguing that his grief is "externalized and pro-
        jected" in the figure of the Black Knight once the dream begins.
        The Dreamer leads the Knight through consolation to self-
        recognition; in this way Chaucer praises Blanche, consoles John
        of Gaunt, and maintains social propriety.

816   BROWN, JAMES NEIL. "Narrative Focus and Function in the Book
        of the Duchess." Massachusetts Studies in English 2
        (1970):71-79.
            Describes the narrator of Book of the Duchess as "socially
        naive," a "would be courtier" who "tries very earnestly to appear
        courtly and sophisticated." Through contrast between this
        persona and the sophisticated Black Knight, Chaucer produces
        humor, praises Blanche and ironically censures excessive grief.

817   CHERNISS, MICHAEL D. "The Boethian Dialogue in Chaucer's Book
       of the Duchess." JEGP: Journal of English and Germanic
       Philology 68 (1969):655-65.
            Parallels the Book of the Duchess and the first two books
       of Boethius's Consolation of Philosophy to suggest that the con-
       solation of Chaucer's poem is incomplete. The grief of the Black
       Knight is therefore unmitigated, so he should not be identified
       with John of Gaunt.

818   _____. "The Narrator Asleep and Awake in Chaucer's Book of
       the Duchess." Papers in Language and Literature 8 (1972):115-
       26.
            The "unspecified spiritual malady" of the narrator in Book
       of the Duchess and the poem's contrast between natural and un-
       natural generalize the consolation of the poem beyond the grief
       of the Black Knight and the misfortune of Alcyone, suggesting
       that we must all accept misfortune as part of the order of
       nature.

819   CONDREN, EDWARD I. "The Historical Context of the Book of the
       Duchess: A New Hypothesis." Chaucer Review 5 (1971):195-212.
            Proposes 1377 (eight years after Blanche's death) as the
       date of composition for the Book of the Duchess, and reads the
       poem as a plea for patronage on the basis of four topical puns.
       Identifies the narrator of the poem as contemporary Chaucer, the
       Black Knight as Chaucer the youthful poet, and Octovyen as John
       of Gaunt. Challenged by Palmer (entry 831).

820   DELASANTA, RODNEY. "Christian Affirmation in the Book of the
       Duchess." PMLA 84 (1969):245-51.
            Identifies a pattern of Christian allusions to suggest that
       Book of the Duchess promises resurrection as part of its conso-
       lation. The exclusion of the transformation of Ceys and Alcyone
       into birds "initiates a process of spiritual epiphany in the
       Dreamer," manifested in apocalyptic images of trumpets and a
       thematic call to resurrection based on the biblical Song of
       Songs.

821   FICHTE, JOERG O. "The Book of the Duchess--A Consolation?"
       Studia Neophilologica 45 (1973):53-67.
            Challenges the traditional designation of Book of the
       Duchess as a consolation by arguing that the Dreamer fails to aid
       the Black Knight. Assesses the poem as an encomnium: Chaucer's
       concern is literary merit, not Christian consolation.

822   FRIEDMAN, JOHN BLOCK. "The Dreamer, the Whelp, and the
       Consolation in the Book of the Duchess." Chaucer Review 3
       (1969):145-62.
            Studies the whelp of Book of the Duchess, surveying past
       criticism and showing how the animal guides the Dreamer to
       consolation. As a traditional figure of guiding, healing, and
       explanation, the dog appropriately suggests the process of

consolation, anticipating the encounter between the Dreamer and
the Black Knight. Compare to Rowland (entry 836).

823   HILL, JOHN M. "The Book of the Duchess, Melancholy, and that
       Eight-Year Sickness." Chaucer Review 9 (1974):35-50.
           Rejects the traditional notion that the narrator of Book of
       the Duchess suffers from love-sickness, suggesting instead that
       his symptoms and the context of their description before the tale
       of Alcyone indicate his illness is "head melancholy," a poten-
       tially fatal illness that can be cured by no "phisicien but oon"
       --sleep.

824   JORDAN, ROBERT M. "The Compositional Structure of The Book of
       the Duchess." Chaucer Review 9 (1974):99-117.
           Applies the compositional criteria of Geoffrey of Vinsauf's
       Poetria Nova to Chaucer's Book of the Duchess, describing the
       poem's "groundplan," noting its inorganic but meaningful digres-
       sions, and identifying its array of poetic devices. These tech-
       niques evince Chaucer's "emotional range and poetic virtuosity."

825   KELLOGG, ALFRED L. "Amatory Psychology and Amatory Frustra-
       tion in the Interpretation of the Book of the Duchess." In
       Chaucer, Langland, Arthur: Essays in Middle English
       Literature. New Brunswick, N.J.: Rutgers University Press,
       1972, pp. 59-107.
           Reads Book of the Duchess autobiographically as a reflec-
       tion of an amorous affair between Chaucer's wife , and John of
       Gaunt, and sketches the development of the medieval psychology of
       the heart from Plato through the Islamic tradition as background
       to the poem. The poem's inner structure of consolation records
       medieval psychology; the outer frame, Chaucer's aspirations.

826   KISER, LISA P. "Sleep, Dreams, and Poetry in Chaucer's Book
       of the Duchess." Papers on Language and Literature 19
       (1983):3-12.
           Equates the narrator's insomnia in Book of the Duchess with
       Chaucer's concern for poetic inspiration, and discovers in the
       work "several important statements" about poetry and Chaucer's
       career: the difficulty of writing a "sincere yet artful lyric,"
       the importance of poetry, and the relative values of the classi-
       cal and French traditions.

827   KREUZER, JAMES R. "The Dreamer in the Book of the Duchess."
       PMLA 66 (1951):543-47.
           Distinguishes between the narrator and the dreamer of Book
       of the Duchess, characterizing the first as mature and sad and
       the other as young and sensitive to the Black Knight's grief.
       Chaucer's separation of the two is an innovation in the use of
       persona in poetry.

828   LAWLOR, JOHN. "The Pattern of Consolation in the Book of the
       Duchess." Speculum 31 (1956):626-48. Reprinted in Chaucer

Criticism, vol 2, "Troilus and Criseyde" & the Minor Poems, ed. Richard J. Schoeck and Jerome Taylor (Notre Dame, Ind.: University of Notre Dame Press, 1961), pp. 232-60.

Analyzes the consolation of Chaucer's Book of the Duchess in terms of the place of courtly love in the poem, its pattern of recognition, and the function of its humor. The narrative pose and the humor keep the courtly grief in proportion.

829   LUMIANSKY, R.M. "The Bereaved Narrator in Chaucer's The Book of the Duchess." Tennessee Studies in Literature 9 (1959):5-17.

Argues that the narrator's eight-year sickness in Book of the Duchess is bereavement rather than love-sickness. His grief is evident in the verbal echoes between his situation and that of the Black Knight. The narrator learns the consolation of natural law from the Ceyx/Alcyone preamble and leads the Knight to similar consolation.

830   MORSE, RUTH. "Understanding the Man in Black." Chaucer Review 15 (1981):204-8.

Argues that much of the supposed stupidity of the Dreamer in Book of the Duchess disappears when we imagine the poem as originally recited by the poet. The Black Knight's song and his complex chess metaphor reflect his grief. The Dreamer is tactful.

831   PALMER, J.N.N. "The Historical Context of the Book of the Duchess: A Revision." Chaucer Review 8 (1974):253-61.

Documents the date of Blanche's death as 12 September 1368 (rather than 1369) by reference to historical documents and argues that Chaucer composed Book of the Duchess in 1368-69. Challenges the evidence for 1377 offered by Condren (entry 819). See Condren's response (Chaucer Review 10 [1975]:87-95).

832   PALMER, R. BARTON. "The Book of the Duchess and Fonteinne amoureuse: Chaucer and Machaut Reconsidered." Canadian Review of Comparative Literature 7 (1980):380-93.

Contrasts Book of the Duchess and Machaut's Dit de la fonteinne amoureuse, clarifying Chaucer's modifications of his source and demonstrating the discontinuity between frame and dream in his poem, a discontinuity that questions the relevance of art to experience and suggests the limits of emotional idealism.

833   PECK, RUSSELL A. "Theme and Number in Chaucer's Book of the Duchess." In Silent Poetry: Essays in Numerological Analysis. Edited by Alistair Fowler. London: Routledge & Kegan Paul; New York: Barnes & Noble, 1970, pp. 72-115.

Studies the numerology that underlies Book of the Duchess, reading the poem as a Boethian recognition of human transience within cosmic permanence. The number three structures the poem, and with one, eight, and twelve, signifies "mind, revelation,

harmony, and repose," linking the poem to its "cosmic background."

834   ROBERTSON, D.W., Jr. "The Historical Setting of Chaucer's
        Book of the Duchess." In Medieval Studies in Honor of Urban
        Tigner Holmes, Jr. Edited by John Mahoney and John Esten
        Keller. Chapel Hill: University of North Carolina Press,
        1966, pp. 169-95. Reprinted in Essays on Medieval Culture
        (Princeton: Princeton University, 1980), pp. 235-56.
            Establishes the historical context of Book of the Duchess
        as a public "funerary" poem and explores the difference between
        medieval/moral and modern/psychological notions of grief and
        consolation. Compares the poem with Boethius's Consolation of
        Philosophy and reads it as a chivalric lament. The Black Knight
        is not John of Gaunt.

835   ROWLAND, BERYL. "Chaucer as a Pawn in the Book of the
        Duchess." American Notes and Queries 6 (1967):3-5
            Explores the imagery of chess in Book of the Duchess in
        light of details of Chaucer's biography, suggesting that the
        narrator's eight-year sickness in the poem may represent the
        poet's anticipation of promotion under John of Gaunt's patronage,
        metaphorically his promotion from pawn to fers.

836   _____. "The Whelp in Chaucer's Book of the Duchess."
        Neuphilologische Mitteilungen 66 (1965):148-60.
            Surveys Chaucer's references to dogs and argues that the
        whelp in Book of the Duchess is best viewed as a modified version
        of the traditional nightmare hound, which lends continuity to the
        dream and introduces the dreamer's encounter with his alter ego,
        the Black Knight. Compare to Friedman (entry 822).

837   SADLER, LYNN VEACH. "Chaucer's the Book of the Duchess and
        the 'Law of Kynde.'" Annuale Mediaevale 11 (1970):51-64.
            Resolves the conflict between authority and experience in
        Book of the Duchess by considering them in the broader context of
        the law of nature. The poem leads its audience to accept death
        as part of this law by showing the Black Knight's recognition of
        the pitiableness of the human condition and the Dreamer's
        development.

838   SEVERS, J. BURKE. "Chaucer's Self-Portrait in the Book of the
        Duchess." Philological Quarterly 43 (1964):27-39.
            Challenges the critical tradition that Chaucer's persona in
        Book of the Duchess suffers from an eight-year sickness for love,
        pointing out that the poem never presents him as a lover and
        often suggests that he is uncourtly. The "phisician" of the poem
        is as likely to be religious as amorous.

839   SHOAF, R.A. "'Mutatio Amoris': 'Penetentia' and the Form of
        the Book of the Duchess." Genre 14 (1981):163-89.

Assesses the formal aspects of confession, autobiography, and dream vision in Book of the Duchess to show how they are historically related and how they inform the poem. The prologue to the work establishes the "thematics" of autobiography, the dream is autobiographical, and the dialogue within the dream is confessional. The interaction of autobiography, confession of love, and the sacrament of penance has precedent in Augustine's Confessions and Roman de la rose. Elegy is only a secondary concern in Chaucer's poem.

840   _____. "Stalking the Sorrowful H(e)art: Penitential Lore and the Hunt Scene in Chaucer's Book of the Duchess." JEGP: Journal of English and Germanic Philology 78 (1979):313-24.
Reads the Black Knight section of Book of the Duchess as an allegory of penance in which the hunt-as-confession follows the allegory of Le livre de seynt medecines, written by Henry of Lancaster, Blanche's father. The hart suggests both heart and penitential self; the whelp suggests the conscience; and as in Chaucer's An A.B.C., the white-walled castle is the renewed self.

841   TISDALE, CHARLES P. "Boethian 'Hert-Huntynge': The Elegaic Pattern of the Book of the Duchess." American Benedictine Review 24 (1973):365-80.
Reads Book of the Duchess as a "psychological" consolation in which the narrator/dreamer, representing reason, aids the Black Knight, representing sorrow, to regain its proper subordinate position, thus redressing psychic balance. The model for this allegory is Boethius's Consolation of Philosophy, and the search for consolation is "figuratively portrayed in the hunt of the hart."

842   WIMSATT, JAMES I. "The Apotheosis of Blanche in the Book of the Duchess." JEGP: Journal of English and Germanic Philology 66 (1967):26-44
Demonstrates that in the allegorical, Marian overtones of the Black Knight's description of his beloved in Book of the Duchess typological symbols and scriptural references combine with traditional conventions of French poetry to correlate the Knight's beloved with the Virgin.

843   _____. "The Book of the Duchess: Secular Elegy or Religious Vision?" In Signs and Symbols in Chaucer's Poetry. Edited by John P. Hermann and John J. Burke, Jr. University: University of Alabama Press, 1981, pp. 113-29.
Argues that Chaucer's Book of the Duchess emulates Machaut's dit amoreaux, yet shows unmistakable similarities to figurative visions like Pearl and Dante's Purgatorio. Chaucer fuses these two traditions in a way that is reminiscent of the Song of Songs, simultaneously conveying erotic and spiritual meanings.

844   _____ . Chaucer and the French Love Poets: The Literary
Background of the "Book of the Duchess." University of North
Carolina Studies in Comparative Literature, no. 43. Chapel
Hill: University of North Carolina Press, 1968, 195 pp.
   Traces the development of French courtly love poetry (dits
amoreux) from Guillaume de Lorris's portion of the Roman de la
rose to Chaucer's contemporaries, detailing its influence on
Chaucer's Book of the Duchess. The Roman pervades Chaucer's
poem. Four poems by Guillaume de Machaut are sources or models
for portions of the poem, while Jean Froissart's Paradys d'amours
"is the main source" of Chaucer's "dream machinery." Such allegories, debates, and poems of complaint and comfort inform the
Book of the Duchess and influence Chaucer's poetic career.

845   _____ . "The Sources of Chaucer's 'Seys and Alcyone.'" Medium
Ævum 36 (1967):231-41.
   Demonstrates the variety of sources from which Chaucer
could have woven his account of Seys and Alcyone in Book of the
Duchess: Machaut's Le dit de la fonteinne amoreuse, Ovid's
Metamorphoses, Statius's Thebaid, Froissart's Paradys d'Amours,
Vergil's Aeneid, the Roman de la rose, and the Ovide moralisé.

   See also entries 7, 47, 133, 154, 157, 233, 237, 806-8,
810. For style: 8, 135, 141; persona: 9, 657, 809, 812;
literary relations: 165, 167, 187, 236, 811.

Parliament of Fowls

846   BENNETT, J.A.W. The "Parlement of Foules": An Interpreta-
       tion. 2d ed. Oxford: Clarendon Press, 1965, 217 pp.
          Reads Chaucer's Parliament of Fowls as a sustained ex-
       ploration of Christian love infused with Neoplatonic thought and
       imagery and inspired by the poetic tradition of Cicero,
       Macrobius, Alain de Lille, Jean de Meun, and Dante. Demonstrates
       the tight verbal structure and the allusiveness of the poem,
       identifying the traditions of its central themes and images, and
       explicating the importance of love to Chaucer's conceptions of
       social and cosmic order. Love, in the Parliament and its tradi-
       tion, is the natural, binding force of the universe, even though
       man can only know this imperfectly.

847   BENSON, LARRY D. "The Occasion of the Parliament of Fowls."
       In The Wisdom of Poetry: Essays in Early English Literature
       in Honor of Morton Bloomfield. Edited by Larry D. Benson and
       Siegfried Wenzel. Kalmazoo, Mich.: Medieval Institute Pub-
       lications, 1982, pp. 123-44.
          Reappraises the evidence for the occasion and date of
       Parliament of Fowls and argues that the poem was written for the
       1380 negotiations of marriage between Richard and Anne of
       Bohemia. The political nature of the poem's Scipio section and
       its central concern with love and selection of a mate corroborate
       the occasion. New evidence suggests that three suitors, like the
       poem's three eagles, vied for Anne's hand and that the astrologi-
       cal reference to Venus was possible in 1380.

848   BRADDY, HALDEEN. Chaucer's "Parlement of Foules" in Relation
       to Contemporary Events. 2d ed. New York: Octagon, 1969, 120
       pp.
          Interprets Parliament of Fowls historically, establishing
       the date of the poem as 1377 by astrological reference, and
       interpreting the poem as a result of Chaucer's involvement in the
       negotiations for the marriage of Richard II and Princess Marie of
       France. Summarizes the contemporary political relations between
       England and France. The dissension among the birds reflects the
       actions of the Good and Bad Parliaments of 1376 and 1377; the

early date suggests Chaucer wrote <u>Parliament</u> before <u>House of Fame</u>, which reflects relatively less Italian influence.

849   BREWER, D[EREK] S.   Introduction to <u>Geoffrey Chaucer:</u> "The <u>Parlement of Foulys</u>."   Old and Middle English Texts. Manchester: Manchester University Press; New York: Barnes & Noble, 1972, pp. 1-64.
       Introduces the topics necessary to a full understanding of Chaucer's <u>Parliament of Fowls</u>: its occasion, literary tradition, sources and background, rhetoric, language, meter, manuscripts, and themes.   Particularly helpful are the discussions of rhetoric and mythology, and the analysis of the poem as a delicate investigation of love and a structure "of opposites balanced if not entirely reconciled."

850   BRONSON, BERTRAND H.   <u>In Appreciation of Chaucer's "Parliament of Foules</u>."   University of California Publications in English, vol. 3, no. 5.   Berkeley: University of California Press, 1935, 30 pp.
       An early recognition of the structural and verbal irony of <u>Parliament of Fowls</u>, identifying the tensions between conventions of love-visions and Chaucer's use of them in the poem.   Assesses the function of Africanus, the depiction of Venus, and the impossible astrology of the narrator's apostrophe to the goddess; regards the birds as "types of humanity" and the satiric focus of the poem as the "unreality of courtly love."

851   BROWN, EMERSON, Jr.   "Priapus and the <u>Parlement of Foulys</u>." <u>Studies in Philology</u> 72 (1975):258-74.
       The allusion to Priapus near the middle of <u>Parliament of Fowls</u> suggests that sensual love is neither wholly commendable nor condemnable.   It is at least slightly ridiculous.

852   CAWLEY, A.C., ed.   "Chaucer's Valentine: The <u>Parlement of Foules</u>."   In <u>Chaucer's Mind and Art</u>.   Essays Old and New, no. 3.   London: Oliver & Boyd, 1969, pp. 125-39.
       Compares the framing dream of Scipio and the dreamer's vision of the garden in <u>Parliament of Fowls</u> to demonstrate the poem's coherent expression of "bewilderingly different kinds of love."   The two dreams are linked by verbal echoes, their common theme of time, and their common source in <u>Roman de la rose</u>.

853   COWGILL, BRUCE KENT.   "The <u>Parlement of Foules</u> and the Body Politic."   JEGP: <u>Journal of English and Germanic Philology</u> 74 (1975):315-35.
       Explores the political allegory of the <u>Parliament of Fowls</u>, discussing the opposition between common profit and social discord, the traditional view of Scipio as a wise temporal ruler, and the literary convention of representing the state as a garden.   The poem teaches that a breakdown in natural law produces social discord.

854   ELDREDGE, LAURENCE. "Poetry and Philosophy in the <u>Parlement</u>
       <u>of Foules</u>." <u>Revue de l'Université d'Ottawa</u> 40 (1970):441–59.
           Explores the relation between Venus and Nature in
       <u>Parliament of Fowls</u>, assessing Venus as a nominalistic represen-
       tation of individual desire and Nature as a realistic depiction
       of concern for the common good. Does not argue that <u>Parliament</u>
       is a philosophical poem, but that the philosophy of universals
       underlies its patterns of thought and imagery.

855   JORDAN, ROBERT M. "The Question of Unity and the <u>Parlement of</u>
       <u>Foules</u>." <u>English Studies in Canada</u> 3 (1977):373–85.
           Describes <u>Parliament of Fowls</u> structurally, identifying its
       "discontinuity and acentricity" of form, and denying that it has
       organic unity. Following medieval rather than modern principles,
       <u>Parliament</u> consists of "sharply articulated," various, and
       "loosely integrated" parts, which critics have unfortunately
       attempted to reconcile into unity.

856   KEARNEY, J.A. "The <u>Parliament of Fowls</u>: The Narrator, the
       'Certyn Thyng,' and the 'Commune Profyt.'" <u>Theoria</u> 45
       (1975):55–71.
           Articulates the "dynamic continuity of Love" in <u>Parliament</u>
       <u>of Fowls</u>, reading the poem's apparent tensions as evidence of the
       narrator's limited perception. Framed by the philosophy of
       Scipio, Nature's resolution to the love debate suggests that the
       plenitude of love is part of God's order.

857   LUMIANSKY, R.M. "Chaucer's <u>Parlement of Foules</u>: A
       Philosophical Interpretation." <u>Review of English Studies</u> 24
       (1948):81–89.
           Surveys criticism of <u>Parliament of Fowls</u> and interprets the
       poem as a unified expression of Chaucer's unsuccessful search for
       a way of reconciling true and false felicity. The poem fulfills
       the poet's immediate need for a love poem for St. Valentine's day
       and embodies his unfulfilled desire to justify love poetry and
       religious truth.

858   McCALL, JOHN P. "The Harmony of Chaucer's <u>Parliament</u>."
       <u>Chaucer Review</u> 5 (1970):22–31.
           Explains how the various types of discord in <u>Parliament of</u>
       <u>Fowls</u> resolve into a "dynamic harmony" once we recognize that
       final reconciliation is heavenly, not earthly. The cacaphony of
       the birds, the duality of the garden, and the diversity of the
       catalogs harmonize in a manner reminiscent of Africanus's vision
       of the spheres.

859   McDONALD, CHARLES O. An Interpretation of Chaucer's <u>Parlement</u>
       <u>of Foules</u>." <u>Speculum</u> 30 (1955):444–57. Reprinted in <u>Chaucer:</u>
       <u>Modern Essays in Criticism</u>, ed. Edward Wagenknecht (New York:
       Oxford University Press, 1959), pp. 309–27; <u>Chaucer Criticism</u>,
       vol. 2, <u>"Troilus and Criseyde" & the Minor Poems</u>, ed. Richard

J. Schoeck and Jerome Taylor (Notre Dame, Ind.: University of
Notre Dame Press, 1961), pp. 275-93.
Shows how the theme of common profit and the figure of
tolerant Nature bridge the opposing views of the high and low
class birds in Parliament of Fowls. The realistic and idealistic
attitudes of the birds are anticipated early in the poem by other
contrastive pairs: the two sides of the gate, Priapus and Venus,
etc.

860   OLSON, PAUL A. "The Parlement of Foules: Aristotle's
       Politics and the Foundations of Human Society." Studies in
       the Age of Chaucer 2 (1980):53-69.
       Reads Parliament of Fowls as "a very great civic poem"
which in its structure and images reflects the fourteenth-century
parliament. "Common profit" and Christian charity are synonymous
in the poem, based on a Christianized form of Aristotle's
Politics, Giles of Rome's De Regimine Principium.

861   PELEN, MARC M. "Form and Meaning of the Old French Love
       Vision: The Fableau dou Dieu d'Amors and Chaucer's Parliament
       of Fowls." Journal of Medieval and Renaissance Studies 9
       (1979):277-305.
       Defines the characteristic structure, imagery, and themes
of Old French love visions and applies these generic features to
the anonymous Fableau dou dieu d'amors and Chaucer's Parliament
of Fowls. Chaucer follows the tripartite structure of the tradition (visionary setting, questing love debate, and Court of Love)
and its humorous, ironic preference for spiritual rather than
earthly love.

862   POLZELLA, MARION L. "'The Craft So Long to Lerne': Poet and
       Lover in Chaucer's Envoy to Scogan and Parliament of Fowls."
       Chaucer Review 10 (1976):279-86.
       Traces the "complex analogy" between the activity of love
and the creativity of art in Envoy to Scogan and Parliament of
Fowls, arguing that the poet affirms both love and poetry even
though he is more concerned with describing love than with enact-
ing it.

863   QUILLIGAN, MAUREEN. "Allegory, Allegoresis, and the
       Deallegorization of Language: The Roman de la Rose, the De
       Planctu Naturae, and the Parlement of Foules." In Allegory,
       Myth, and Symbol. Edited by Morton W. Bloomfield. Harvard
       English Studies, no. 9. Cambridge, Mass.: Harvard University
       Press, 1981, pp. 163-86.
       Contrasts the literary modes of Chaucer's Parliament of
Fowls and its sources, Jean de Meun's Roman de la rose and Alain
de Lille's De planctu naturae, demonstrating how Chaucer's oral,
dramatic presentation differs from their overt "textuality" and
how his mimesis differs from their allegories even though he
shares their concern with the analogy between writing and
sexuality.

864   ROTHSCHILD, VICTORIA. "The Parliament of Fowls: Chaucer's
       Mirror up to Nature?" Review of English Studies, n.s. 35
       (1984):164-84.
            Explores the numerological significance and astrological
       allegory of Parliament of Fowls which date the poem to 1384.
       Reads the poem as a celebration of the Boethian, Neoplatonic
       world view, ordered and governed by Divine Love, a hierarchy from
       the cosmic to the mundane in which the birds represent various
       classes of creatures. Suggests that this symbolic dimension in-
       spired Edmund Spenser's emulation of the poem in his Mutability
       Cantos.

865   SMITH, FRANCIS J. "Mirth and Marriage in the Parlement of
       Foules." Ball State University Forum 14, no. 1 (1973):15-22.
            Impressionistic reading of Parliament of Fowls that empha-
       sizes its energy and humor and suggests that the discontinuities
       of the poem reflect the nature of dreams and the nature of love.

866   VON KREISLER, NICHOLAI. "The Locus Amoenus and Eschatological
       Love in the Parliament of Fowls, 204-10." Philological
       Quarterly 50 (1971):16-22.
            Identifies the "reminiscence of popular eschatological
       literature" in the description of the park of love in Parliament
       of Fowls, associating it with the tradition of locus amoenus, and
       suggesting that it colors the "allegorical conception of love" in
       the poem.

            See also entries 7-8, 47, 154, 157, 201, 214, 249, 806-10,
       812. For style: 135, 137, 141; for date and occasion: 88, 221-
       22, 228; for literary relations: 167, 185, 192, 196, 225, 236,
       802, 811.

House of Fame

867   ALLEN, ROBERT J. "A Recurring Motif in Chaucer's House of
Fame." JEGP: Journal of English and Germanic Philology 55
(1956):393-405.
     A seminal discussion of Chaucer's literary self-conscious-
ness that traces the "sustained interest in the nature of
literary art" throughout House of Fame. Through the dream of
Troy, the contrast between Geffrey and the eagle, and the houses
of Fame and Rumor, Chaucer explores the literary artist's
"indifference to the world of facts."

868   BENNETT, J.A.W. Chaucer's "Book of Fame": An Exposition of
the "House of Fame." Oxford: Clarendon Press, 1968, 205 pp.
     Explicates Chaucer's House of Fame by identifying the
imagery, allusions, and verbal echoes he derived from preceding
literature, especially Vergil's Aeneid, Ovid's Metamorphoses,
Alain de Lille's Anticlaudianus, and Dante's Commedia. Colored
by "Boethian sentiments," Chaucer's manipulation of this
material and his iconography of poetic authority in book 3
constitute a "vindication of poetry" even while he ironically
proposes to "eschew the poetic art" within his fiction. The
Dreamer's passage through the temple of Venus and the palace of
Fame suggest a quest for "new poetic matière," resolved perhaps
in the house of Rumor where he encounters the "ceaseless movement
and miscellanity of the ordinary life"--the subject matter of
Chaucer's later poetry.

869   BOITANI, PIERO. Chaucer and the Imaginary World of Fame.
Chaucer Studies, no. 10. Cambridge: D.S. Brewer; Totowa,
N.J.: Barnes & Noble, 1984, 263 pp.
     Studies Chaucer's House of Fame in the context of the
Western idea of fame, emphasizing the imagery that accrued to
fame, its etymological similarity to fate and fable, and its
network of associations ranging from glory to vainglory. Traces
the idea of fame from Gilgamesh to the Scholastics and isolates
the importance of Vergil's Aeneid to the fourteenth-century
Italian explosion of concern with fame. Identifies French and
English medieval traditions of fame, but focuses upon Chaucer's

relation to Italian tradition. House of Fame appropriates many
images from the tradition of fame: wind, labyrinth, letters
written in ice, etc. Its dream-vision frame and self-conscious
concern with poetry derives from the same tradition. House of
Fame follows the tradition of fame in its imagery, mythography,
and association of subjects; it goes beyond tradition by
investigating the role, that the language of fame has as a
repository and arbiter of human culture.

870   DAVID, ALFRED. "A Literary Satire in the House of Fame."
       PMLA 75 (1960):333-39.
           Examines the "planned chaos" of House of Fame to show how
       "one major purpose of the poem is literary satire." Chaucer
       satirizes the dream vision by substituting the palace of Fame for
       the court of Love and modifying the conventions of invocation,
       the lover-narrator, and courtly atmosphere.

871   DELANY, SHEILA. "Chaucer's House of Fame and the Ovide
       Moralise." Comparative Literature 20 (1968):254-64.
           Documents verbal parallels between Chaucer's House of Fame
       and the early fourteenth-century Ovide moralise, suggesting that
       this allegorization of Ovid inspired Chaucer's characterization
       of Fame as a judge and influenced his poem's concern with con-
       flicting literary authorities.

872   _____. Chaucer's "House of Fame": The Poetics of Skeptical
       Fideism. Chicago: University of Chicago Press, 1972, 143 pp.
           Attributes the incongruities of Chaucer's House of Fame to
       the narrator's skeptical inability to find truth, and argues that
       the poem transcends such skepticism by fideism. The medieval
       philosophical tradition of "double truth"--logical versus
       religious--parallels the poem's epistemology: the truth of
       dreams, the validity of the classical tale of Dido and Aeneas,
       the accuracy of science, and the conflicting claims of history
       and fiction. Such issues reflect the narrator's anxieties in the
       poem, clarifying the poet's notion of the "potential sterility of
       being unable to choose." Traces the presence of similar concerns
       in Chaucer's later works.

873   DICKERSON, A. INSKIP. "Chaucer's House of Fame: A Skeptical
       Epistemology of Love." Texas Studies in Literature and
       Language 18 (1976):171-83.
           Argues that House of Fame poses a skeptical view about the
       reliability of love rumors and hypothesizes that the poem was
       written to answer some "accusation against Chaucer as a lover."

874   FRY, DONALD K. "The Ending of the House of Fame." In Chaucer
       at Albany. Edited by Rossell Hope Robbins. New York: Burt
       Franklin & Co., 1975, pp. 27-40.
           Argues that Chaucer ended House of Fame with the man of
       "gret auctorite" to undercut humorously literature and other
       kinds of traditionalism. The Dido episode and the Eagle's

disquisition establish the distorted and unreliable nature of
Fame's minions.

875   GRENNEN, JOSEPH E. "Chaucer and Calcidius: The Platonic
       Origins of the House of Fame." Viator 15 (1984):237-62.
       Reads House of Fame as a parody of the philosophical epic,
specifically Calcidius's version of Plato's Timaeus, identifying
verbal echoes and similarities of detail that anticipate, for
example, Chaucer's wicker house of Rumor and the rock beneath
Fame's castle. Chaucer substitutes unpredictibility and confusion for the "arithmetical harmony of Timaeus."

876   JEFFREY, DAVID LYLE. "Sacred and Secular Scripture: Author-
       ity and Interpretation in the House of Fame." Chaucer and
       Scriptural Tradition. Edited by David Lyle Jeffrey. Ottawa:
       University of Ottawa Press, 1984, pp. 207-28.
       Reads House of Fame as an exploration of the authority of
history. The poem's three-part structure, its concern with
epistemology, and its lack of conclusion reflect the version of
the story of Aeneas that it includes and the vision of Ezechial
to which it alludes. Like the biblical vision, the poem offers
the eschatological hope of knowing truth, but it asserts the
futility of pursuing truth through secular authority.

877   JOYNER, WILLIAM. "Parallel Journeys in Chaucer's House of
       Fame." Papers on Language and Literature 12 (1976):3-19.
       Compares the similarities of pattern and detail in
Geffrey's journey in House of Fame and the journey of Aeneas re-
called at the beginning of the poem, noting echoes of Dante's
Commedia in the parallels and comparing Aeneas's diversion from
his goal to Geffrey's diversion in the court of Fame and the
digressive technique of the poem.

878   KELLEY, MICHAEL R. "Chaucer's House of Fame: England's
       Earliest Science Fiction." Extrapolation 16 (1974):7-16.
       Demonstrates that the Eagle's disquisition on sound and his
ascent with Geffrey in House of Fame accord with medieval acous-
tical and cosmological science, suggesting that by virtue of this
contemporary plausibility the work can be read as science fiction. Reflects the range of Chaucer's learning.

879   KENDRICK, LAURA. "Chaucer's House of Fame and the French
       Palais de Justice." Studies in the Age of Chaucer 6
       (1984):121-33.
       Points out several similarities between the architecture of
the French Palais de Justice, which Chaucer visited, and the
architectural details in House of Fame, especially the pillars
surmounted by statues in Fame's court.

880   KOONCE, B.G. Chaucer and the Tradition of Fame: Symbolism in
       the "House of Fame." Princeton: Princeton University Press,
       1966, 293 pp.

Reads <u>House of Fame</u> as an allegorical exploration of the
"vanity of worldly fame," establishing the literary and theological tradition of fame in the Middle Ages, interpreting the poem's
pattern of scriptural and literary allusions, and assessing the
influence of Dante's <u>Commedia</u> upon it. The dream-vision frame of
the poem, its "symbolic date," and its invocation of Dante's work
signal allegory. The Aeneas/Dido episode initiates thematic contrast between heavenly and earthly varieties of love and fame,
represented in the traditionally dualistic figure of Venus. The
flight of the eagle suggests the pursuit of true love and true
fame by grace-aided reason. Fame's court is rich with apocalyp-
tic symbolism, and the love tidings pursued by Geffrey are the
twofold tidings of spiritual and earthly love.

881   LEYERLE, JOHN. "Chaucer's Windy Eagle." <u>University of
       Toronto Quarterly</u> 40 (1971):247-65.
       Assesses the function and significance of the eagle in
Chaucer's <u>House of Fame</u>. The eagle's associations with 10
December—the internal date of the poem—are many. The figure of
the eagle has roots in mythology, bestiaries, Dante, Boethius,
and the iconography of St. John. Its disquisition on sound including scatological puns, unifies the poem by emphasizing the
irrepressibility of sound, and, therefore, of private or secret
love.

882   OVERBECK, PAT TREFZGER. "The 'Man of Gret Auctorite' in
       Chaucer's <u>House of Fame</u>." <u>Modern Philology</u> 73 (1975):157-61.
       Proposes that the "man of gret auctorite" at the conclusion
of <u>House of Fame</u> is the God of Love. Petrarch's <u>Triumph of Love</u>
is an analogue, perhaps a source.

883   ROWLAND, BERYL. "The Art of Memory and the Art of Poetry in
       the <u>House of Fame</u>." <u>Revue de l'Universite d'Ottawa</u> 51
       (1981):162-71.
       Summarizes classical and medieval techniques of visual
memory and argues for their structural importance in Chaucer's
<u>House of Fame</u>. The poem externalizes the poet's journey through
his memory, showing how memory creates poetry and how it mediates
between authority and experience.

884   STEVENSON, KAY. "The Endings of Chaucer's <u>House of Fame</u>."
       <u>English Studies</u> 59 (1978):10-26.
       Surveys the various suggestions and theories about
Chaucer's ending of <u>House of Fame</u>, assessing them in light of the
oppositions in the earlier portions of the poem and the endings
to his other poems. Argues that the most "inconsequential" ending is most appropriate to the rest of the poem.

885   TISDALE, CHARLES P. "The <u>House of Fame</u>: Virgilian Reason and
       Boethian Philosophy." <u>Comparative Literature</u> 25 (1973):247-
       61.

Investigates the unifying combination of Vergilian narrative and Boethian thought in Chaucer's House of Fame. The
dreamer of Fame reenacts the role of Aeneas from book 4 of the
Aeneid, extending the narrative implications of Vergil's epic
into a Boethian rejection of fascination with the world.

886   WATTS, ANN C[HALMERS]. "Amor gloriae in Chaucer's House of
       Fame." Journal of Medieval and Renaissance Studies 3
       (1973):87-113.
       Identifies the Christian and classical attitudes toward
fame expressed in House of Fame, book 3: fame as a desire of the
proud, as the just reward for great poetry, and as a neutral
record of the past. Boethius's Consolation of Philosophy may be
the source of the poem's "ambivalent attitude," but the autobiographical references in the work indicate the attitude is
Chaucer's own.

       See also entries 3, 7-9, 47, 154, 157, 190, 192, 249, 806-
7, 809-10, 812. For persona: 67, 84-85; literary relations:
166-67, 225, 373, 811.

Legend of Good Women

887   AMY, ERNEST F. <u>The Text of Chaucer's "Legend of Good Women."</u>
Princeton: Princeton University Press, 1918. Reprint. New
York: Haskell House, 1965, 118 pp.
    Describes how the eleven manuscripts and Thynne's 1532
edition of <u>Legend of Good Women</u> fall into two independent
families, each with its own version of the prologue, designated
"F" from the Fairfax manuscript and "G" from Cambridge Gg.
Provides no complete text of the poem but assesses two early
editions line by line, comparing their readings to the
manuscripts.

888   ESTRICH, ROBERT M. "Chaucer's Maturing Art in the Prologues
to the <u>Legend of Good Women</u>." <u>JEGP: Journal of English and
Germanic Philology</u> 36 (1937):326–37.
    Compares Chaucer's early (F) and later (G) versions of the
Prologue to <u>Legend of Good Women</u> to argue that Chaucer's revision
was largely a process of reducing "conventional courtly love
material" with a "concomitant heightening" of ironic comedy at
the expense of these conventions.

889   FISHER, JOHN H. "The Revision of the Prologue to the <u>Legend
of Good Women</u>: An Occasional Explanation." <u>South Atlantic
Bulletin</u> 43, no. 4 (1978):75–84.
    Assesses the G version of the Prologue to the <u>Legend of
Good Women</u> as a commemoration of Richard's marriage to Isabelle
in 1397, arguing that the event accounts for Chaucer's revision.
The changes in detail and tone all reflect "how distant and
dream-like" the ideal of the F version had become.

890   FRANK, ROBERT WORTH, Jr. <u>Chaucer and the "Legend of Good
Women</u>." Cambridge, Mass.: Harvard University Press, 1972,
228 pp.
    The first full-length study of <u>Legend of Good Women</u>, read-
ing it as important to understanding Chaucer's development as a
narrative artist, and as a self-conscious innovation in genre,
theme, technique, and verse form. The Prologue, a playful
farewell to the love-vision, introduces and justifies the legends

and earnestly questions the proper subject matter of poetry and
its allowable subjects. The tales are "essentially alien to the
code of courtly love" and reflect Chaucer's growing dexterity
with brief, straightforward narration that requires quick summary
and deft characterization, more typical of Canterbury Tales than
Troilus and Criseyde. Through the legends, Chaucer explored his
poetic freedom and developed the ability to write emotionally
charged tales. Critical accusations that Chaucer became bored
with the legends misconstrue their tone and rhetorical use of
occupatio.

891   . "The Legend of Good Women: Some Implications." In
       Chaucer at Albany. Edited by Rossell Hope Robbins. New York:
       Burt Franklin & Co., 1975, pp. 63-76.
          Assesses the narrative virtues of Chaucer's Legend of Good
Women and John Gower's Confessio Amantis, particularly their
"unimpeded succession of events" which makes for bare stories
that benefit from clear events, sharp sequence, memorability, and
meaning—the "magnetic power of a simple story."

892   GAYLORD, ALAN T. "Dido at Hunt, Chaucer at Work." Chaucer
       Review 17 (1983):300-315.
          Contrasts the Dido account of Chaucer's Legend of Good
Women with its Latin and French sources, assessing the prosody of
the works and demonstrating how Chaucer's new decasyllabic line
creates a "literary colloquial"—a new voice.

893   HANSEN, ELAINE TUTTLE. "Irony and the Antifeminist Narrator
       in Chaucer's Legend of Good Women." JEGP: Journal of English
       and Germanic Philology 82 (1983):11-31.
          Reads Legend of Good Women as a parody of literature that
falsely idealizes female passivity and stupidity, arguing that
Cupid and perhaps the narrator ironically prefer such an ideal,
that the legends individually reflect the absurdity of the
notion, and that the incomplete state of the text underscores
Chaucer's rejection of the false ideal.

894   KISER, LISA J. Telling Classical Tales: Chaucer and the
       "Legend of Good Women." Ithaca: Cornell University Press,
       1983, 169 pp.
          Reads Legend of Good Women as a poem about poetry,
especially about the artist's responsibility to his classical
sources. The Prologue clarifies the author's conviction that
poetry need not be abstract and that it should not be distorted
by Christian moralization. The legends reflect both these
concerns and Chaucer's role as a "translator" of traditional
sources rather than as an original maker or poet.

895   KNOPP, SHERRON. "Chaucer and Jean de Meun as Self-Conscious
       Narrators: The Prologue to the Legend of Good Women and the
       Roman de la Rose 10307-680." Comitatus 4 (1973-74):25-39.

Compares patterns and details of Chaucer's Prologue to the
Legend of Good Women with Jean de Meun's meeting with Amours in
Roman de la rose, demonstrating how Chaucer emulates Jean's
ironic self-portrait and inverts his view of love, both compli-
menting and parodying Jean's depiction.

896   KOLVE, V.A. "From Cleopatra to Alceste: An Iconographic
       Study of The Legend of Good Women." In Signs and Symbols in
       Chaucer's Poetry. Edited by John P. Hermann and John J.
       Burke, Jr. University: University of Alabama Press, 1981,
       pp. 130-78.
            Argues that Cleopatra, the first tale in the Legend of Good
       Women, provides a paradigm for the major motif of the collection
       as it stands—fruitless pagan tragedy. Had Chaucer finished the
       series, he would have transcended the motif in the tale of
       Alceste as an icon of Christian resurrection. The full design of
       the poem, implied in the Prologue, reflects Chaucer's respect for
       the pagan past and for women, locating "within pagan history
       certain possibilities of human loving that Christian history
       would later confirm and redeem."

897   LOSSING, MARIAN. "The Prologue to the Legend of Good Women
       and the Lai de franchise." Studies in Philology 39 (1942):15-
       35.
            Challenges the tradition that that Deschamps' Lai de
       franchise was the primary source of Prologue F of the Legend of
       Good Women by demonstrating the conventional nature of their
       verbal parallels. As a result, questions the pre-1385 date for
       the Prologue.

898   LOWES, JOHN LIVINGSTON. "The Prologue to the Legend of Good
       Women as Related to the French Marguerite Poems and to the
       Filostrato." PMLA 19 (1904):593-683.
            Defines the French tradition of marguerite poetry, and
       demonstrates its pervasive influence upon Chaucer's two versions
       of the Prologue to the Legend of Good Women. Takes account of the
       influence of Boccaccio's Filostrato on the poem and establishes
       that the B [F] version of the Prologue preceded A [G].

899   _____. "The Prologue to the Legend of Good Women Considered
       in Its Chronological Relations." PMLA 20 (1905):749-864.
            Using internal and external evidence, dates the early, F
       version of the Prologue to the Legend of Good Women as "not
       earlier than 1386." Compares this version with other Chaucerian
       works, proposing the following chronology: House of Fame about
       1379; the early version of Knight's Tale, Troilus and Criseyde,
       and the early version of the Legend of Good Women Prologue and
       most of its tales by 1386; revised Prologue, 1394.

900   PAYNE, ROBERT O. "Making His Own Myth: The Prologue to
       Chaucer's Legend of Good Women." Chaucer Review 9 (1975):197-
       211.

223

Assesses the place of the second, G version of Prologue to the Legend of Good Women in Chaucer's career, reading it as a personal valediction to his book-inspired love-visions. Its narrator is an "imaginative reconstruction from Chaucer's early poems," but closely aligned with the historical Chaucer. Structurally, the work reflects Chaucer's self-conscious search for an ars poetica.

901   TAYLOR, BEVERLY. "The Medieval Cleopatra: The Classical and Medieval Traditions of Chaucer's Legend of Cleopatra." Journal of Medieval and Renaissance Studies 7 (1977):249-69.
        Reads the account of Cleopatra as a signal of pervasive irony in Chaucer's Legend of Good Women, demonstrating its deviation from traditional condemnations of Cleopatra and its ironic assertion of her virtue. As the first legend, it sets an ironic tone for the rest of the collection.

        See also entries 3, 10, 47, 67, 96, 154, 162, 190, 216, 221, 235, 563, 807, 810. For literary relations: 167, 373, 775, 811.

Short Poems, Lyrics,
and Lyrical Technique

902   CHERNISS, MICHAL D. "Chaucer's Anelida and Arcite: Some
        Conjectures." Chaucer Review 5 (1970):9-21.
            Hypothesizes that the fragmentary Anelida and Arcite was to
        be a dream vision, structurally similar to Chaucer's other dream
        visions, and suggests that conflicts of plot and purpose between
        the poem and the early version of the Knight's Tale compelled
        Chaucer to stop where he did.

903   CLOGAN, PAUL M. "The Textual Reliability of Chaucer's Lyrics:
        A Complaint to His Lady." Medievalia et Humanistica, n.s. 5
        (1974):183-89.
            Challenges editorial emendation of Chaucer's Complaint to
        His Lady, arguing that the poem is unfinished and experimental,
        valid as an example of Chaucer at work and better left unemended.

904   CROSS, J.E. "The Old Swedish Trohetsvisan and Chaucer's Lak
        of Stedfastnesse--A Study in a Mediaeval Genre." Saga-Book 16
        (1965):283-314.
            Assesses the genre and purpose of Chaucer's Lak of
        Stedfastnesse, comparing it to the Old Swedish Trohetsvisan as a
        conventional example of moralizing complaint. Even though its
        envoy and manuscript rubrics suggest several occasions for the
        piece, Chaucer's poem follows the genre's traditional conventions
        of thought and expression. Includes a valuable line-by-line
        schematic analysis of Chaucer's poem.

905   DAVID, ALFRED. "An ABC to the Style of the Prioress." In
        Acts of Interpretation: The Text in Its Context, 700-1600:
        Essays on Medieval and Renaissance Literature in Honor of E.
        Talbot Donaldson. Edited by Mary J. Carruthers and Elizabeth
        D. Kirk. Norman, Okla.: Pilgrim Books, 1982, pp. 147-57.
            Reads Chaucer's An A.B.C. as a careful piece of artifice
        rather than a mere translation of its French model and, comparing
        this artifice to the style of the Prioress's character and tale,
        shows how both reflect a contemporary "sentimentalized
        religiosity that worships beauty as a version of truth."

906   ____. "Chaucer's Good Counsel to Scogan." <u>Chaucer Review</u> 3 (1969):265-74.

      Explains Chaucer's <u>Envoy to Scogan</u> as a playful ballad of good counsel with autobiographical overtones and an implicit serious moral: human accomplishment, including poetry, is transitory.

907   FINNEL, ANDREW J. "The Poet as Sunday Man: <u>The Complaint of Chaucer to His Purse</u>." <u>Chaucer Review</u> 8 (1973):147-58.

      Argues that Chaucer wrote <u>Complaint to His Purse</u> while avoiding debts in the sanctuary of Westminster close some months after the accession of Henry IV, explicating the poem as a cogent plea for funds.

908   GALWAY, MARGARET. "Chaucer among Thieves." <u>Times Literary Supplement</u>, 20 April 1946, p. 187.

      Reads Chaucer's <u>Fortune</u> autobiographically, suggesting that the date of the poem and its details match well with the events of early September 1390 when the poet was robbed twice and beaten. His embarrassment at these events is punningly presented in the poem.

909   LAIRD, EDGAR S. "Astrology and Irony in Chaucer's <u>Complaint of Mars</u>." <u>Chaucer Review</u> 6 (1972):229-31.

      Argues in astrological terms that Venus's abandoning of Mars for Mercury in <u>Complaint of Mars</u> is anthropomorphic, a cosmic enactment of Criseyde's betrayal of Troilus.

910   LAMPE, DAVID E. "The Truth of a 'Vache': The Homely Homily of Chaucer's <u>Truth</u>." <u>Papers on Language and Literature</u> 9 (1973):311-14.

      Surveys the interpretations of the reference to "Vache" in Chaucer's <u>Truth, Balade de Bon Conseyl</u> and reads "vache" as "ox," a tropological figure of the "necessity of worldly renunciation." The poem encourages humanity to leave the world for heavenly truth.

911   LENAGHAN, R.T. "Chaucer's <u>Envoy to Scogan</u>: The Uses of Literary Conventions." <u>Chaucer Review</u> 10 (1975):46-61.

      Reads <u>Envoy to Scogan</u> in its court context of the 1390s, comparing it to contemporary conventional verse by Deschamps, Machaut, and Gower, and arguing that the poem reflects the urbane and ironic atmosphere of the court.

912   LUDLAM, CHAS. D. "Heavenly Word-Play in Chaucer's <u>Complaint to His Purse</u>." <u>Notes and Queries</u>, n.s. 23 (1976):391-92.

      Identifies two puns and demonstrates three levels of imagery in Chaucer's <u>Complaint to His Purse</u>: financial, amatory, and heavenly.

913   NICHOLS, ROBERT E., Jr. "Chaucer's <u>Fortune, Truth,</u> and <u>Gentilesse</u>: The 'Last' Unpublished Manuscript

Transcriptions." <u>Speculum</u> 44 (1969):46–50.
Transcribes <u>Fortune</u> and <u>Truth</u> from the Leiden Manuscript,
also known as MS Vossius 9, and <u>Gentilesse</u> from Cambridge
University Library MS Gg 4.27.1(b), making available in print for
the first time these versions of the poems.

914   NOLAN, CHARLES J., Jr.   "Structural Sophistication in the
       <u>Complaint unto Pity</u>."   <u>Chaucer Review</u> 13 (1979):363–72.
       Demonstrates the structural and verbal parallels between a
portion of Chaucer's <u>Complaint unto Pity</u> and contemporary legal
bills of petition, showing how the poet blended legal and amorous
styles to produce "resonance" in his poem.

915   NORTON-SMITH, J.   "Chaucer's <u>Anelida and Arcite</u>."   In <u>Medieval</u>
       <u>Studies for J.A.W. Bennett, Aetatis Suae LXX</u>.   Edited by P.L.
       Heyworth.   Oxford: Clarendon Press, 1981, pp. 81–99.
       Against critical trend, argues that <u>Anelida and Arcite</u> is a
complete poem influenced formally and thematically by Italian
humanistic verse more similar to <u>Troilus and Criseyde</u> and <u>Legend</u>
<u>of Good Women</u> than to Knight's Tale, and therefore probably
written fairly late in Chaucer's career.

916   PACE, GEORGE B.   "The Chaucerian Proverbs."   <u>Studies in</u>
       <u>Bibliography</u> 18 (1965):41–48.
       Presents the evidence necessary to assess whether the
short poem, <u>Proverbs</u>, is Chaucer's.   Collates the four available
versions, commenting on their variations.   Reworks the manuscript
stemma, assessing the evidence of Stow's edition which is based
on none of the three extant manuscripts.

917   ROBBINS, ROSSELL H[OPE].   "Chaucer's <u>To Rosemounde</u>."   <u>Studies</u>
       <u>in the Literary Imagination</u> 4, no. 2 (1971):73–81.
       Surveys critical opinions of <u>To Rosemounde</u> and reads the
poem as the aging Chaucer's humorous flattery of the young
Isabelle of France, new child-queen of England.   The poem was
composed on the occasion of Isabelle's entry into London, 1396.

918   SCATTERGOOD, V.J.   "Chaucer's Curial Satire: The <u>Balade de</u>
       <u>bon conseyl</u>."   <u>Hermathena</u> 133 (1982):29–45.
       Places Chaucer's <u>Balade de bon conseyl</u> (<u>Truth</u>) in the
tradition of epistolary curial satire, comparing it to examples
of the genre by Horace, Seneca, Walter Map, Alain Chartier, and
William Dunbar.   Suggests that the conventions and ideas of the
poem come from this tradition rather than from Boethian
philosophy.

919   SCHMIDT, A.V.C.   "Chaucer and the Golden Age."   <u>Essays in</u>
       <u>Criticism</u> 26 (1976):99–115.
       Explicates the poetic technique of Chaucer's <u>Former Age</u>,
demonstrating the quality of its rhetoric, metrics, imagery, and
diction, and its successful adaptation of its Boethian source.

920   SCOTT, FLORENCE R.   "A New Look at the <u>Complaint of Chaucer to</u>
       <u>His Empty Purse</u>." <u>English Language Notes</u> 2 (1964):81-87.
          Reads Chaucer's <u>Complaint to His Purse</u> in light of contem-
       porary records and argues that, written at the time of Henry's
       accession, the poem was not an earnest claim of poverty, but a
       successful and somewhat ironic reminder of loyalty from Chaucer
       to his new king.

921   VASTA, EDWARD.   "To Rosemounde: Chaucer's 'Gentil' Dramatic
       Monologue." In <u>Chaucerian Problems and Perspectives: Essays</u>
       <u>Presented to Paul E. Beichner, C.S.C.</u> Edited by Edward Vasta
       and Zacharias P. Thundy. Notre Dame, Ind.: University of
       Notre Dame Press, 1979, pp. 97-113.
          Reads Chaucer's <u>To Rosemounde</u> as a satire on poetic
       language and bourgeois aspiration to courtly sentiment. The
       poem's images of a tub of tears and a wallowing fish, its clumsy
       paradoxes, and its incompetent structure establish a bathetic
       voice for a mediocre lover.

922   WIMSATT, JAMES I.   "<u>Anelida and Arcite</u>: A Narrative of
       Complaint and Comfort." <u>Chaucer Review</u> 5 (1970):1-8.
          Compares Chaucer's unfinished <u>Anelida and Arcite</u> to French
       <u>dits</u> of complaint and comfort, showing how the extant complaint
       portion of the poem parallels French models in style and detail,
       and suggesting that the poem would have ended with a structurally
       similar section concerned with comfort--the "reunion of the
       lovers."

          See also entries 3, 5, 22, 39, 46-47, 233, 236, 243. For
       lyrics and lyrical technique: 38, 183, 188-89, 240, 379, 734,
       773; moral ballads: 170, 187, 482, 555; complaints: 88, 165,
       806; <u>An A.B.C.</u>: 32, 208, 806, 840; <u>Anelida and Arcite</u>: 46, 137,
       373, 806, 809; <u>Complaint of Mars</u>: 165, 210, 217, 221-22, 224,
       243, 774, 806, 809; <u>Scogan</u>: 67, 862.

Boece

923 ECKHARDT, CAROLINE D. "The Medieval Prosimetrum Genre (from
Boethius to Boece)." Genre 16 (1983):21-38.
Studies the prosimetrum tradition from Boethius to Chaucer
in order to understand why Chaucer translated Boethius's verse-
and-prose Consolation of Philosophy into prose only. While "no
characteristic" of the tradition explains Chaucer's motive, his
desire for clarity may have been the cause.

See also entries 39, 163-64, 170, 187.

Treatise on the Astrolabe

924 LIPSON, CAROL. "'I N'am But a Lewd Compilator': Chaucer's
Treatise on the Astrolabe as Translation." Neuphilologische
Mitteilungen 84 (1983):192-200.
Challenges the traditional assumption that Chaucer's
Treatise on the Astrolabe was largely translated from sources
like Massahalla's Astrolabe and suggests that it is mostly
Chaucer's own composition.

See also entries 16, 18, 56, 163-64, 221.

Equatorie of the Planets

See entries 15, 18, 56, 105, 221.

Index

References are to entry numbers; names, titles, and topics analyzed in the table of contents are not listed here, most notably, works by Chaucer.

Boulger, James D., 636
Bowden, Murial, 57, 330
Boyd, Beverly, 21, 205
Boyd, Heather, 277
Braddy, Haldeen, 47, 97, 108,
    524, 754, 848
"Bradshaw shift," 270, 274, 328
Bradwardine, Thomas, 213, 494
Bratcher, James T., 377
Brenner, Gary, 725
Brenner, John P., 601
Brewer, Derek S., 47, 65-66,
    153, 189, 194, 244, 247-48,
    294, 390, 475, 706, 849
Brinton, Laurel J., 619
Brodie, Alexander, 666
Broes, Arthur T., 637
Bronson, Bertrand H., 87, 815
    850
Brooks, Douglas, 355
Brown, Emerson, Jr., 501-5,
    558, 675, 851
Brusendorff, Aage, 26
Bryan, W.F., 252
Bugge, John, 506
Burbridge, Roger T., 391
Burlin, Robert B., 154
Burnley, David, 98-99
Burnley, J.D., 507, 765
Burrow, J.A., 67, 356, 612-14
Burton, T.L., 423

Caie, Graham D., 403, 424
Cahn, Kenneth S., 508
Calcidius, 875
Cambridge University, 56
Campbell, A.P., 684
Campbell, Jackson J., 660, 667
Carruthers, Mary J., 425, 455
    476, 533
Carton, Evan, 785
Cary, Meredith, 426
Cassian, John, 626
Catullus, 174
Cawley, A.C., 852
Caxton, William, 21, 269
Chamberlain, David, 226
Chanson de geste, 612
Chartier, Alain, 918
Chaucer, Philippa, 74, 76, 825
Chaucer, Thomas, 74, 76
Chaucer Society, order of

Canterbury Tales, 23, 274;
    publications of, 45
Cherniss, Michael D., 477, 817-
    18, 902
Cherry-tree Carol, 516
Chrétien de Troyes, 759, 782
Christianity, 1, 3, 77, 205-8,
    229, 258
Cicero, 646, 803, 811, 846
Clanvowe, John, 200
Clark, George, 215
Clark, Roy Peter, 467
Clark, Susan L., 404
Claudian, 174
Clawson, W.H., 295
Clemen, Wolfgang, 806
Clogan, Paul M., 405, 653, 903
Clough, Andrea, 726
Coghill, Nevill, 1, 245, 277A
Collette, Carolyn P., 602
Collins, Marie, 232
Colmer, Dorothy, 427, 541
Comedy, genre and theory, 258,
    307, 315, 388. See also
    Humor
Common profit, theme of, 250,
    480, 853, 856, 859-60
Condren, Edward I., 571, 819
Conley, John, 615
Contemptus mundi, theme of, 402,
    798, 802. See also Innocent
    III, pope, De contemptu
    mundi
Cook, Albert Stanburrough, 357
Cook, Richard G., 786
Cooke, Thomas D., 309
Cooper, Geoffrey, 378
Corrigan, Matthew, 766
Corsa, Helen Storm, 2, 708
Costanza of Castille, 88
Cotten, Michael E., 709
Cotter, James Finn, 428
Coulton, G.G., 58
Courtney, Neil, 278
Cowgill, Bruce Kent, 358, 853
Cox, Lee Sheridan, 266
Cox, Robert C., 218
Crampton, Georgia R., 359, 710
Crawford, William R., 43
Crosby, Ruth, 134
Cross, J.E., 904
Crow, Martin S., 63, 68